ETHNOSOCIOLOGY

ALEXANDER DUGIN

ETHNO SOCIOLOGY

THE FOUNDATIONS

ETHNOSOCIOLOGY VOL. I

ARKTOS
LONDON 2019

ΛRKTOS

🌐 Arktos.com 👍 fb.com/Arktos ✆ 📷 arktosmedia ✖ arktosjournal

ISBN
978-1-917646-35-2 (Softcover)
978-1-912975-00-6 (Hardback)
978-1-912975-02-0 (Ebook

Translation
Michael Millerman

Editing
Arkacandra Jayasimha
Martin Locker

Layout and Cover
Tor Westman

THE FOUNDATIONS

The Foundations

CHAPTER ONE

Ethnosociology: Definition, Subject Matter, Methods

SECTION ONE
A Brief Excursus into Classical Sociology

The Basic Concepts of Sociology: The General and the Particular

Ethnosociology studies the ethnos with the help of the sociological apparatus, and for that reason we will need the basic concepts of the discipline of Sociology. We shall now make a short excursus into the fundamentals of Sociology.

Sociology is a discipline that examines society as a *whole* preceding its parts, as an *organic*, not a mechanical phenomenon; it is a discipline that emphasizes the *common*, or the social, and not the particular, or the individual. Psychology concerns itself with the person. Sociology, on the other hand, studies society as a whole. The fundamental principle of sociology can be summed up thus: *the particular derives from the common.*

Social Strata and Groups

The fundamental framework of sociological knowledge is two axes, x and y, on which are arranged social strata (*x-axis*) and social groups (*y-axis*).

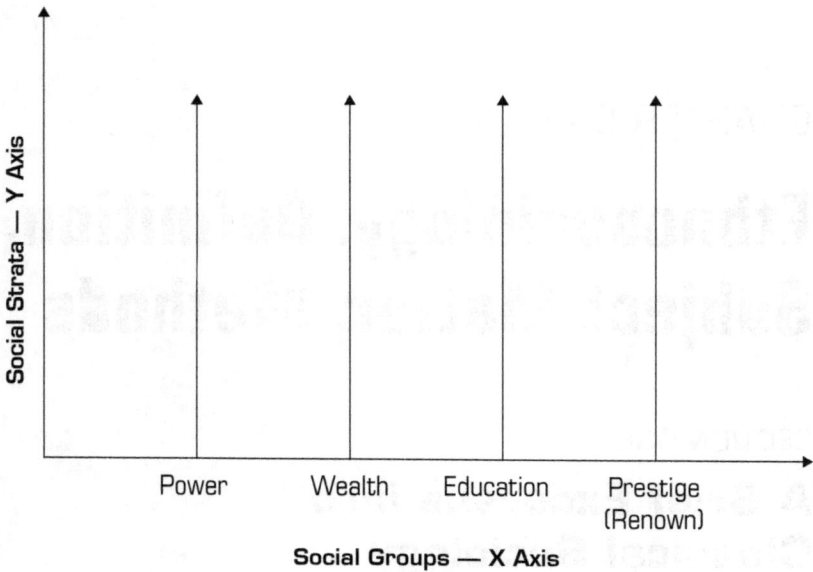

Figure 1. The basic model of sociology.

Of course, Sociology is a well-established scientific discipline. It has many theories, concepts, and methods for the study of society, but the fundamental meaning, scientific paradigm, and *episteme* of Sociology can be reduced down to this very simple diagram.[1]

A person's position with respect to these two axes determines his *status*. Status consists in a set of roles.

The *y*-axis, on which strata or classes (understood sociologically) are arranged is called *the axis of social stratification*. From the sociological point of view, strata are primary in relation to other forms. On the *x*-axis, social groups are arranged. This is the amalgamation of people by markers of their belonging to a profession, gender, age, geographic area, ethnicity, or administrative position, drawn up in accordance with a non-hierarchical principle. Strata, for their part, imply a hierarchy.

---

1   See Kravchenko, S. A. *Sociology: Paradigms and Themes*. Moscow: 1997.

The superimposition of these two axes provides a basic representation of the structure of a society and the place of any unit in it taken for consideration, whether collective or individual. Each social phenomenon, institution, and personality can be resolved into its components through these axes. Such resolution is *sociological analysis*, the main professional activity of the sociologist.

Sociology operates with the concept of inequality, the quantitative indicator of which is placed along the y-axis. The qualitative indicator is marked on the x-axis: belonging to one or another social group or to a few groups at once.

The strata define a *social hierarchy*, for which reason the y-axis is vertical. In themselves, groups do not yet say anything about a higher or lower position, which is why the axis on which they are arranged is horizontal. The fact that someone belongs to the group of pensioners, Orthodox Christians, or Muslims in no way makes a pensioner or a Christian higher or lower than one another. Hence groups are arranged horizontally or are at times superimposed on one another. Someone can be a pensioner or a Christian or both one and the other at the same time.

From the point of view of strata, a person can be either a rich, educated, and famous director, or a subordinate, poor, undereducated, and entirely unknown local. By a certain relativity of approach, society as a whole can be mapped onto this scale of stratification. Sociologists usually distinguish between three main classes: the upper, the middle, and the lower. Membership in each of them is evaluated according to entirely precise criteria: one's income, number of subordinates, years of education, academic level, and index of citations. A man who has thirty dollars in his pocket and sees a poor person begging might consider himself to be "rich," but the sociologist will swiftly return him to reality if he asks about his monthly income. The same principle applies to renown: it might seem to someone that he is "famous" if he is known by two or three groups of his peers and he enjoys success among them, but a measurement of the index of citations will put him in his place if it proves that there is no mention of this person among relevant sources.

Metaphor of the Theater

From the point of view of Sociology, *man is nothing other than his status or the totality of statuses, a status-set*. Contained within the status is a *set of roles*. The totality of statuses, the carrier of which is the same individual, is a totality of role-sets. For that reason, the *metaphor of the theater* lies at the basis of the sociological method. In Shakespeare's words: "All of the world's a stage, / And all the men and women merely players." The personal life of the actor does not exist. The actor lives in his roles. These roles can vary. The same actor can play the villain or the hero, a love-struck youth or a greedy loan shark. That which lies beneath the mask, beyond the limits of the stage, normally interests neither the theater, nor the audience, nor the producers.

It is exactly the same thing in Sociology. The sociologist studies roles and whether they are played well or not. The question "By *whom* are they played?" does not interest him. In any girl, for instance, the sociologist sees an actor and her ability to cope with the roles of beloved, wife, bride, mother, daughter, secretary, future scientist, gymnast, swimmer, cook, etc. In other words, the sociologist sees in a person a set of social statuses.

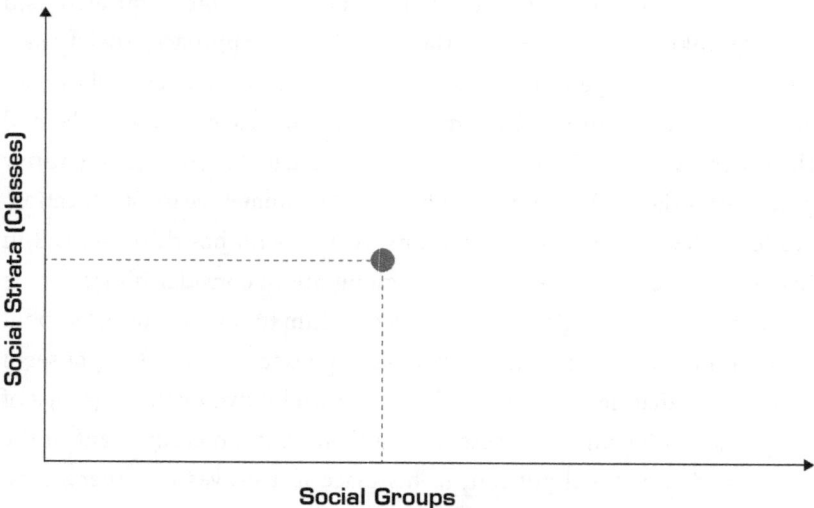

Figure 2. Status in the sociological coordinate axes.

Man as a Derivative from Society

From a sociological point of view, a person is *a derivative of the two axes*. The essence of the sociological person is defined depending on where on the diagram we put the dot. In Sociology, status prevails over personal qualities.

The person is derived because, being a set of statuses, he does not himself create it. He takes it over. He is inscribed into it. It is always created by *something else*.

In Sociology, the person is a product, a result, a detail in an enormous construction. He does not write the drama, nor is he the director. He merely plays roles, which someone else always writes. The person does not build the theater. The theater is unquestionably built: it is called "society." Sociology does not set before itself the task of discovering the originator of society. This is too abstract and philosophical a question. There is an obvious fact: when we look at history, when we deal with people, we always see *society*. We come across it everywhere — in archaic, primitive, and highly-developed peoples. Furthermore, society is always built up on collective, super-individual foundations. Everywhere — both in very complex and in very primitive societies — there exist strata and groups.

Who invented society? Sociologists do not know and do not ask this question. Society is absolute. Society always was, and it was always primary in relation to the person. The person is a product of society, a sociological convention. A person outside of society does not exist as a phenomenon. We know a person only as a *social person*, i.e., as the bearer of social statuses.

Taking this fundamental principle into consideration, we begin to study the "ethnos."

SECTION TWO

Introducing the Concept of "Ethnos"

The Etymology of the Word "Ethnos" and its Synonyms

Ethnos (ἔθνος) is a Greek word meaning "people," along with other Greek synonyms, such as γένος (*génos*), φυλή (*phylé*), δῆμος (*démos*), and λαός (*laós*), all of which have certain semantic nuances.

Ethnos is another name for the *narod*, which gradually became a scientific term.[2] The Greek word *éthnos* is close to the Russian word этос (*etos*), from which the concept of "ethics" is formed. Этос means "disposition," "behavior," "morality." Ethics is a semantic synonym of morals. The archaic Greek root ἔθ (éth-), from which both the words *ethnos* and *ethos* are both descended, meant a populated locale, "a locale in which villages or settlements are found," or "rural settlement," but not "city," inasmuch as the city is a πόλις, a *polis*, from which the term "politics" is derived.

Thus, in the concept of *ethnos* there is combined a spatial notion of a populated (rural) country (ἔθ), the concept of "disposition," "morality" and "custom" (ἔθος) just as it is in the meaning of narod (ethnos). *The ethnos is an organic society, located on a defined territory and distinguished by a common morality.*

A society can be varied: from the intricate (complex) to the simple (primitive). *The ethnos is a simple society, organically (naturally) associated with a territory and bound together by common morality, customs, and symbolic systems.*

---

2   TN: I often transliterate the Russian term "narod" into English as a technical term.

Definition of the Ethnos

In Russian, the term "ethnos" was introduced into scientific use by Sergei Mikhailovich Shirokogoroff (1887–1939), the great Russian ethnologist, founder of Russian Ethnology, who influenced the Russian historian, ethnologist and Eurasianist Lev Nikolaevich Gumilev (1912–1992). This is how Shirokogoroff defined an ethnos:

> An ethnos is a group of people who (1) Speak the same language, (2) Acknowledge their single origin, (3) Possess a complex of customs, ways of life, and preserved and sanctified by tradition, differing from the customs of other groups.[3]

The criterion of customs, sanctified by tradition and differing from other groups, very evidently points to the ethos. That is, the presence of specific traditions, customs, and mores comprises one of the main definitions of an ethnos. Thus, a moral basis is one of the essential aspects of an ethnos, which is based on a unity of mores, on the synchronism of moral valuations.

Let us recall Friedrich Nietzsche's (1844–1900) wonderful observation in his book *The Genealogy of Morals*, wherein he draws attention to the extent to which the mores of different peoples differ from one another.[4] For Christian ethnoses there are truths such as "love your neighbor" and "do not murder." But for the Iranians, for example, the understanding of what is ethical is expressed differently: "it is good to shoot with a bow and to speak the truth." That is to say: *different ethnoses have different ethoses.*

In Shirokogoroff's definition, the complex of customs, way of life, and traditions that characterize a given ethnos necessarily *differ* from those of other ethnoses. In the very definition of ethnos and ethos there is contained the idea of *a plurality of* ethnoses and *a plurality of* ethoses, mores and morals. For that reason, the expression "universal ethnos" is deprived

---

3   Shirokogoroff, S. M. *Ethnos: A Study of the Basic Principles of Change of Ethnic and Ethnographic Phenomena.* Shanghai: 1923.

4   Nietzsche, F. *Genealogy of Morals.* Moscow: Azbuka, 2007.

of any sense, since it has nothing to *oppose* to it. There is no universal ethnos. The ethnos is always concrete.

One can speak of a *global socium* as an artificial sociological and political construction, but it is not possible to speak of a *global ethnos*. It is theoretically possible to imagine a *socium* as something global and universal, but an *ethnos* is always concrete and particular. At the center of the ethnos, as at the center of morality, there always lies the assertion of *a specific system of values*.

Unity of language is another qualitative feature of the ethnos. People, speaking one language, living in the same system of signs, senses, and meanings, delineate a specific *terrain* in the sphere of ideas, mores, psychology, and social relations, which unites them and integrates them along a cultural trait. The ethnos thereby creates a spiritual world, all the participants of which dwell in a *shared space of meaning*.

There is such a phrase as "the Russian world." It describes the borders within which communication in the Russian tongue is possible. Language, as Martin Heidegger said, is "the house of being."[5] And *this house is always ethnic*. Language, the commonality of language, constitutes the unity of a common terrain in the sphere of the spirit. It is not important whether this terrain belongs to one or two countries, or whether political or religious borders lie between ethnoses. If people speak and think in one language, then they find themselves in the space of that ethnos to which the language belongs.

Shirokogoroff spoke of the *acknowledgement* by an ethnos of its single origin. Does a community of people have a single origin or not? From the point of view of sociology and history this is a very difficult question, because almost always peoples, ethnic cultures and traditions turn to the theme of their mythical origins. Plato, for instance, considered himself a descendent of the god Poseidon.

At the source of an ethnos there always lies myth. For instance, Tibetans think that their ancestors were red monkeys and for this reason Tibetans

---

5   Heidegger, M. *Elucidations of Holderlin's Poetry.* SPB: Academic Project, 2003.

are those who consider themselves descendants of red monkeys.[6] Each people has its first-ancestors in culture, and what is important is not whether this ancestor in fact existed or not: nobody knows. Something else is important: how, with what degree of intensity, the ethnos is *aware of* and *experiences* its common origin (be it purely mythological). Many who call themselves ethnically "Russian" are representatives of other (most often indigenous) peoples of the Russian Empire, and this "Russianness" forms an ethnos together with the Russian language and a sense of belonging to Russian culture.

The Ethnos as an Open Community

The reality of the genetic commonality of the roots of descent does not have a big influence on ethnic self-consciousness. For this reason, Shirokogoroff does not speak of a community of people "having a single origin," but specifically of their *"acknowledging"* one. In other words, the ethnos, as it appears from Shirokogoroff's definition, is to a significant extent *a question of choice*. One can *change* ethnoses, because having acknowledged a different origin, expressed loyalty to different first-ancestors, begun to speak in a different language, and taken part in other rituals and customs, a person executes an act of ethnic *transgression*, he moves from one *ethnos* to another.

If a person acknowledges descent from a first-ancestor, a red monkey, professes the Buddhist tradition, learns Tibetan, settles in Tibet and turns the Buddhist prayer wheel, then, from the point of view of the ethnos, he is Tibetan, even if this happened after he completed a degree in Sociology at Moscow State University and set out on an ethnological and religious-studies expedition, deciding never to return from it.

A person can integrate into an ethnos. *The ethnos is an open field.* Even the most closed and most hierarchical ethnos has paths, customs, and normative scenarios for integration into it. *It is possible to enter into an ethnos.*

---

6   Kychanov E.I. & Melnichenko, B.I. *The History of Tibet from Ancient Times to Today.* Moscow: Vost. Lit, 2005.

Let us imagine a situation in which the members of one ethnos lost a little child in the woods, and the members of another ethnos found him, pitied him, and took him into theirs, after which he became a member of *that* ethnos. His ethnic identity will be formed in the new ethnos to which he belongs.

A Definition of Ethnicity

Max Weber, one of the earliest pioneers of sociology, gave a second definition of the ethnos or ethnicity. He asserted that *ethnicity is belonging to an ethnic group, united by cultural homogeneity and belief in a common origin.*[7] We see here a definition analogous to Shirokogoroff's definition, with the only exception being the omission of the theme of language. It is characteristic of Weber's definition, as with that of Shirokogoroff, that the ethnos is defined not simply by a common origin, but by a belief in a common origin. The ethnos is a concept and a volitional decision of the human spirit, and not a biological predetermination (incidentally, the very notion of "biology" demands careful sociological analysis: are explanations of communal regularities through reference to the bodily, zoological or physiological specifics of organisms all that reliable?).

Theories of the Ethnos in Russian Science: Lev Gumilev's Theory of Ethnogenesis

The eminent ethnosociologist and researcher of the ethnos, Lev Nikolaevich Gumilev, was on one hand a follower of Shirokogoroff and, on the other, an adept of the Eurasianist philosophical and culturological school. Nikolaevich called himself "the last Eurasianist."[8] Few have

---

7   Weber, M. *Selected Works*. Moscow: Progress, 1990.

8   Gumilev, L. N. *Historico-Philosophical Works of Prince N. S. Trubetskoi (Notes of the Last Eurasianist)*; Trubetskoi, N. S. *History, Culture, Language*. Moscow: Progress, 1995; *Notes of the Last Eurasianist, Interview with L. N. Gumilev // Our Heritage*. 1991, no. 3.

made as significant a contribution to the study of the ethnos and to the popularization of the concepts "ethnos" and "ethnicity" as Gumilev did.

Gumilev and Shirokogoroff's approaches to the ethnos can be considered tendencies in the framework of one school, which (in contrast to the classical Marxist approach) thinks of the ethnos as an *"organic, vital unity."* It treats the ethnos as a *living being,* a collective, distinct from the separate individual, large and living in the course of an extended period of time. A person is limited by his body, but the possibilities of an ethnos are much broader: it can produce many different bodies. Just as with a living person, however, according to Gumilev, the ethnos has a beginning, an ascent, maturity, a decline, and old age. The lives and fates of the ethnos are composed of such cycles.

Gumilev's main work dedicated to the ethnos is the book *Ethnogenesis and the Biosphere of the Earth.*[9] From the point of view of an approach to Ethnosociology, this is his most serious, profound and consistent writing. Gumilev touched upon the theme of ethnoses in practically all of his historical works, which is why they carry great interest and are fundamental for Ethnosociology.

Yulian Vladimirovich Bromley's Theory of the Ethnos

Another direction in Russian Ethnosociology is connected with the works of the academic Yulian Vladimirovich Bromley (1921–1990), who studied the problems of the ethnos in the context of official Soviet science, based on the dogma of the class-based and economic nature of societies (including archaic ones).[10] In order to stay within the bounds of the acceptable, he had to adjust his studies of ethnic phenomena to the tune of Soviet Marxism, the specifics of the political moment, internationalist rhetoric, and the idea of progress, from which it followed that a phenomenon like the "ethnos" did not exist in the USSR at all, and perhaps, does not in principle exist at the contemporary stage of development of social

9   Gumilev, L. N. *Ethnogenesis and the Biosphere of the Earth.* Moscow: Progress Publishers, 1992.

10 Bromley, Y. V. *Outlines of a Theory of the Ethnos.* Moscow: 1983.

relations in capitalistic—and even more so in socialistic—countries. Bromley's works are practically impossible to read nowadays, since it is unbelievably difficult to break through the very complicated references to Marxist dogma (the meaning of which is almost lost) to reach what he himself wanted to say. Regrettably, this "inarticulateness" is inherent also to the following generation of "ethnologists" in Bromley's school, who are distinguished by a complicated and baseless scholastic terminology and an increased dependence on the political state of affairs (since the ethnic problem is a fairly painful topic for the leadership and society also of contemporary Russia as well), which greatly detracts from the scientific content of their work.

We will look more closely at the Russian sources of ethnosociological sciences and their structure in a separate chapter.[11]

Foreign Ethnosociology

Foreign sociology goes back to one of the early founders of the field, the German sociologist, Max Weber, who introduced the concept of "ethnicity" (*Ethnizität*) into scientific circles.

The first properly ethnosociological school, which also arose in Germany, started to use the term "Ethnosociology." Its founders were Richard Thurnwald (1869–1954) and Wilhelm Mühlmann (1904–1988), who laid down the conceptual basis of this discipline.

A direct analogue to the German school was the American school of *Cultural Anthropology*, founded in the USA by German emigrant Franz Boas (1858–1942). The American school produced a whole constellation of first-rate ethnologists, sociologists, and anthropologists with names recognized world-wide.

In England, Ethnology and Sociology were also inseparably intertwined with the sociological approach. This tradition is connected with Bronisław Malinowski (1884–1942) and Alfred Radcliffe-Brown (1881–1955).

---

11   See Chapter 5.

In France, closest of all to Ethnosociology stands the ethnologist and philosopher, Claude Lévi-Strauss (1908–2009), the founder of "Structural Anthropology."
A more detailed analysis of their ideas will be carried out in a separate chapter.[12]

Ethnos and Race

In some languages ethnos is thought of as a synonym of "race," and ethnic belonging as a synonym of racial belonging. For instance, in German the word "race" (*Rasse*) and "ethnos" (*Ethnos*) have approximately the same meaning. But in a strict sense and in commonly accepted scientific use "race" necessarily indicates *biological cohesion*, the certified fact of belonging to a progenitor. For that reason, a strict definition of "race" does not refer to "belief in a common origin."

For instance, if we are talking about members of a "yellow race," then the persons studied should have a yellow-colored skin, narrow eyes, broad cheekbones, a round face, a specific mark on the sacral bone, noticeable right after the birth of a child (the so-called "Mongolian spot"), firm black hair, and so on. But whether the studied individual considers himself a member of the "yellow race" or not means nothing. In the concept of "race," emphasis is placed on the aggregate of physiological, phenotypic and genetic characteristics. Belonging to a race implies the physiological identification of a bodily organism, proven by some scientific means.

There exist many different methods for determining racial belonging. In the 19th century, theories were based on visual observation (skin color, height, proportions of the limbs of the body, characteristic hair growth and their structure) and measurements of bodily proportions.[13] Within the framework of such an approach, called "Anthropometry," the skull is measured, and the structures of the ears, muscles, and the face are described. Anthropometry includes in itself Cephalometry (measurement

---

12   See Chapter 4.

13   Gobineau, G. A. *Experience of the Inequality of Human Races*. Moscow: Samoteka, 2007.

of the skull), Osteoscopy (the study of the length and breadth of bones) and so on. In the 20th century serologic means started to be employed, based on the study of the structure of blood serum.[14]

More broadly spread at the present time is genetic theory, which traces the racial origins of various people to a common ancestor (the Human Genome Project).[15]

But, however we might relate to these methods from a scientific point of view (and many scientists contest their reliability), they have absolutely nothing to do with the way the ethnos is understood in Ethnology, Ethnography, and Ethnosociology. The ethnos of ethnosociology has no relation to the scientifically (with the help of whatever methods) verified biological and physiological qualities of a person. In a scientific context, the term "ethnos" is used without reference to race. It is not accidental that for both Shirokogoroff and Weber the issue is precisely about "acknowledgement" [TN: avowal] by a human collective of a common origin.

For example, a person considers himself Russian. It is entirely possible that, from a racial point of view, he may belong to an anthropological type altogether uncharacteristic for the main population of Eastern Slavic-Great Russians. But from an ethnic point of view, there can be no doubt that he will be Russian if he considers himself Russian, speaks Russian, thinks in Russian, and is a co-participant in Russian culture. His biological or racial belonging may be extremely vague. But from the point of view of Ethnosociology we are undoubtedly dealing with a member of the Russian ethnos.

Let us now put the question differently: does the ethnos exclude biological cohesion? Of course not. Moreover, when people live near one another, speak the same language, relate to one another closely and often over the course of many generations, start families, and produce children, obvious similarities appear in their features. In ethnic societies, where ethnicity (in the sociological sense, as a unity of language, belief in

---

14 Lenz, F. *Die Rasse als Weltprinzip. Zur Erneuerung der Ethik.* Munchen: Lehmann 1933; Bauer, E., Fischer, E., Lenz F. *Grundriss der menschlichen Erblichkeitslehre und Rassenhygiene.* Munchen: Lehmann, 1921.

15 http://www.ornl.gov/sci/techresources/Human_Genome/home.shtml.

a common origin, common traditions and a shared way of life) is strong, those entering into this ethnos as a rule reproduce others who look like them. But Ethnosociology does not ascribe any substantial or semantic indication to physical resemblance. It studies the structure of society and only society. And the society it studies is an ethnic society, a specific kind of society as ethnos. Moreover, the physiological, biological, zoological and anthropometric components of this society are not only *not* the cornerstone; they are not studied at all, since there are no reliable studies (besides racist nonsense) about their credible connection with social peculiarities.

Ethnos and Nation

Not being a racial category, the ethnos is also neither a political nor a legal category. It is no less important to distinguish the ethnos from the nation than to distinguish it from race.

In Shirokogoroff and Weber's definitions of the ethnos, there is no indication of its political belonging or of its relation to one or another state or any other kind of administrative unit. In the classical understanding of the term, "nation" signifies citizens, united politically into a unified state. For this reason, in French there is an established political term *État-Nation*, "nation-state," which shows that the nation is inseparably connected with the political system of the state, and unites in a specific formation [TN: образование, which can also mean "education" and "constitution"] the citizens of that state.

Not every kind of state is a "nation-state." Nation-states (or national states) are contemporary states of the European type, most often secular and based on the political dominance of the bourgeoisie. Only with respect to the citizens of such a contemporary, secular (non-religious) bourgeois state can we employ the designation "nation" with complete justification. In other situations, this will be an unauthorized transference of one semantic complex onto an entirely different one.

We see the signs of the ethnos in all societies, archaic and contemporary, Western and Eastern, those organized politically and those living communally. But the signs of the nation are found only in contemporary, Western (in their organization), and politicized societies.

We will speak in more detail about the phenomenon of the nation and its relation to the ethnos in a separate chapter.[16]

Ethnos and Society

Now we will look at the relationship between the ethnos and society, which will bring us directly to that fundamental reality studied by Ethnosociology.

Shirokogoroff calls the ethnos "a group of people," and a group of people is a form of organization of society. Thus, we can consider the ethnos a specific form of society. But it is worth paying attention to the following circumstance. Max Weber, who introduced the concept of "ethnicity" into sociological circles, did not give it a special significance and even stated that the category of "ethnos" is in some respects unnecessary, inasmuch as it adds nothing to the classical methods of Sociology. Sociology studies any societies whatsoever, including ethnic ones, with the help of identical scientific instruments, and for that reason the ethnos, as also any other form of society, is considered by it on a universal basis.

Moreover, if we apply to the ethnos the system of coordinates of classical Sociology (see Figure 1), we notice a very interesting regularity. Ethnic society, taken in its pure guise, possesses, as a rule, minimal differentiation (degree of difference) along both axes (X and Y). This means that in the ethnic community both hierarchical stratification (i.e. differentiation according to *strata/classes*) and differentiation according to groups are minimal. The ethnic group equalizes and unites all its members into something whole, single and indivisible. In such a group both differences and hierarchies are brought down to a minimum, and even if they are present, they do not determine ethnicity and its structure, but that which unites the members into a single and indivisible whole does; hence, the equality and unity of all with all in the structure of the ethnos.

---

16   See Chapter 5 of *Ethnos and Society*. London: Arktos, 2018.

The ethnos is a society in which collective identity is maximal, total, and all-embracing. This collective identity completely subordinates to itself all other forms of differentiation.

Weber did not give great significance to "ethnicity" for precisely this reason. His Sociology ("understanding Sociology"), based on the study of individual behavior in the main, is focused on highly differentiated types of society (ancient and contemporary). The ethnos, however, is neither individual nor differentiated. If we place the ethnos on the sociological system of coordinates (see Figure 1) then we get an interesting picture: along both axis y and axis x all values will tend toward zero — in the ethnos, stratification and division into groups is minimal.

From this we can draw two conclusions.

The first conclusion (in the spirit of Weberian or Marxist Sociology, focusing its main attention on class-based and economic differentiation) is this: the ethnos does not merit the special interest of the sociologist since the basic characteristics of society as such are minimal and tend toward zero in it.

The second conclusion, on the other hand, proceeding from the ethnos as the principal matrix on which is built (and from which arises) all of the more complex and differentiated types of society, affirms the ethnic society as basic and fundamental, deserving, for this reason precisely, privileged study. Ethnosociology and Cultural Anthropology hold this position. This very position forms the basis of the discipline of Ethnosociology, which, being conceived of in this way, becomes not an incidental and instrumental branch of general Sociology, but rather opens up as the most important and principal part of sociological knowledge.

The ethnos is the primordial society, which lies at the basis of all societies. In order to underscore the character of the ethnos, fundamental for humanity, the founder of Ethnosociology Richard Thurnwald called his main scientific work *Human Society in its Ethnosociological Foundations.*[17]

---

17   Thurnwald, R. *Die menschliche Gesellschaft in ihren ethno-soziologischen Grundlagen,* 5 volumes. Berlin: de Gruyter, 1931–1934.

Ethnos as Koinon

We can liken the ethnos as the basic form of society to a geometrical point, which, on one hand, gives rise to a plane (space consists of an infinite number of points), and on the other hand does not itself have an area (hence its definition as not having an area). The function of a geometrical point in the formation of space is paradoxical: it gives rise to space, but it is not itself space, since it has no area (or extent).

The relationship of the ethnos to society on the whole is approximately similar. The ethnos gives rise to society and its structures (based on vertical and horizontal differentiation), which possess, correspondingly, non-zero indicators; it lies at the foundation of society and its structures. But the ethnos itself does not have habitual social structures, i.e.; it is society with null-differentiation, similar to a mathematical point with a null-area.

Of course, any physical point that is depicted or taken as a model will have both an area and an extent. But they will be so small that they can be neglected during measurement. It is exactly the same in the case of the ethnos. Any concrete ethnos will have a minimal amount of stratification and division into social groups, but in comparison with other types of society it is possible to disregard them and, theoretically, to think of them as absent. The purport of society is to emphasize and assert collective identity not only as a goal, a project, or a cohesion of separate parts, but as a given, organic fact and the sole possible form of self-identification. Another definition follows from this:

The ethnos is society, the differentiation of which is minimal and tends toward zero or (theoretically) is altogether absent.

In different disciplines, there are special terms that describe the main elements, not resolvable into parts, from which more complex structures are produced. In Physics, they are called "atoms" (literally, "indivisibles"); in linguistics, "semes" (from the same Greek root from which is formed the word "semantics," "the science of meanings"). In phonetics, the "phoneme" is the smallest atom of the acoustic expression of speech. Lévi-Strauss, who studied the structure of myths, proposed the similar term "mytheme," i.e. the minimal and indivisible core of mythological storytelling. A myth is composed of a combination of mythemes. Continuing this line, we can introduce a neologism: "*koineme.*" It is formed from the Greek word κοινόν (*koinón*), which signifies "common," "universal," and also κοινωνία (*koinounía*) — "society," "community." Koineme in this case will mean that indivisible origin that lies at the basis of society, just as a mytheme does at the basis of myth and a seme at the basis of semantics.

In this conception, *the ethnos is a koineme.* Society in the broad sense is formed on an ethnic basis and grows from an ethnic core (most often from several cores) as from a seed.

Holomorphism of the Ethnos

All societies are arranged according to the principle of functionality, also called "*holomorphism*" (from the Greek root ὅλος (*hólos*), "whole," and μορφή (*morphé*), "form"). This means that society contains in itself the paradigm of its own structure in its integral aspect, and if some part is removed from society (one of its members), after some time it will re-establish the missing elements, as a lizard re-establishes its tail. As opposed to mechanisms, holomorphism is inherent to organisms, which are composed of a totality of functions and not details; the shortage of a concrete element is replaced due to the fact that its functional significance is preserved. Society is capable of itself re-establishing its own integrity with reliance on itself and on the basis of its inner resources. That is how the lizard's tail, the newt's leg, and a person's hair or nail grows.

Holomorphism is present in different types of societies to different degrees. But in some societies the processes of the functional replacement of elements occurs quickly and easily, while in others it happens slowly and problematically. The more complex the structure of a society — the higher the level of differentiation of strata and groups — the more complex the question of functional replacement becomes and the more mechanical its procedure. Simple societies re-establish holomorphism automatically. In complex societies, a managing apparatus is required for this.

The ethnos is a type of society in which holomorphism is total and absolute. The ethnos is so trans-individual that it can fail altogether to take note of the loss of an individual or group of individuals, and also not distinguish one individual from another. The being of the ethnos is purely functional; any sign, subject-matter, phenomenon or event is integrated into a general holomorphic structure, in which the whole predominates. Europeans were struck by this characteristic of archaic tribes, capable of trading away their riches for bric-a-brac, or fertile land for cheap ornaments. "Bric-a-brac" and "ornaments" were interpreted in the holomorphic structure of the former's society as something important, whose functional significance could be enormous — something the Europeans missed, having approached the question from their more differentiated and mechanical point of view.

This functionalism of archaic societies was studied in detail by Malinowski and Radcliffe-Brown. Essentially, their reconstructions describe the extreme forms of holomorphism.

Functionality and holomorphism in their extreme expression are the key distinguishing features of ethnic societies. In them the whole (*hólos*) prevails absolutely over the parts, and the particular exists only as a function of the whole; outside the whole, the particular has no meaning, and hence also no being.

SECTION THREE

Ethnos as Concept and Ethnos as Phenomenon

The Subject-Matter and Object of Ethnosociology

In the Russian scientific tradition, there is a rule to divide the subject-matter and object of any scientific discipline. To the extent of the convergence of our scientific approach with the Western one, this rule is constantly called into question, because in the majority of European languages the word "subject-matter" is in meaning and significance entirely identical to the word "object" and is most often denoted by the same expression, derived from the Latin *objectum* (literally, "that which is thrown before [us]"). In German, there is a specific word, *Gegenstand* (literally, "that which is found before [us]"), denoting the same concept, but this is a pure calque from the Latin language. The same is true of the relatively late Russian scientific neologism "subject-matter" (*pred-met*, literally, "that which has been thrown before [us]"). This must be taken into consideration if we are to approach strictly to the definition of Ethnosociology in an international scientific context, at international conferences, symposia, congresses, etc.

In the framework of the European scientific tradition *the object (or subject-matter) of Ethnosociology is the ethnos, studied by sociological methods.*

In the framework of the Russian one, however, we can say that *the object of Ethnosociology is society* and *the subject-matter is the ethnos as a form of society.*

However, the structure of Ethnosociology is not exhausted by the simple application of the sociological method to ethnic societies. The ethnos is not simply another form of society: it is a form that lies at its basis, i.e., a koineme. This is the main thesis of Ethnosociology, as a consequence of which, it can be stated that Ethnosociology is the study by society of its own deepest and most basic foundations, of that point from which space is made, or that seme on which rests the grand edifice of cultural and linguistic meanings. For that reason, we can give yet another definition of the object and subject-matter of Ethnosociology. *The object of sociology is the deep foundations of society, identified as ethnic societies, koinemes; its subject-matter is the structure and arrangement of these foundations.* In the European context, the object and subject-matter can be combined, giving us the following definition: *the object (objectum) of Ethnosociology is the pure, radical structure of society or basic society with a null-dimension, on the basis of which other, more complex types of society historically unfold.*

Thus, Ethnosociology studies the ethnos–not separately but as the basis of society itself— tracing the transformation of the ethnos at different historical stages, including its various dialectical derivatives, which sometimes are not proper ethnoses, but in one way or another (often in the form of direct antagonism) remain connected with it.

Definitions of Ethnosociology That We Should Reject

The contemporary English sociologist Anthony Giddens gives a definition of Ethnosociology as "a form of dual hermeneutics — sociological and ethnomethodological simultaneously."[18] "Ethnomethodology" is a sociological approach, developed by the contemporary American sociologist Harold Garfinkel, which has no direct relation to the ethnos and proposes merely that at the basis of the behavior of members of a society (in a "people" or "the masses") there lies not the chaos of accidental circumstances, experiences and emotions, but a peculiar sociological model, which can be studied scientifically.[19] In his youth, Garfinkel bumped up against the sociological problem of a systematic explanation of the behavior of jurymen, their motivations, logics, etc. In the apparent spontaneity, fortuitousness and groundlessness of decisions Garfinkel saw in the actions of a group of random simple people, not professionals and not specialists, a peculiar logical structure, entirely subject to study. The "ethnos" in this case is nothing more than an extended metaphor for a group of random laymen, connected with one another by practically nothing.

The combination of the classical sociological method and the ethnomethodology of Garfinkel (as Giddens interprets Ethnosociology) is a very productive and promising approach in Sociology, on par with the phenomenological approach developed by the sociologist Alfred Schutz.[20] But this has no relation to the classical conception of Ethnosociology. The ethnos is something entirely different from an accidentally gathered group of laymen for the decision of some artificial (for them) problem.

---

18 Giddens, A. *Central Problems in Social Theories.* London, MacMillan Press, 1979.

19 Garfinkel, H. *Studies in Ethnomethodology.* Englewood Cliffs, NJ: Prentice-Hall, 1967.

20 Schutz, A. *The Phenomenology of the Social World.* Evanston, IL: Northwestern University Press, 1967.

Another famous sociologist, Pierre Bourdieu (1930–2002), under-standing "Ethnosociology" to be something close to Garfinkel's scheme and contrasting Ethnosociology as a discipline, turned to a concrete, em-pirical unit of society, with all its anomalies, deviations, and forms of be-havior, unable to be subsumed under general rules, to forms of Sociology that operate with highly abstract theoretical and normative constructs. Although Bourdieu offered to "erase the borders between Sociology and Ethnology," not only did he not consider the ethnos as the basic instance of society (koineme), but he did not even make it an object of sociological study.

We should recognize the definitions of Giddens and Bourdieu, and others similar to them, as the private opinions of well-known sociologists, all the more so since none of them dedicated a separate book or even a full-fledged essay to Ethnosociology.

The Ethnos as a Phenomenon and the Phenomenological Method

Ethnosociology in its fullest expression operates with the ethnos as a basic *social phenomenon*. The ethnos is both a theoretical concept (the object of Ethnosociology) and a phenomenon that can be observed in real life. For this reason, Ethnosociology bases its conclusions on perceptions of the ethnos as a given and derives theoretical constructions from the study of this given.

If we return to Shirokogoroff's definition, then in the ethnos are dis-tinguished: 1) language, 2) belief in a common origin, 3) the presence of common customs and traditions, culture. In all societies, there are neces-sarily all three components of the ethnos. We know of no society, neither in current period nor in the historical chronicles of its past, that did not have at least one of these three components. For this reason precisely, the ethnos is a basic phenomenon. All societies known to us are, to one degree or another, ethnic.

The phenomenological essence of the ethnos is extremely important to the method with the help of which Ethnosociology studies it. These methods, based on a reliance on the ethnos and its structures and *empathy* ("living into," "feeling into"), are necessary in order to describe, study, and understand the structures of ethnos as adequately as possible.

Different historical schools study the sources of society's origin differently. Aristotle thought that society is built on the basis of the family. Evolutionists see as the source of society a form of development of feral (animal) flocks or herds. Marxists think that society is formed as a superstructure over economic relations, and at its basis lie the phenomena of labour and its instruments. All of these theories suppose that human society as we know it is a product of some other factors.

Ethnosociology approaches this problem differently, phenomenologically speaking. Society is a phenomenon, and at its roots this phenomenon is ethnic. All forms of society known to us today and about which reliable information has been preserved have always had common structural roots. In concrete lived experience these roots are *the society as ethnos*, i.e., a group of people united by language, belief in a common origin, and common traditions. This is confirmed by observation and all forms of verification.

But we cannot see the process of the expansion of the family to the extent of the ethnos (according to Aristotle), trace the transformation of a herd of monkeys into a human collective, or fix the role of the instruments of labour in the establishment of social forms. Ethnoses are simple and complex, archaic and developed, but they are always something other than an extended family, evolved animals or autonomous products of economic activity. For the existence of even the smallest tribe-ethnos at least two lineages (i.e. two big families) are required, as a minimum, as Lévi-Strauss shows. But as concerns the evolutionary hypothesis or Marxist dogma, they are purely theoretical constructions. And on the contrary, the ethnos is an easily verified phenomenon. We see this phenomenon everywhere and always. And it is precisely the ethnos which we see at the sources of the most complex and differentiated societies. It makes itself known even at the most complex stages of development.

For this reason, Ethnosociology, focusing its attention on the ethnos, is dealing with something unconditionally existing, i.e., with a phenomenon.

Phenomenology, both philosophical (Husserl and Fink) and sociological (Schutze), is the privileged method of ethnosociological study. This appears especially clearly in the works of one of the founders of Ethnosociology, Wilhelm Mühlmann, who considered Shirokogoroff his teacher.[21]

Examples of an Ethnos: Contemporary Chechens

Let us give some examples of the ethnos in the contemporary world. We will look at the Chechen ethnos in today's Russia.

What characteristics must Chechens possess, in order to be considered an ethnos? Let us turn once again to Shirokogoroff's definition.

1. Language. There is a Chechen language, which the Chechen people speak. It relates to the Vainakh linguistic group and is very close to the Ingush language. Nevertheless, Chechens themselves, like the Ingush, consider their ethnic languages distinct (despite their objective resemblance), and this is a not insignificant factor in their ethnic self-definition.

2. Chechens believe that they have a common origin, that all of them are descendants of the same tribes, which separated gradually into a few branches. Some Chechens think that they are the direct descendants of Noah, interpreting the self-styling of Chechens *Nokhchi* as "descendants of Noah" (in Arabic, *Noi* [Noah] is pronounced as *nuakh*).[22]

3. Chechens possess a common complex of customs, which are a specific mixture of properly ethnic and religious, Islamic, customs. To this we should add the mystical orientation in Islam of Sufism, which possesses its owns mores, rituals and doctrines. The community of Sufis in Chechnya is called the *wird*. The celebrated round-dances that the Chechens dance is the *zikr*, a

---

21 Mühlmann, W. *Rassen, Ethnien, Kulturen*. Neuwied, Berlin: Luchterhand, 1964.

22 Nukhaev, H.A. *Vedeno or Washington?* Moscow: Arktogaia-Center, 2001.

form of collective Sufi prayer, which is different in every *wird*. The mores, customs and culture of Chechens are a unique combination of purely ethnic, Islamic, and Sufi elements. In the self-consciousness of Chechens themselves, this cultural complex distinguishes them from all other ethnoses and comprises their identity.[23]

At the same time, is it possible to discover in the Chechens a clear expression of a shared racial type? This is impossible. Chechens are tall and short, dark and swarthy, blue-eyed and red-haired, recalling classical Indo-Europeans, and even red-bearded. There is a Mediterranean type, spread over all the Caucasus. There are brachycephalic Chechens, but there are also dolichocephalic ones. It is likely that from the point of view of race, various biological lines and different racial groups combined to form the contemporary Chechen population, as is the case in the overwhelming majority of ethnoses, coming across in waves, one over another, and "settling" in the difficult to reach mountains of the Northern Caucasus. However, Chechens themselves practically do not record the phenotypic differences and variation of types as a decisive or significant factor in the recognition of themselves as an organic unity, i.e., an ethnos.

From the point of view of Ethnosociology, this is the deciding factor. Chechens recognize themselves as an ethnos. Other ethnoses living alongside them also consider them an ethnos. At the same time, all of the signs of the ethnos, according to Shirokogoroff, are present. Hence, we are dealing with an ethnic phenomenon and can study it by ethnosociological means.

Another question: is it possible to consider the Chechens *only* as an ethnos? This assertion will be imprecise, since in addition to ethnic identity there also exist civil, national (the majority of Chechens, excluding the members of the diaspora, are citizens of the Russian Federation), territorial-administrative (they live in the Chechen Republic), and religious (Chechens are predominantly Muslim) identities. But all of these

---

23 Ilyasov, L. *The Culture of the Chechen People*. Moscow: UNESCO, 2009.

other identities are built on top of the ethnic identity. In diverse people these superstructures have diverse meanings, but all who consider themselves Chechens and who consider Chechens different are in the first place united on the deepest level precisely by their ethnic commonality. This is an empirical fact. Through it we meet the *phenomenon of the ethnos* directly. To the extent to which they are, Chechens truly are an ethnos.

What we have said relative to Chechens can be applied to all ethnoses, whether they live in Russia or beyond her borders. They are a phenomenon, and should be studied as such.

The Main Rules of Ethnosociology: The Plurality of Ethnoses and Their Classification

In the course of Ethnosociological research we must follow a set of rules, which are of paramount importance:

On the one hand, when we study an ethnos specifically *as* an ethnos, we apply general criteria to it. Any ethnos in its pure guise is a *simple* society, with the domination of a collective identity, a synchronism of ethnic reactions and exceedingly weak vertical and horizontal differentiation, which corresponds to Shirokogoroff's three indicators. That is, we are dealing with a koineme.

But this common quality of all ethnoses expresses itself in practice in the most variegated and often unexpected forms. Even the simplest ethnoses have a different structure of their simplicity, precisely as the languages humanity speaks have something in common (after all, they are all languages), but at the same time contain a tremendous number of differences.

Consequently, after identifying some ethnos as an ethnos, the ethnosociologist is dealing with a koineme. But this does not yet mean that a koineme in the case of one ethnos will be exactly the same as a koineme in the case of another one. Even the most archaic and simple tribes differ from one another substantially.

Consequently, ethnosociology does not deal with the ethnos but with *ethnoses in the plural*. A koineme differs from more complex social systems, and, at the same time, from other simple koinemes, with other structures of this simplicity.

The first rule of Ethnosociology is to recall the plurality of ethnoses, even in their most radical and simplified foundation.

The second rule concerns the classification of ethnoses. To speak of more or less "developed," "civilized," or "progressive" ethnoses means to take a racist approach in relation to them, to separate them into "higher" and "lower." And even if this racism is not dogmatic or biological and is based on an analysis of technical, economic, or some other kind of criteria, it nevertheless remains racism (even in a veiled and cultured form). This is absolutely unscientific, since in doing so we approach the study of one ethnos from the position of another one, evaluating its condition, values, and social structures with an aloof, extraneous gaze. Such an approach is inadmissible, since the entire structure of the ethnic phenomenon becomes invisible as a result.

Thus, the founder of American Cultural Anthropology (an analogue to Ethnosociology) Franz Boas wrote in his letters from the expedition to the Eskimo-Inuit: "I often ask myself what the superiority consists in which 'developed' society possesses over a society of 'savages,' and I find that the more I study their habits, the more I understand that we simply have no right to look down on them from above. We do not have a right to judge them for their forms and prejudices, however absurd they might seem to us. We 'highly educated people' are much worse than they are..."[24]

The sole correct form of the classification of ethnoses is their placement on the scale "simple–complex." At the same time, the concepts of "simplicity" and "complexity" should not carry anything at all positive or negative; these are two neutral constants, founded on the description of a phenomenon. There are "simple societies" and "complex societies." Neither one is better or worse than the other. They are simply different.

---

24   Cole, D. (ed.) "Franz Boas' Baffin Island Letter-Diary, 1883–1884" / *Stocking, George W. Jr. Observers Observed. Essays on Ethnographic Fieldwork.* Madison, WI: The University of Wisconsin Press, 1983. p. 33.

This is a non-hierarchical classification, fixed on the state of affairs and in no way evaluative of it.

Here we should notice that the simpler a society is, the more ethnic it is, and the more complex it is the less ethnicity comes forth by itself, both on the surface and at a glance. In a simple society ethnicity is obvious; in complex society, it must be looked for. The more complex a society is, the deeper ethnicity is hidden in it and the less apparent it is to superficial familiarity.

The simplest society is a purely ethnic society, which has no content besides the ethnic. Using our terminology, we can say that it is practically identical to the koineme.

The most complex society is one in which the ethnic factor is found on a fundamental level, over which are built a few floors, imposing and striking to the imagination. The attention of the observer is drawn to these floors, and few lower their gaze to the foundation or take an interest in the construction of the basement.

These two rules — the rule of the plurality of ethnoses *and* the rule of the non-evaluative criteria "simple-complex" *are the basic principles of ethnosociology.*

The Ethnos and the Lifeworld

The ethnos cannot be considered in isolation from the surrounding environment. The ethnos always lives in a concrete space, and this space is integrated into its own structure; it is apprehended, transformed, and dwelt in by it.[25] Gumilev referred to it as "[an] accommodating landscape," emphasizing that the ethnos in its existence is a single whole with the surrounding environment, and their interaction [TN: inter-influence] lies at the basis of the different phases of an ethnos' transformation.

The philosopher and founder of phenomenology Edmund Husserl introduced the very important concept of a "lifeworld" (*Lebenswelt*), which is a set of arrangements and acts of consciousness that are not subject

25 Lefebvre, H. *La production de l'espace*. Paris: Anthropos, 1974. See also Dugin A.G. *Geopolitics*. Moscow: Academic Project, 2010.

to logical verification along the lines of subject-matters and phenomena found opposite a person, i.e., objects.[26] The "lifeworld" is contrasted with the "scientific world," with its conception of *what* is "real" or "objective," and *what* "imaginary" or "subjective," where consciousness ends and material begins, etc. The "lifeworld" does not know such stringency and simply identifies thought with reality, representations and models with that which actually is. For this reason, the "lifeworld" does not distinguish between a person and that in which he lives, i.e., his surroundings, understanding both one and the other as an *integrated whole*.

The "lifeworld" is the *only world* in which the ethnos lives. Simple society (the koineme) is built precisely in this manner. There are no borders in it between culture and nature, the inner and the outer. A person and his surrounding environment comprise an indissoluble unity, a common "living space." The "lifeworld" is that floor on which the ethnos dwells. In simple societies, this floor is the sole one; in complex ones, other floors are built on top of it.

From the point of view of ethnosociology, the identity of the "lifeworld" with the ethnic space is fundamental.[27]

An Example of the Space of the Ethnos: The Lezghins

Let us see how this is expressed in practice. We'll take the contemporary Caucasian ethnos of the Lezghins as our example.

The Lezghins have their own language, belief in a common origin and shared traditions: we are dealing with a classic ethnos.

The space in which today's Lezghins live is from an ethnic point of view something *unified* (*edinoe*). It is an accommodating landscape, "native places" for the Lezghins, situated in the mountainous regions of the Caucasus.

---

26 Husserl, E. "Philosophy as a Rigorous Science" / *The New Yearbook for Phenomenology and Phenomenological Philosophy II*. London: Routledge, 2002. Pp. 249–295.

27 See Chapter 1 of *Ethnos and Society*. London: Arktos, 2018.

But according to a territorial-political division, the Lezghins today reside partly in Dagestan and partly in Azerbaijan. Dagestan is a subject of the Russian Federation. In Azerbaijan, the Lezghins are citizens of Azerbaijan, subject to its laws and are considered Azerbaijanis from the point of view of the nation. Lezghins living in Dagestan are citizens of Dagestan and accordingly of the Russian Federation. These Lezghins are Russians (by citizenship), the others, Azerbaijanis (by citizenship).

Legally, Russians (by citizenship), whether they are Lezghins or Great Russians, and Azerbaijanis (by citizenship), whether they are an ethnic majority of Azerbaijanis or ethnic minority, are entirely different categories, which comes about as a result of their being two different sociopolitical organizations, the Azerbaijani and the Russian (i.e. as politico-legal nations, not ethnicities). The legislation of the Russian Federation and of the Republic of Azerbaijan are such that in neither of these countries is it written in the passport of Lezghins that they are Lezghins. It turns out, then, that a Lezghin who lives on one side of the border and his own brother living on the other side of the border are legally members of two different societies and two different political, national, and administrative spaces, while their kinship is not recorded anywhere. One group must know Russian in order to be normal citizens; the other, the Azerbaijani language. Legally the house and lot of one group of Lezghins is anchored to one territorial-administrative unit; the house and lot of the other, to a completely different one. Furthermore, they live according to different laws, in different societies, and in different spaces. The fact that they are Lezghins finds no expression anywhere.

Nevertheless, outside of direct legal rules and legislations the Lezghins themselves clearly recognize their ethnic unity, their integrity and indivisibility. And the earth on which they live — on both sides of the border — is considered by them as a common earth, as "native places," the Motherland. Surrounding ethnoses on both the Russian and Azerbaijani sides and in Dagestan also recognize the Lezghins as an ethnic unity, by their silence, and they develop special relations with them and with the territories in which they traditionally dwell.

Thus, a structured ethnic space is independent of legal, national, and administrative-territorial borders.

A question arises. If we should want to formalize the Lezghin ethnos, to interpret and describe the structure of Lezghin territories, to which means should we have recourse? The status of the ethnos is not registered in any legislation of the national governments and is not a legal category. But this means that the ethnic space, too, has no legal meaning. Nor is the ethnos (in our case, the Lezghins) a political category. The sole instrument for the description, study and understanding of the ethnos and ethnic spaces is *Ethnosociology*. No other discipline is able to cope with this problem correctly and by means of a strictly scientific apparatus.

CHAPTER TWO

The Fundamental Concepts, Instruments, and Methods of Ethnosociology

SECTION ONE

The Basic Concepts of Ethnosociology (Types of Society)

The Concepts and Terms of Ethnosociology

Ethnosociology operates with a set of specific concepts and terms, which in other contexts, and all the more so in common use, might have an entirely different meaning. Thus, we should emphasize these terminological peculiarities and describe the semantic structure of these basic concepts. Then it will merely be a technical problem to correlate the terms and concepts of ethnosociology with classical sociology and political science. Otherwise, a confusion of concepts might arise.

In this chapter, we shall describe the basic concepts and terms of ethnosociology and give their definitions.

The Problem of a Synonymous Set

Let us begin with the concept of the ethnos, the definition of which we gave in the previous chapter. The definitions of Shirokogoroff and Weber, and also the group of additional examples given, reveal the ethnos as a phenomenon with which Ethnosociology operates. The ethnos understood in this way is a scientific concept. At the same time, this concept has as its referent in the world surrounding us a concrete phenomenon. In other words, the concept of the ethnos is phenomenological and is developed not as an abstraction but as the product of scientific observation, as something derived from the phenomenon itself. In a certain sense the ethnos is an empirical concept. We live in a world in which there are ethnoses and we take them as the basis of our theorization.

At the same time, in common use, the term "ethnos" is used very loosely: as a synonym of people, peoplehood, the nation, nationality, and race. We add to this the shades of meaning that these words acquire in their translation into European languages. In the last chapter, we listed the set of Greek synonyms of the concept "ethnos": *génos, phylé, démos, laós.* Latin gives us two words, populus and natio, from which are formed the majority of the corresponding words of contemporary European languages (the English "people" and "nation," the French *peuple* and *nation,* the Italian *popolo* and *nazione,* and the Spanish *pueblo* and *nación,* as well as the German *Nation,* etc.). The synonymy of this set, to which we could add various derivatives, is rather subtle: all its members indicate approximately the same phenomenon, but in each case and in each linguistic context there occurs semantic shifts, which essentially change the meaning of the word. All of this gives rise not only to numerous problems in political journalism, debates, and discussions, where this terminology is employed freely, but also in scientific circles, in particular in sociology, where the meaning of these words is also modified substantially depending on the national context, the school, or even the specific author. Sometimes different phenomena are indicated by the same term; other times, the same phenomenon is given different names.

The Structure of Basic Ethnosociological Terms and Concepts

Ethnosociology establishes in its sphere a strict semantic structure and gives each term only one concrete meaning. This allows for the systematization of ethnosociological studies as a whole and gives them the necessary scientific rigor.

In Ethnosociology, the above-listed synonyms are not synonyms at all. Each word is a term and indicates an entirely distinct phenomenon. Thus, we get a specific ethnosociological taxonomy of social phenomena and a structure, which lies at the basis of the entire discipline.

The basic concepts of the ethnosociological taxonomy are the following chain:

Ethnos — narod (the Greek *laós*, the German *Volk*) — nation (the Latin *natio*) — civil society — global society — post-society or post-modern society.

Each of these concepts has a strictly defined meaning and sense, which does not overlap with any of the others. This chain can be depicted in the form of *logical* succession, which in the case of Western society coincides on the whole with historical succession:

Ethnos → narod → nation → civil society → global society → post-society

In order to elucidate the structure of the ethnosociological method, we should also arrange these concepts hierarchically. But inasmuch as this hierarchy, as we showed in the previous chapter, describes only the degree of complexity of a society and nothing else, it is built on the principle "from simple to complex," from less differentiated to more differentiated. At the same time, we can describe this hierarchy as a vector directed from the organic and integral to the mechanical, combined, and complex.

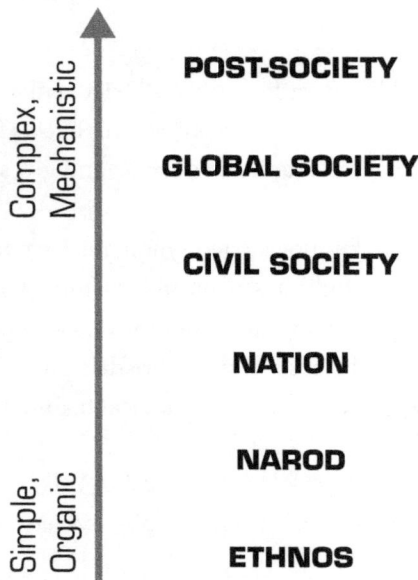

Figure 3. The main ethnosociological concepts in their hierarchical order.

Identity and Identification

For an introduction into the essence of the ethnosociological problematic we offer a preliminary description of the basic ethnosociological concepts, which will be considered in detail in the corresponding chapters and sections of the book.

It is convenient to do this through a consideration of the way the identity of a society changes during transition from one ethnosociological category to another.

But first let us define *identity* and the process of *identification*.

Identity is a form of identification of an individual, social group, or entire society with a certain independent structure — whole, collective, or individual. The term "identity" is formed from the Latin pronoun *id*, "that" (*to*). Hence the Russian copy "тождество" (*tozhdestvo*). The "identical" is the "то же (самое)," (we might say the *id-enti*, the being-that-thing).

The structure of identity is based on the act of "identification," i.e., the conscious or unconscious act, in the course of which someone (an individual, group, or society) asserts, "I (we) am that." In the process of identification there is asserted the content, structure, meaning, and significance of "that" with which the unit identified itself, and through this act the unit that identifies itself with something describes its own content, structure, meaning, and significance. Identity is a property of human consciousness; animals and other forms of life do not know this operation. A bird is a bird, but this fact is not for it a fact of consciousness; a bird does not assert in a voluntary and conscious manner its belonging to the type "bird." Being a bird, it does not have a "bird identity." Only man executes an act of identification — first and foremost of self-identification. He determines himself, his being and his meaning through appeal to "that" (id); he invests "that" with content, and directs this content towards himself. He can reflect upon this process or carry it out unconsciously, but in either case, it is consciousness that is active in this process, whether actively (with the involvement of reason), or passively (automatically).

Ethnic Identification: *Do Kamo*

The basic form of collective identity, inherent in all types of societies, from the simplest to the most complex, is ethnic identity. This means that a person answering the question "Who am I?" responds "I am an ethnos." In this case, the "that" (*id*) coincides with the concept of the *ethnos*.

The peculiarity of ethnic identity is its utter impersonality. In the ethnos, there are organic ties between all members; all share a language, belief in a common origin, and common customs. In the ethnos, the collective identification of all its members with one another and with common (often mythological) ancestors (totems, spirits, chiefs, fetishes, etc.) is so great that the individual principle almost does not exist at all. The ethnos itself as the "that" prevails entirely over all other possible responses to the question "Who am I?" This very question is formulated in the structure of the ethnos as "Who are we?," and the substance of the answer indicates a sort of all-embracing, indivisible and global *whole*. This whole is the ethnos.

Such ethnic identification manifest itself must vividly in some archaic tribes with a very specific, systematic notion of their own beginning. The ethnologist and sociologist Maurice Leenhardt (1878–1954) studied this theme in detail in his famous book dedicated to the phenomenon of *Do Kamo*.[1]

Leenhardt studied the Melanesian ethnos of the Kanak in New Caledonia and discovered that among the Kanaks there was no word for the indication of the individual "I." In different cases when the majority of languages proposes the utterance "I," "to me," "mine," etc., the Melanesians utter *Do Kamo*, which means "a living being," "that which lives." *Do Kamo* is the person, the group of people, the clan, the fetish-snake on the head gear of the chief, whose wife addresses him also as *Do Kamo*.

Then Leenhardt noticed that Melanesian youths never walked around alone, but always in groups. And speaking of themselves, they always appealed to *Do Kamo*, which indicated their group as a *common, indivisible being*. Even when they met with girls the Melanesian youths went in small groups, as did the girls. The Kanaks do not have a notion of the individual body; for them the body is the "clothing of *Do Kamo*."

If we were to ask a Melanesian what *Do Kamo* represents and what he is like "in himself," he will shrug his shoulders in perplexity. *Do Kamo* is *he who is*, he is not explained through anything else. But it is possible to be deprived of *Do Kamo*. If a person carries out some crime or offence, he is thrown out of the social structure, he loses his status. After this he has no name, no being. This is the most frightening thing for a Melanesian, to become a social outcast, to lose *Do Kamo*. This is much worse than death, since in the social context a deceased member of society becomes a spirit and continues to live in other parts of the clan; i.e., *Do Kamo* is preserved. To lose *Do Kamo* means *to disappear without a trace,* even if biological individuality still remains.

---

1   Leenhardt, M. *Do Kamo la personne et le mythe danse le monde melanesien*. Paris: Galimard, 1947.

In this case by the figure of *Do Kamo* the tribe of the Kanaks describes the phenomenon of the ethnos, the synthesizing "that" with which they identify themselves. The Melanesian tribe has its name for that which ethnosociology calls the ethnos and ethnic identification.

The Inner Structure of the Ethnos: Family, Lineage,[2] Clan

Before we move to more complex types of society than ethnic society, let us consider the structure of the inner core of the ethnos.

Ethnosociology equates the ethnos with the koineme, since there are no independent societies that might have a scale smaller than the ethnos. But this does not mean that the ethnos has no divisions within itself. It has them, but these divisions — which are various and often placed on top of one another — do not yet form an independent social structure. They always remain part of something else, from which they draw the fundamental paradigms and meanings of their existence. The most minimal form of society is precisely the ethnos, while those parts into which it is divided are not autonomous or self-sufficient; that is to say, they are not full-fledged societies in their own right, but only parts of a larger whole (the ethnos).

A koineme may have parts and, moreover, must have them, but it is not *composed* of these parts mechanically. A koineme is holomorphic and holistic in itself, but its inner divisions are properties of its organism.

Let us take for example the biological structure of a human organism. This organism necessarily has organs, but these organs have meaning only in a whole organism. Independently the organs are not organisms. Parts of the body do not grow from one another, for instance the head from the neck, the neck from the shoulders, etc. They exist all together as the structure of an integrated organism, which lives fully only when all its organs are present.

---

2   TN: The Russian word is *rod.*

It is the same with the ethnos. This is the primary social unit. It is autonomous and vital, but inside of it function various vitally important elements.

We can distinguish as functional instances in the ethnos *the lineage, the clan, and the family.*

There are various taxonomies of the inner segmentation of the ethnos. Thus, L. N. Gumilev distinguishes the *"subethnos," "consortia,"* and *"convictia."*[3] Certain schools of anthropologists and sociologists make more detailed and nuanced taxonomies, but we will limit ourselves to the most common.

The most basic social cell of the ethnos is the *family*, consisting of a husband and a wife, along with their progeny (the nuclear family), and in some cases their parents and relatives (extended family). Family types vary widely: monogamous (one husband, one wife), polygamous (one husband, numerous wives), and polyandrous (one wife, numerous husbands). The types of extended families can also vary widely, depending on where the newly married couple traditionally dwells (in the house/village of the husband's parents, or with the wife's parents, etc.).

The structure of the family in all societies, without exception, is based on an *exogamous* principle. This is fixed in common for all types of societies by the fundamental socio-generative *prohibition of incest*, i.e., marriage between the members of one family. We do not know of any societies built on another principle. And partial deviations from this norm are met with only as episodes of social history, most often in specific castes (Egyptian Pharaohs) or specific religious cults (some forms of Iranian Zoroastrianism). We should consider separately *levirate* and *sororate*, specific marriage institutions, securing the rights of the remaining brothers to the wife of one of them and the symmetrical right for the husband of one of a number of sisters.

The exogamous principle of the family assumes the existence of at least *two lineages*, without which it is not possible. (The Russian word *rod* corresponds terminologically exactly to the Greek *génos* and the Latin

---

3   Gumilev, L.N. *Ethnogenesis and the Biosphere*. Moscow: Progress Publishers, 1990.

genus). It is for this reason precisely that the family is not considered the primary cell of society. In order to get one family, it is necessary to have two *lineages* and an exogamous rule of marriage. But two lineages and the exogamous rule is the minimal format of the ethnos as that instance which precedes both the lineage and the family. *A family can be formed only on the basis of two unrelated lineages.* This is the absolute law of society as such.

The family and the lineage are connected by a fundamental *regularity*, which, according to Lévi-Strauss, comprises the unique figure of each concrete society with all its original cultural characteristics — myths, rites, basic attitudes relating to the surrounding environment, taxonomy of things, social institutions, etc.[4] Lévi-Strauss asserts that in illiterate societies the institution of marriage makes of the basis of "text" and the paradigm of culture. The concrete way in which the problem of the relationship between the family and the lineage is decided, which kinds of marriages are considered permissible and which not, how which lineage one's progeny belong to is determined (whether by a matrilineal model or a patrilineal one), where a young couple is placed (in the genus of the father — patriarchal model — or in that of the mother — matriarchal model), what norms exist in the relations between brother-in-law and sister-in-law, etc. — all this is the key to the myths and rituals, the philosophy and culture of the ethnos.

The ethnos as a koineme in its most minimal version consists of two lineages. This duality of lineages comprises the fundamental feature of the ethnos. For this reason, the majority of ethnoses preserve this duality even in the case that the scope of the ethnos is increased. The ethnos is divided into two halves in order to preserve the conditions for exogamy — one half must be *alien* for the other half, in order to assure a legitimate marriage.

It is customary in ethnosociology and anthropology to call the union of a number of lineages a *clan*. The word "clan" derives from the Celtic *clann*. Its closest analogue is the Greek φυλή (*phylé*).

---

4   Lévi-Strauss, C. *Les structures élémentaires de la parenté*. Paris: Mouton, 1967.

Clans can be organized in several different ways: as a number of lineages within which marriages are forbidden (in which case a clan is an expanded mode of a genus), or as a number of lineages within which marriages are permitted (in which case the clan represents the ethnos in miniature). Despite the fact that the presence of clans in the ethnos complicates its structure, it does not introduce into it anything substantial. This complication does not bear a decisive ethnosociological load and only increases the scale of the lineage or ethnos. The presence of clans and the structures is necessary must be taken account of, but their significance should not overshadow the identification of the most important elements to which ethnosociological analysis reduces — the detection in the ethnos of the deep organization of the structure of kinship (*rodstvo*).

We can propose the following structural formula:

Exogamous clan = *lineage* (expanded)
Endogamous clan = *ethnos* (minimal)

For this reason, the category of clan is useful, but it is not fundamental for the structure of ethnosociological knowledge.

The inner structure of the simplest ethnos can be represented by the following figure:

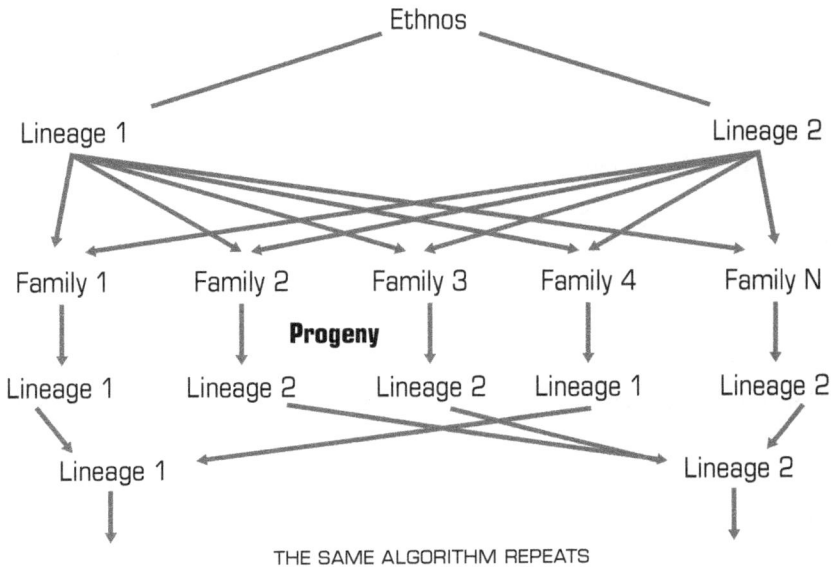

Figure 4. The structure of kinship in the simplest ethnos.

The Ethnos and the Lineage-Identity: Twin-Myths

We spoke in the first chapter about the differences in the definitions of ethnos and race. On the basis of the analysis of the inner structure of the ethnos, always consisting of two halves, we can introduce yet another additional consideration concerning the problem inherent in the notion of a "common origin."

A person born into an ethnos and identifying himself entirely with it at the same time identifies himself necessarily with some single lineage, which is foreign with regards to another lineage. Consequently, inner ethnic identity, presupposing belief in an ancestor *common to all,* is superimposed on lineage-identity, which presupposes *belonging* to the posterity of the founder of one lineage and *non-participation* in the posterity of the founder of another one. If ethnic identity integrates all the members of an ethnos, the lineage-identity differentiates them.

This is often expressed in the veneration of the figure of twins, but also in diverse figures and signs in which a dual symmetry is traced. Twins resemble one another, and for the archaic consciousness this is the same as their being identical. But, at the same time, they are different as individuals. In the figure of twins, we are dealing with the most universal symbol of a double identity. Half of the tribe are the progeny of one twin; the other half of the other. The primordial twins find themselves in a complicated relationship to one another: they are brothers and for that reason are united in their genus. But in order to give rise to two foreign (non-lineage) lineages, they must be antagonistic. Hence, the variety of plot-lines about twins, one of whom was a god, the other a person (for instance Castor and Pollux in Greek mythology). Many myths tell of a deadly battle of twins with one another and of the murder of one by the other. Herein lies the origin of the rather frequently encountered rite of the murder of one of two twins immediately after birth in archaic tribes and the many legends that give supernatural powers to the twins.

In totem models this is manifested in the erection of two exogamous halves of the tribe to different mythical ancestors, between whom there was most often enmity, rivalry, or at least a certain degree of imbalance: hierarchy, for instance.

The paradigm of the dual origin (as a minimum) of all its members is already contained within a tribe. And care concerning the maintenance of exogamy as the guiding paradigm of the ethnos as a whole is constantly shown in the fact that this distance between lineages was preserved and was not erased. Thus, the myth of a common origin at the level of the ethnos was doubled into a myth of different origins at the level of the tribe.

The ethnos integrated, the genus differentiated, creating on the level of the koineme, i.e., the simplest social form, a dialectic of identity, where commonality and difference were joined with one another.

But in exactly the same way as it is difficult to prove by strictly scientific means the physiological proximity of the members of an ethnos to one another, it is sometimes difficult also to prove difference of lineage. The problem is that belonging to a lineage is a social, not a biological category.

A child is born to a couple, each member of which surely belongs to different lineages. With which of the lineage the child should be associated is a complicated problem, constituting the basis of the cultural paradigm of the ethnos. Different ethnoses have different opinions about this matter. But in being associated with the lineage, for instance, of the father, a person becomes a "stranger" in relation to the lineage of his mother; "stranger" [TN: foreigner, alien] in the sociological sense, whereas biologically he is a relative of both the paternal and maternal lineages. For this reason, for justifications of differences of lineage there is recourse to belief in different ancestors, to myth and rites, called upon to aggravate this difference.

All of this finds rich expression in twin plot-lines and in the even more extensive domain of dual myths, which most often have a social function in the organization of an exogamous marital structure.

The all-ethnic myth of kinship, which most likely never factually was, is doubled into lineage-myths of foreignness (which is equally doubtful). And even if it is difficult to prove both one and the other on the physical and genetic (i.e., racial) level, on the level of social fact they remain irrefutable and absolute. The ethnos as the most basic form of society is built on the dialectic of a dual ethno-lineage identity.

Narod as an Ethnosociological Category

In ethnosociology the concept of *narod* differs essentially from the concept "ethnos." The narod is a social organization of society, qualitatively more *complex* than the ethnos.

We shall use the Greek word λαός (*laós*), since it is the most suitable in its meaning for the description of the narod as an ethnosociological category. For the Greeks, the concept of *laos* was the notion of a group of people united either by common participation in a military campaign or simply organized for some particular purpose.

The ethnos is static. The laos is mobile. The laos is a more artificial, goal-oriented, and organized community than the ethnos. The laos can be likened to a militia. That is, to a group of people mobilized for the attainment of some historical and most often military goal. It is the Greek term laos which most of all corresponds to the German *Volk* and the Russian *narod*. It is significant that the Russian word *polk* ("regiment") is related to the German in its derivation. The meaning of an organized collective, in the first place a military one (regiment), corresponds exactly to the concept of "narod."

Some ethnosociologists, for instance Shirokogoroff, do not use this term, considering it unnecessary, but we will see later that it is so helpful in regularizing various ethnosociological constructs, that it is indispensable and crucial. Moreover, the absence of this concept in ethnosociological theories results in many terminological and conceptual misunderstandings, contradictions, and unjustified semantic shifts. The introduction of the concept of the "narod" (λαός, *populus*, *Volk*, etc.) is necessary for the orderliness of the whole ethnosociological theory. Without this key concept there shall inevitably occur the interference of meanings, which creates insurmountable noise on the path of development of a full-fledged and high-quality scientific theory.

The presence of the concept of "narod" is of principal importance for Ethnosociology. Where this term is introduced in the corresponding way with a strictly defined meaning, we are dealing with Ethnosociology as a full-fledged scientific discipline and independent theory. Where it is absent, however, in the best case we are dealing with a prolegomenon to real Ethnosociology, and in the worst case, with recycled, patchy, fragmented, and disorganized studies and methods at the conjunction of Classical Sociology, Ethnology, and Ethnography. But such syncretism does not yet represent a scientific discipline, possessing a scientific character. The delayed institutionalization of Ethnosociology in Russia and elsewhere is connected to this very fact. Lowering from sight the category of the narod, we deprive ourselves of the possibility of developing a full-fledged theory. We shall see later why this is the case.

The integrity of the *ethnos* is disturbed in the *narod*. The structure of society becomes qualitatively ten times more complex. Social stratification and the separation of distinct social groups arise. In the narod there are classes and differentiated professional and other social gradations. The process of the division of labor begins.

The narod is the ethnos that has stepped into history. Instead of *eternal return*, a perpetual cycle supported by myth, other forms of temporality emerge. The most striking of these is *linear time.*

In the narod the separation of different social strata, which are isolated from one another, begins. In each stratum, there develops its own sociological idiosyncrasies. Often the strata acquire the form of fixed castes. To move from one caste to another is difficult and almost impossible. The institute of slavery and the practice of wage labor take place.

The system of myths and rituals changes qualitatively. They are also differentiated according to the caste principle. *If tales and myths are characteristic of the ethnos, then the epic is so for the narod.*

The distinctions between the sexes become more distinct, often in the form of a patriarchy that becomes standard.

In the formation of the narod there necessarily always participate a few ethnoses — two or more. The narod is never formed by way of the quantitative growth of an ethnos. The specific character of the narod consists in the fact that at its basis lies the contact between at least two ethnoses (and most often, many more than two). In the course of complex sociological, political and economic procedures one of the ethnoses or groups of ethnoses forms the higher stratum; another ethnos (or group of ethnoses) forms the lower one. Thus, the basis of the sociological categories elite and *masses* are formed.

The Narod Is the First Derivative of the Ethnos

Though it is not the ethnos in its purest form, the narod yet maintains an organic connection with it. In the narod there is an ethnic slice, an ethnic dimension, but henceforth it is not the sole component. The narod as a specific historical form of society contains in itself the ethnos (as the timeless form of society), but it is not encompassed by it. We can imagine the narod (or the laos) as a two-floored building. The first story is the ethnos as a concept, and most often ethnoses as phenomena (in the plural). The second floor is the narod proper, i.e., that new thing which is contained only in it and not in the ethnos.

"Narod" is an ethnosociological category, determined by a number of parameters.[5]

Identity in the narod is more complicated than identity in the ethnos. If impersonality and the collective, an authority containing everything in itself (for instance *Do Kamo* in the Melanesian tribes) were dominant in the ethnos, in the narod there is both a collective and an individual identity. The individual identity, however, is not thought of as something common, but as exclusive, as a prerogative of heroes, chiefs, outstanding personalities — generally, of the elite. In the structure of the narod the collective identity is the most widespread and popular,, while the individual identity is rare and elite.

Thus, the process of self-identification for the society as a whole becomes significantly more complicated. The model of the ethnos as a whole and of the lineage as a part is supplemented by a scale of stratification and division into social groups, which becomes additional instances of identity.

Now, besides the identity of the ethnos and the lineage, a response to the question "Who am I?" or "Who are we?" (the question "Who am I?" now has validity) needs to make reference to caste, profession, and location.

From a koineme a socium is formed, as a myth of formed of mythemes. Mythemes, koinemes, or the words of a language are quantitatively limited, but the number of their combinations in myths, societies, or speeches is limitless.

---

5   See Chapter 4 of *Ethnos and Society*. London: Arktos, 2018. See also Dugin, A. G. *Sociology of the Imagination: Introduction to Structural Sociology*. Moscow: Academic Project. Pp. 338–344.

The Narod's Three Forms of Creation: The State, Religion, & Civilization

The ethnosociological category "narod," when it appears as a historical phenomenon, necessarily produces the following forms:

- The State

- Religion

- Civilization

These forms can exist in sequence (history provides examples of every sequence), or they can exist all together or in any other combination whatever. The presence of society as a narod allows for the transition from one form to another. Precisely the narod provides these forms with continuity, steadiness and actuality.

Every time a narod lets its existence be known, it does this by means of the creation of one of these forms or a few of them simultaneously. The narod does not show itself independently, but only through these forms. As a result of this, circumstances are such that many historical and sociological schools lose sight of the narod as an ethnosociological phenomenon, since its essence and its structure are concealed behind other phenomena, more obvious and worthy of study: states, religions, and civilizations. The narod is hidden behind these forms, and in order to uncover it, it is necessary to undertake certain efforts, which are sometimes shattered against the dogmatic devices of one or another scientific or ideological school. Marxists gravitate towards an economic interpretation of the nature of the state. Liberals see individuals, market institutions, and contracts in everything. Political scientists and historians throw themselves into the study of political regimes. Theologians focus on dogmas and institutions. Culturologists immerse themselves in the comparison between civilizational styles. In the course of all these approaches, the unity of the social system (society as narod) standing behind all of these phenomena disappears. If other disciplines also elaborate consistent constructions, ignoring the category of "narod," then for Ethnosociology this omission is fatal and represents the missing link because of which Ethnosociology as a discipline is destroyed.

Reversibility of the Relations of Ethnos and Narod

We see in history that the relations between two forms of society, the ethnos and the narod, are interconvertible. The emergence of the narod out of the ethnos (out of numerous ethnoses) is one direction of the ethnosociological process. But the narod can also disintegrate into ethnoses — as a rule, new ones. This is the reverse direction. Thus, the correlation "ethnos-narod" is *reversible*.

The process of the emergence of the narod from ethnoses and the disintegration of narods into new ethnoses is a system of historical cycles. The ethnos is a koineme, i.e., the most basic structure of society. The narod is a more complex structure, consisting of a few koinemes arranged in a hierarchical sequence. The disintegration of a narod (state, civilization, and religion) into its elements brings new koinemes to life. At the same time, we should note that in the composition of a narod ethnoses often change to such an extent that after the disintegration of the narod there occurs not a return to the old ethnoses, but the appearance of new ethnoses, although in some cases the old ethnoses are preserved. Concurrently at least one ethnos is changed irreversibly, the one that was the *core* of the formation of the narod. After existing as the core of the narod the ethnos does not return to its previous historical form, and new ethnoses are formed instead of it.

We can trace this in the example of the Greek civilization. Ancient Greeks were a narod, consisting of a number of ethnoses and having produced a specific Mediterranean civilization. When the civilization disintegrated, various new ethnoses appeared in its place, but the core of the Greek civilization (the population of the Peloponnesus and Balkans) was transformed into an entirely new ethnos, of whom modern Greeks are the representatives.

The narod that created the Roman Empire was built around three ethnic groups (Ramnes, Tities, Luceres — *tribus*, which later became the

English word "tribes") and gradually received the general name "Roman" or "Latin," i.e., "residents of Latium," the "core" of the Roman Empire. The history of Rome knew many very complex ethnic transformations, but after its disintegration, entirely new ethnoses appeared in its borders, including Italy. The disintegration of a massive structure, formed by a narod, engendered an entire series of new koinemes, although some ethnoses (as a rule, on the periphery of the empire) were preserved from ancient times unchanged (for instance, the Basque).

Narodnost Is Not an Ethnosociological Category

If "narod" is a crucial ethnosociological category, then the concept of "narodnost'" derived from it (in the sense of a "minor" or "small narod") has no special significance. For ethnosociology it is not important whether a narod is quantitatively large or small: in any case, it is always bigger and more complex both qualitatively and quantitatively than the ethnos. The ethnos is a koineme; the narod (laos) is derived from it. And it does not matter whether we are talking specifically about a big or small narod. The narod is an ethnosociological status. From the point of view of ethnosociology, narodnost is an empty term. It can have a certain contextual meaning, strictly one of two: either people mean by it "ethnos," or indeed the "narod" (in the ethnosociological sense), but small in its quantitative composition or having lost some of its qualitative characteristics (statehood, religiosity, civilizational identity). But in the case of its having lost its qualitative characteristics a "narod" or its fragments (parts) can be transformed anew into an "ethnos," since the processes of complication and simplification of social systems is in principle reversible. Thus, strictly speaking, in the majority of cases when the word narodnost is used, it should be replaced with the more concrete, substantial and unambiguous term "ethnos." If in some specific cases it is necessary to indicate the small quantitative parameters of the narod, then we can use the sociological formula proposed by Augustin Cochin, "little narod."

The Nation: The Second Derivation from the Ethnos

Another concept with many interpretations which provokes heated disputes is that of the **"nation."** Here the spread of definitions is so great that the topic demands a separate analysis.[6] For now, we will give a schematic description of the content of this concept.

As the first derivative of the ethnos, the narod produces a state and/or religion, and/or civilization. In the case that the ethnos creates a state, we are dealing with a specific type of society, in which political structures, institutions, forms, and codes are clearly traced. This is a feature of all states.

A certain type of state, namely the modern European state, produces a historically specific model of political arrangement, based on fundamentals and principles different qualitatively from all other states. It is customary to call these radically new type of states and the societies corresponding to them "national states" or "nation-states" (*État-nation* in French). A society presenting itself as the content of a "national state" is a nation.

"Nation" is a strictly political concept, inseparably connected with the state; what is more, with a concrete state, the current-day European bourgeois state of Modernity.

In ethnosociology, "nation" is one of the most fundamental concepts. *It is interpreted as the second derivation from the ethnos.* The nation is a society qualitatively even more complex and differentiated than the narod.

Just as the ethnos was the matrix for the narod (laos), so too is the narod a matrix for the nation. But there is an obvious dialectical moment here. The narod, manifesting itself in history, displaces the ethnos, carrying it off into the sphere of implication, into the lowest floor or the basement, hiding it behind its façade.

There is the exact same dialectical moment in the nation, too. The nation, manifesting itself in the political history of Modernity (since in other epochs we do not find traces of the nation in such an understanding),

---

6   See Chapter 5 of *Ethnos and Society*. London: Arktos, 2018.

replaces the narod, carrying it off into the sphere of implication, shifting it to a lower floor (this time to the second floor, since the first is occupied by the ethnos), and sealing it off with its façade.

On a superficial level, when there is a narod, there is no ethnos; when there is a nation, there is no narod. But if we look deeper, then under the narod we discover the ethnos (koineme) and under the nation, the narod (as the first derivative from the ethnos).

If there were two models of identity in the narod, the ethnic (collective, popular) and individual (minimal, elite), then in the nation only one becomes the norm, the individual identity, which is spread out over all the members of the nation. In the narod, the individuals were the "heroes" of the aristocracy. In the nation, the individuals are "merchants," i.e., the third estate, and normatively everyone.[7]

Individual identification lies at the basis of the nation and is expressed in a concrete legal attribute, *citizenship*. The citizen of a given state is an element of the nation. This form of identity is legal, political, and strictly fixed.

At first glance, it appears to supplant and abolish other forms of identity, the ethnos and the narod. From a legal point of view, this is certainly the case; neither the ethnos, the narod, estate-hood, profession, nor place of residence count as legal categories in classical nations, nor do any of them figure in any official documents or legal codes. But on a deeper level the factors of ethnicity and belonging to a narod as a historical whole, including its structure of stratification, is preserved and makes itself known in certain circumstances.

In a nation, the city (politicized) population, to which the Greek term δῆμος (*démos*) corresponds most of all, predominates. The "demos" in contrast to the ethnos and the "laos" signified in Greek history the "population," the residents of the "city limits" without a clear ethnic or estate identity. For this reason, Aristotle considered democracy a negative model

---

7   The sociological notion of the types "heroes" and "merchants" was proposed by the German sociologist Werner Sombart. See Sombart, W. *Merchants and Heroes*. Munchen: Dunkler & Humblot, 1915.

of political arrangement, in contrast to the "polity." In both democracy and the polity, according to Aristotle, we are dealing with a government of *the majority* (as opposed to aristocracy, monarchy, tyranny, and oligarchy). But the polity is a quality, socially competent, organic majority (which we can correlate with the narod), and democracy is the rule of the "city limits" where all live indiscriminately, i.e., the rule of the poor majority.

The nation consists of citizens, the totality of whom are the population (*demos*).

Thus, we can illustrate the diversity of identities of different types of societies as follows:

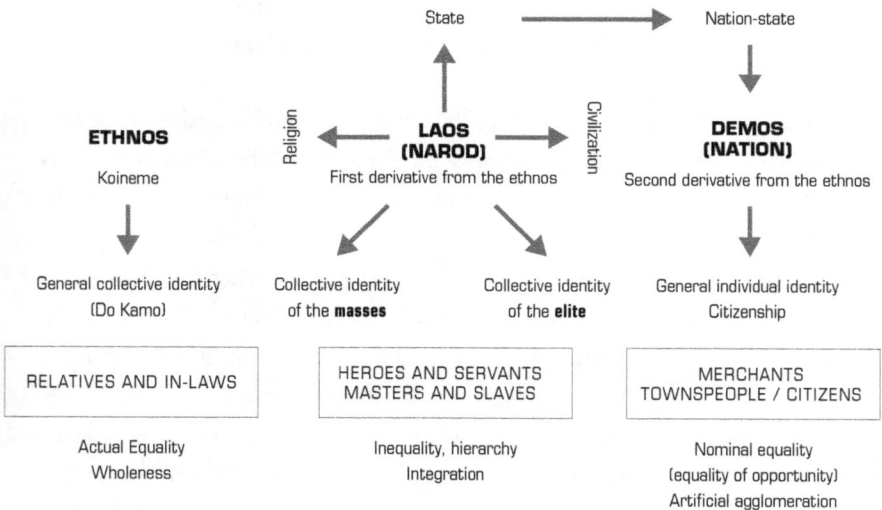

Figure 5. Identity in various types of societies.

The Nation and Reversibility

In the relationship between the ethnos and the narod we see *reversibility*: from the ethnos (more precisely, from ethnoses) a narod is formed, which disintegrates anew into ethnoses. Does the principle of reversibility also apply to the nation?

Here everything becomes more complicated. The nation, in contrast to the ethnos, is not an *organic* community, and, in contrast to the narod, not a *historical* community, i.e., one that depends on the realization of a project, advanced by a heroic elite (in the sociological sense). The nation is conceived as a purely rational and contractual phenomenon, and in the very idea of a contract is contained the possibility of its dissolution and the conclusion of another. Thus, theoretically, the nation, in disintegrating, begets new nations, on the basis of new agreements with other groups of participants. But in practice the matter is somewhat different. The disintegration of national governments, for instance Czechoslovakia or Yugoslavia in the 1990s, which were formed as nations almost a hundred years ago on the fragments of the Austro-Hungarian and Ottoman Empires, while formally introducing a new contract, gives way in practice to new nations based on a return either to an ethnic koineme or to the narod that had historically created a government formed as a nation.

Czechoslovakia was divided peacefully and by agreement into two national governments, the Czech Republic and Slovakia, but at the basis of such a division there lay an ethnic and ethno-confessional principle. The Czechs are mainly Protestant; the Slovaks, mainly Catholic. Religion is a sociological marker of the narod, and the separation of two so closely related Slavic cultures, the Czech and the Slovak, with a very similar, if not identical language, indicates the exposure of a purely ethnic source, the koineme.

In the former Yugoslavia, the narod was formed around the Serbian ethnos, which had tried to consolidate the other ethnic and cultural groups of Yugoslavia. The Serbs were an ethnos with the ambitions of a narod, but one formed as a nation. When the vertical of federal power weakened in Yugoslavia, ethnoses in the various republics — Croats, Slovenes, Macedonians, Bosnians, Albanians and Montenegrins — started to undermine the national state. The Serbs, considering themselves a narod and Yugoslavia their state, opposed this desperately. This ended tragically: almost all the ethnic regions separated and formed new national governments, and the Serbs were thrust back from the identity of a narod to the identity of an ethnos. The majority of these processes were accompanied by massacres, battles, and the interference of external nation-states: the countries of NATO and Russia.

Here we see that superficially the Yugoslav nation reconsidered its contract for the creation of new national combinations. And from a legal point of view that is what happened. In practice, however, in this tragic and bloody process there occurred first:

- The partial rehabilitation of ethnoses (except for the Serbian), i.e., the reverse disintegration of the nation into ethnoses (return to koinemes).

- The accelerated (artificial) transformation of ethnoses into nations, bypassing the stage of the narod, since the entire process was determined by the legal European context of Modernity, in which the norm of the establishment of a society only along the lines of the nation-state principle is acknowledged.

Thus, from an ethnosociological position we can discern reversibility also in the case of the disintegration of the nation.

Nationality Is Not an Ethnosociological Category

Even more than with *narodnost*, a problem arises with the concept of "*nationality*." This is complicated by the fact that the term nationality received a specific semantic burden only in the Russian-speaking context (scientific and legal), while in other European languages the meaning of this term is unambiguous and does not evoke any confusion: nationality (the French *nationalité*, the German *Nationalität*) signifies belonging to some national state, i.e., "citizenship." This is a legal category and it is registered in documents.

In Soviet history in connection with a series of circumstances, which we shall consider in detail in the corresponding chapter, the concept of nationality acquired a completely different meaning and started to signify "belonging to an ethnos." Thus, a significant confusion of two sociological concepts, separated by a great distance, occurred: between the ethnos (koineme) and nation (the "second derivative" of the ethnos, a political and artificial construction).

In ethnosociology as a strict discipline such use of the term nationality is ruled out to an even greater degree than use of the term *narodnost*. The sole meaning that should be ascribed to this term is the generally accepted European use, indicating only and strictly "citizenship" and nothing else.

Nationality in our case is citizenship in the Russian Federation, existence as a Russian citizen. But "Tartar," "Great Russian," "Chechen" or "Yakut" — this is ethnicity, ethnic belonging. In the exact same way, any citizen of France, both an ethnic Frenchman and a naturalized African or Arab, have one and the same "nationality": they are all "Frenchman according to nationality" (*leur nationalité c'est la nationalité française*). They are ethnically, religiously, phenotypically, and visually distinct, but this distinction is neither juridical nor legal; it is not associated with the nation. Even the most ordinary observers can take note of it, but only ethnosociology can correctly interpret, describe, and classify it (as we said in the previous chapter).

So as to avoid confusion, we will not use the term "nationality" in the course of ethnosociology.

Civil Society as an Ethnosociological Concept

Let us move on to the topic of *civil society*. This is another derivative, this time from the nation. It is based, on one hand, on the same principle on which the nation is built, on the principle of individual citizenship, but in contrast to the nation, it denies the fixity of the structure of agglomeration, i.e., the historical justification (on the contemporary level) of the state as a political (although also a constructed and mechanical) whole.

Taken by itself, in isolation from the nation, civil society is a sociological abstract, representing citizens' project of existence without a national state, i.e., content without form. This society is thought of as based exclusively on individual identity, opposite all forms of collective identity — ethnic, narodni, class, religious, and even national.

The theory of civil society was created by the philosopher Immanuel Kant (1724–1804) in the spirit of pacifism and anthropological optimism. Kant thought that people will eventually realize that it is unreasonable to fight among themselves, defending the nation-state, and that it is much more advantageous and profitable to cooperate.[8] At that point, civil society, based on reason and morality, comes to be. Kant's ideas lie at the basis of the main orientation of the liberal and bourgeois democratic politico-social tradition.

Civil society is thus thought of from the beginning as passing beyond the limits of national governments and is opposed to them as forms of organization subject to gradual abolishment. *The form of agglomeration of national identity must give way to an exclusively individual identity.* And only then will we have a society of individuals, in which no forms of collective identity remain.

In a certain sense, "civil society" is an abstraction, since empirically we do not know a contemporary society which exists outside of statehood and is post-national. Nevertheless, behind this concept stands a completely understandable system of thought, which continues the main vector of sociological transformations that have occurred with society in Modernity and draws a theoretical horizon to which, following such a path, we must arrive sooner or later. This path is thought of as a departure from collective identity and individual heroic identity (in an estate society) in the direction of a purely individualistic identity and is announced as the meaning of history and the direction of progress.

For Western culture and Western society such a path of thought is altogether natural and justified. For this reason, in Ethnosociology one can perfectly well use the category "civil society."

Civil society as a concept is the third derivative of the ethnos. In a certain sense, civil society is the complete antithesis of the ethnos, since all relations, structural symmetries, values and forms of identification between them are inverted. Civil society is a sociological model which

---

8   Kant, I. *Perpetual Peace, and Other Essays on Politics, History, Morals.* Indianapolis, IN: Hackett Pub. Co, 1983.

presupposes the absence of the ethnos, even in a deep, unconscious dimension.

The Reversibility of Civil Society

This raises the question: is civil society reversible? We cannot answer this question unambiguously, since the process of the creation of civil society is not complete, and we have no precedents on which to rely. The sole thing that we can do in this regard is trace the reversibility of preceding societies, studied from the point of view of Ethnosociology. In the narod the ethnos remains even after the collapse of the former and is rediscovered anew after the disintegration of those forms that the narod historically produces. The disintegration of the nation shows that in national states, too, the ethnic factor and the narodni factor are not abolished and can again become very important social forms of identification. Thus, reversibility is found in practice in all phenomenologically observable forms. The "first" and "second derivatives" from the ethnos are again "traced back to the argument," to put it in terms of the differential calculus. On this basis, we can suggest that reversibility is one of the laws of ethnosociology and is applicable to all types of society, both those that are known historically (we can convince ourselves of this at a glance) and those future ones that need only to be realized.

Hence, we can say cautiously that a civil society, when (and if) it will be built, *most likely* also has the prospect to transition backward to less complex ethnosociology models, such as the nation, narod, and ethnos.

Global Society as the Apotheosis of Civil Society

If we place the concept of civil society in a concrete historical context, we will see that this society cannot but be global, super-national, and post-state in character. That is, civil society proposes that ultimately it necessarily becomes global. Thus, we can consider global society as the highest form of civil society, as its most optimal and concrete realization.

In its formation, *global society* has the following stages:

1. It begins with the *strengthening of individual identity inside the framework of national states.* This is called "democratization" and "social modernization." Collective identity with the nation and, correspondingly, with the state gradually cedes its place to a strictly individual identity. Civil society gains strength. Democratic national states become *more and more* democratic and *less and less* national.

2. Then, after reaching a high level of democratization and modernization of the nation-state, several of them merge into one super-national formation, which transforms into the basis of a post-national, democratic super-state, which we see realized in practice in today's European Union.

3. The second stage lasts until finally all societies and states reach the highest level of democratization and unite into a *single world state* (Global State) with a single world government. The citizens of this planetary state, this "Cosmopolis," will be citizens of the entire world, and the very *status of a citizen will be entirely equated with the status of man.* This ideology has received the name of "the rights of man." It implies precisely the concept of global citizenship or the global society.

From a sociological point of view, we should pay attention to the main point of the concept of global society (and civil society as well): this society disclaims all forms of *collective identity* — ethnic, historical, civilizational, cultural, class, national, etc.

Real civil society can only be global.

From the point of view of the taxonomies of the ethnosociological disciplines, global society does not represent a separate social paradigm; it should rather be considered as the completed form of civil society. It is possible to look at this distinction differently, however. If we take global society as the end goal and the paradigm, then civil society can be considered a transitional stage from the nation to global society. In this case, all the qualitative signs of civil society (in the first place, a purely individual identification) are automatically carried over to global society.

Post-Society and the Sociology of Postmodernity

All the models of societies we have looked at, from the ethnos (as a koineme) to global society, are versions of "human society."[9] We meet with ethnoses, narods, and nations, and also certain forms of "civil society," empirically in the surrounding world. And we can imagine global society by extending into the future certain tendencies that undoubtedly exist already today. All these types of society presuppose man as their participant. All notions of a transition from the stage of beast to primordial human society remain hypothesis. These hypotheses remain rather popular, however, even in sociology (for instance, the Social Darwinism of the famous sociologist Herbert Spencer [1820–1903], which influenced one of the most authoritative schools of Sociology, the Chicago School).

Other hypotheses are popular nowadays, which are not just hypothetical glances back into the pre-human past, but equally hypothetical glances *forwards* into the post-human future. This trend is known as Postmodernism.

There are postmodern reconstructions that try to reconstruct the next horizon of the future society, beyond the limits of global society. The purpose of such constructions is based on the wish to extend the vector of sociological tendencies existing today not only into "tomorrow" (global society), but also to the day after tomorrow. This hypothesis, even more abstract than the concepts of civil society and global society, is symmetrical with respect to the human society view of the animal "foreword" to human sociality, but can be called a "machine 'afterword.'" This is the idea of the post-human, who must come to replace the human as an individual.

The post-human is a concept that extends the vector of the breaking-up of identity (which we can see in the figure showing the transformations of identity from collective to individual and the ethnos to global society)

9   Thurnwald, R. *Die menschliche Gesellschaft in ihren ethnosoziologischen Grundlagen.* Berlin: Walter de Gruyter & co., 1935.

to yet another qualitative level and proposes to divide individuality into its components. The human individual can also be thought of as something whole and organic, similar to the ethnos. And as social history (at least of Western societies) is the aspiration to crush this wholeness down to the atomic level, so post-history or the concept "post-human" proposes to crush man himself, replacing him with the machine, cyborg, clone, or mutant. The very idea of the decoding of the gene already contains in itself a quest for the machine code of man, which it will be possible to improve and which it will be possible to control and manipulate. Man himself is considered a machine, a mechanism, whose functioning it is possible to interfere with and to perfect.

On the basis of such a sociological hypothesis, made much use of in contemporary science fiction (fragments of which gradually become reality in accordance with the extent of the progress of genetic engineering, cloning, nanotechnology, etc.) we can construct the last purely theoretical model, transcending the bounds of human society.

The last derivative from the ethnos will be the *post-human society* or *post-society*. If within the framework of the human the maximum antithesis of the ethnos is global society ("the third derivation" from the ethnos, as is civil society), then beyond its limits in the projection of post-people (already dividuals, not individuals) we can outline with a dotted line a conditional "fourth derivation" from the ethnos, an association of cyborgs, mutants, clones and machines.

This is the logical limit in which ethnosociology rests in the analysis of man's hypothetical future.

The main concepts of ethnosociology are exhausted by this taxonomy.

We see a consolidated model of all these types of societies in Figure 6.

SECTION TWO

The Instrumental Concepts
of Ethnosociology

The Stereotype — The Ethnic Stereotype

Now let us move to an overview of the fundamental instrumental concepts of ethnosociology, with the help of which we will later describe and interpret the basic ethnosociological phenomena: the ethnos, the narod, the nation, civil society, and post-society.

The concept "stereotype" (from the ancient Greek στερεός, "solid," "spatial" and τύπος, "mark") was introduced into scientific use by the sociologist Walter Lippmann (1889–1974). Lippmann himself gives the following definition: "*a stereotype is a model adopted in a historical society of perceiving, filtering, and interpreting information during the cognition and recognition of the surrounding world, based on previous social experience.*" The purpose of introducing this concept is exceedingly important for the understanding of the essence of society and, in particular, of social opinion, since any society is inclined to explain the *new* through the *old* and the unfamiliar through the familiar. For that reason, the stereotype shows the structure of the social consciousness, which always relates to the surrounding world and its transformations selectively, accepting that which corresponds to its settled notions, and approaching the new with distrust (which often leads to the unreliable interpretation of this "new" or to its being ignored).

Society thinks in stereotypes, i.e., in notions that often conflict with processes unfolding inside and outside of society. But more often than not stereotypes prove stronger than the givens of direct experience, since, being lodged in consciousness, they are processed again in agreement with already established stereotypes. Everything that contradicts these stereotypes is rejected or reinterpreted.

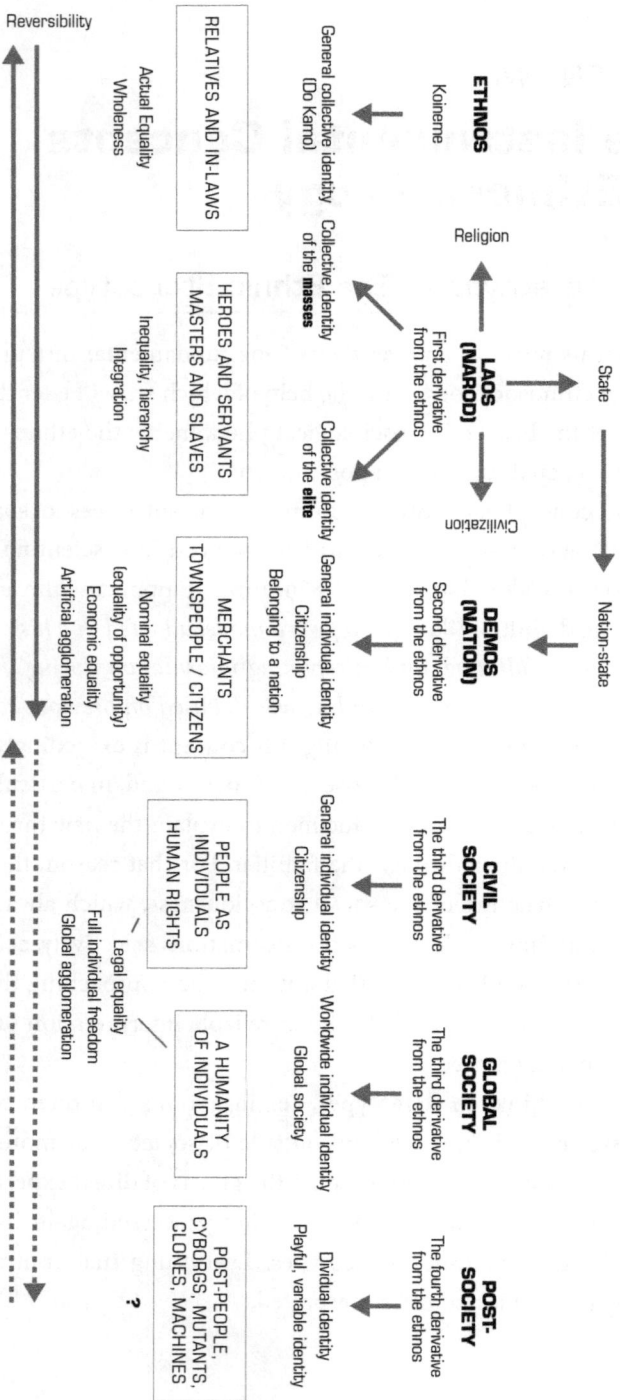

Figure 6. Identity in various types of society.

Reversibility

ETHNOS
Koineme → General collective identity (Do Kamo)

RELATIVES AND IN-LAWS
Actual Equality
Wholeness

Religion

LAOS (NAROD)
First derivative from the ethnos
→ Collective identity of the **masses**
→ Collective identity of the **elite**

State

Civilization

HEROES AND SERVANTS
MASTERS AND SLAVES
Inequality, hierarchy
Integration

DEMOS (NATION)
Second derivative from the ethnos
→ General individual identity
Citizenship
Belonging to a nation

Nation-state

MERCHANTS
TOWNSPEOPLE / CITIZENS
Nominal equality (equality of opportunity)
Economic equality
Artificial agglomeration

CIVIL SOCIETY
The third derivative from the ethnos
→ General individual identity
Citizenship

PEOPLE AS INDIVIDUALS
HUMAN RIGHTS
Legal equality
Full individual freedom
Global agglomeration

GLOBAL SOCIETY
The third derivative from the ethnos
→ Worldwide individual identity
Global society

A HUMANITY OF INDIVIDUALS

POST-SOCIETY
The fourth derivative from the ethnos
→ Dividual identity
Playful, variable identity

POST-PEOPLE, CYBORGS, MUTANTS, CLONES, MACHINES

?

In Ethnosociology the concept of the *stereotype* finds the broadest application. For instance, it can be applied to various types of society.

At the level of the *ethnos*, stereotypes will be the most settled and rigid; everything new is rejected or ignored.

At the level of the *narod* the structure of stereotypes becomes more complicated and is created by a field (of history), in which the new is admitted; although again this new is interpreted most often with the help of the stereotype.

The *nation* puts as its goal to generate stereotypes artificially and rationally. The production of stereotypes and their inculcation society comprises the sphere of ideology, politics, and propaganda.

Civil society strives to transfer stereotypes from the collective level to the individual level. *Global society* proposes a complete eradication of collective stereotypes.

Post-society (and this is a very important program of postmodernism) is thought of as the kind of sphere in which stereotypes will be subject to decomposition even on an individual level.

In a narrower sense, we can speak of ethnic stereotypes, i.e., of one or another society's settled notions about an ethnos, narod, or nation.

Stereotypes can be separated into two kinds: *autostereotypes* and *heterostereotypes*. An autostereotype is a group's system of stereotypes concerning itself. A heterostereotype is this same group's system of notions concerning other groups. In ethnosociology studies, the method of revealing auto- and heterostereotypes is widely employed.[10]

The American sociologist William Sumner (1840–1910), one of the founders of American sociology, formulated the sociological concept of the "we-group" and "they-group" as an instrument for the study of the structure of identity.[11] Sumner also introduce the term "ethnocentrism," in order to emphasize the specific character of the structure of social identity, where the "we-group" (in this case taken as the ethnos) is always found in

---

10   Soldatova G.U. *Psihologiya Mezhetnicheskoy Napryazhennosti.* Moscow: Smysl, 1998.

11   Sumner, W. *Folkways; A Study of the Sociological Importance of Usages, Manners, Customs, Mores, and Morals.* New York, NY: New American Library, 1960.

the center, and the "they-group" always on the periphery. The structure of the "we-group" is determined by autostereotypes; that of the "they-group," by heterostereotypes.

Attitude: Ethnic Attitudes

Another very important instrument of ethnosociological analysis is the sociological concept of *attitude*.

Attitude is the psychological condition of the predisposition of a subject to a certain activity in a certain situation. The phenomenon was discovered by the German psychologist L. Lange (1863–1936). The American sociologists W. Thomas (1863–1947) and F. Znaeskty (1882–1958) applied it to the sphere of Sociology. The defined social attitude as a "psychological process considered in relation to the social world and taken first and foremost in connection with social values." Value, according to them, was "the objective side of attitude. Consequently, an attitude is the individual (subjective) side of social value," they affirmed.[12]

Attitude *precedes* social action and is found on the borderline between the inner and outer as an instance, where is formed the strategy of social behavior and even social perception even before the moment of direct contact with the social milieu arrives.

The American sociologist Milton Rokeach (1918–1988) showed that attitude is of two types: *towards the object* and *towards the situation*. An attitude towards the object is a *knowing relation* (basic stereotype) to some phenomenon, social, or ethnic group. Within this attitude there is no reverse connection; it is projected onto the external world without taking account of its specifics. An attitude towards the situation includes a *reverse connection*, since it puts the subject in a concrete, individual moment, with which he must reckon.

In Sociology, Lapiere's experiment, which has ethnosociological significance, is famous. In the early 1930s, the American sociologist Richard Lapiere (1899–1989) undertook a trip to a number of American cities with

---

12   Shihirev P.N. *Sovremennaya Sotsialnaya Psihologiya*. Moscow: Nauka, 1979, p. 86.

two Chinese assistants. At that time in America there was a rather careful relationship towards the Chinese. When Lapiere sent out correspondence to the inn-keepers with a request to book a room for his and his pair of Chinese assistants, in the majority of cases he did not receive a response, or else he was told that no rooms were available. But when he arrived to a hotel together with his Chinese assistants, the majority of innkeepers agreed to accept them without any particular problems. The "attitude towards the object" (the Chinese) was negative (activated ethnic heterostereotypes), but the "attitude towards the situation" depended on many factors (the personal charm of the professor, the neat outer appearance of the Chinese students, the possibility of earning money on a client, etc.) and more often than not overpowered the "attitude towards the object."

Assimilation

In the study of the contact of two ethnoses with one another, one often finds the process of ethnic assimilation. This signifies the gradual absorption of one ethnos by another right up to its disappearance. Under the influence of one ethnos (stronger, more energetic, more active, more tenacious) another ethnos (weaker, passive, languid) can lose its specific features and merge with the first one. At the same time, there occurs the loss of language, belief in a common origin, and the specific traditions that distinguished the given ethnos from the one with which it is assimilated.

Assimilation can bear a smooth or abrupt character, can be relatively voluntary and strictly compulsory, planned or spontaneous, and can occur in conditions of war or peace. The situation often arises when a conquered ethnos assimilates the conqueror (for instance, today's Bulgarians are a Slavic ethnos who originated in present-day Bulgaria and were conquered in ancient times by the Turks under the leadership of Khan Asparukh, and who gradually assimilated the Turkic elite, which had lost its language, the memory of its origin, and its ethnic traditions in the Slavic masses).

During assimilation, which is considered from without as a unidirectional process — the disappearance of one ethnos and its dissolution into another — a much deeper interaction of the ethnoses occurs. The absorbed ethnos often introduces into the other ethnos its original features, which are capable of influencing the structure of the more active, absorbing ethnos.

Thus, the autochthonous residents of India (mostly its own Dravidian tribes), conquered by Indo-European nomads, after accepting the ethnic culture of the Hindus, their traditions, language, and beliefs, fundamentally transformed the original Vedic culture and imported to it an entirely unique orientation.

Ethnic Conservation

The opposite of assimilation is *ethnic conservation*. Conservation means the preservation of an ethnos in the face of a massive impact with another ethnos, resisting assimilation. But in certain circumstances the weaker ethnos is able to dodge assimilation and to preserve its identity.

Most often the conservation of an ethnos occurs at the cost of the ethnos' retreat to the peripheral zone of influence of the stronger ethnos, areas hard to access and difficult to master: mountains, forests, deserts, tundra, ices, etc. In these territories, difficult for habitation, it is often possible to meet the members of ancient ethnoses, which had undergone in conditions of conservation not a few waves of stronger and more aggressive newcomers. Eskimos, Chukchi, Evenki, and other small ethnoses of the North are examples of such archaic ethnoses. Some highland narods have many ancient features: the Ossetians, Avars, Dargins, Svans, Chechens, Ingush, Tabasarans, Lezgins, etc.

Acculturation

Another form of interethnic influence is acculturation. This process does not affect the entire society, but one a specific section of it. Acculturation is the transfer of the cultural code of one ethnos to another, as a rule without taking account of the specific model of ethnic arrangement of that society towards which acculturation is directed.

In the process of acculturation there occurs the cultural transformation of that social group towards which it is directed, but this does not lead (as in assimilation) to the complete merger of the two groups or to the absorption of one of them by the other.

In the 19th century acculturation was thought of only in the form of the transmission of the cultural code of a more complex society to a simpler one (for instance, from the narod or nation to the ethnos). That is how it happens in most cases. However, the ethnologist F. Boas underscores that there is no such society (simple or complex) as would not be subject to the cultural influence of other societies. Thus, he gives the example of the form of harpoon of Norwegian fishermen, which are exact reproductions of the much older fishing instrument of the Eskimos of Greenland.[13]

Acculturation can be understood broadly, as the cultural impact of one society on another without their mixing in the course of cultural exchange (the formula of the ethnosociologists R. Redfield, R. Linton, and M. Herskovits further developed the approach of F. Boas), or more narrowly as the uni-directional impact of a more complex culture on a less complex one.[14]

Integration

Another form of interethnic influence is *integration*. It is a kind of inclusion of one ethnic group in another, most often voluntarily. The process of integration differs from assimilation by its conscious character and ritual formalization, and also in that it affects the individual members of the other ethnic group. There are a number of rites that serve this purpose.

The main forms of integration are:

1. Adoption
2. Blood brotherhood

13   Boas, F. *Race, Language, and Culture*. New York, NY: Macmillan, 1940.

14   Redfield, R. & Linton, R. & Herskovits, M.J. *Memorandum for the Study of Acculturation* / American Anthropologist. 1936. Vol. 38, No. 1.

3.   The patron/client model

Adoption is a rite of acceptance into an ethnic community by a member of another ethnic community (as a rule, on an individual basis and with the request of the accepted person). In the course of rites of adoption (which have many variants) the initiate imitates "birth" into the ethnos, attests to his faith in an ancestor common to the tribe (i.e., an ancestor of the tribe becomes his own ancestor), and becomes familiarized with traditions and customs. It is intended that the adopted member will live among the given ethnic community and will speak its language.

Blood brotherhood is also connected with a ritual, the point of which is the mixing of blood of two individuals, which symbolizes integration into one and the same tribe (which one precisely is necessarily specified). Having become "blood brothers" with a member of another tribe, a person is henceforth subject to all social forms — taboo, marriage rules, rewards and punishments: he is accepted by all as a full-fledged member of that community. He belongs to the same lineage as his "blood brother," exactly as though he were his blood brother [TN: by birth]. From a sociological point of view, ritual forms of "blood brotherhood" are entirely identical in their results with real family ties.

In some cases, a relationship taking the form of patron/client is established between two ethnoses. This proposes that one ethnos (the patron) takes another under its cover, is obliged to guard it against the possible attack of an enemy, and in exchange the other ethnos (the client) undertakes to supply the patron-ethnos with various material objects, most often food-products or other types of goods. Sometimes the integration of ethnoses along the patron/client model becomes very stable and lasts for centuries, being depicted in myths, social institutions and rites. Ethnoses influence one another, dwelling together in inseparable symbiosis, but all the while without losing their particular features.

In more complex societies the difference between integration and assimilation consists in the fact that integration allows for the preservation of a set of special ethnic signs, while assimilation intends their full displacement by the characteristics of that society which implements the assimilation.

The Applicability of Ethnosociological Methods to Complex Societies

Ethnosociology studies the ethnos as a koineme, the simplest form of society. More complex types of society — the narod, state, religion, civilization, nation, civil society, etc. — are derivations from the ethnos. A more detailed study of the qualities of these derivations and their sociological meaning will be given in the following chapters. It is already possible, however, to outline the most important vector of the ethnosociological approach: those sociological and instrumental concepts which we met with at the level of the ethnos we shall also be able to discover easily in more complex systems of society and to apply them to the study thereof. The structure of these concepts will change somewhat in parallel with the transformations of identity (from collective to individual, and even "dividual"); hence, they can be called **instrumental derivatives**.

For instance, the process of assimilation can be seen in the case of two societies of an ethnic order (two ethnoses), and also in the formation of a narod (wherein assimilation plays a crucial role), but also in the formation of the nation (naturalization). There is a form of assimilation characteristic to civil society, expressing itself in the propaganda of the ideology of liberalism, the principles of tolerance and political correctness, and in the condemnation of national and state structures, which form the means of incorporating a person into the structure of a "civil society." In all cases, we are dealing with assimilation, but its quality and structure are different each time. For this reason, we speak of instrumental derivatives.

That which is transparent and obvious on the level of the koineme becomes more veiled on the level of complex models of society. Ethnosociology is called upon not to reduce the complex to the simple, but to trace the following:

- How the structuration of complex societies on the basis of simple ones occurs.

- What happens in the meantime to simple societies and what their place is in the general context of more complex ones.

- What is common between simple and complex societies.

- What in them is principally different.

CHAPTER THREE

The Theoretical Paradigms of Ethnosociological Methodology

Primordialism

The Fundamental Methods of the Interpretation of Ethnic Phenomena

In Ethnosociology it is customary to distinguish three approaches to the understanding of the essence of the ethnos.[1] These approaches are Primordialism, Constructivism, and Instrumentalism.

Primordialism derives from the Latin word *primordialis*, "primordial," "primary."

Constructivism is from the word *constructio*, i.e., "something artificially produced."

Instrumentalism is from the word *instrumentum*, the use of something for instrumental ends.

---

1   Arutyunyan, Yu.V., Drobizheva, LM, Kondrat'ev, VS, Susokolov, A.A. *Ethnosociology: objectives, methods, research results.* Moscow, 1984.

Primordialism comes close to "Essentialism" (from the Latin *essentia*, "essence"), and "Constructivism" to "Modernism." Sometimes to these three fundamental methods is added also the school of the "ethnosymbolists" (E. Smith).

Some ethnosociological writers present the matter as if it dealt with diverse views of the essence of the ethnos.[2] We shall show that in the course of the correct distinction of the ethnos and its derivations this problem disappears by itself, inasmuch as it is necessary to approach different types of society with different criteria, which automatically removes the contradiction.

For convenience of exposition let us take as our basis the three approaches — Primordialism (Essentialism), Constructivism (Modernism), and Instrumentalism — and on their foundation, show the methodological peculiarities of the interpretation of ethnic phenomena and ethnic processes. Later we shall look at the approach of "*Ethnosymbolism*" separately.

The Essence of the Primordialist Approach

The **primordialist approach** in its broadest interpretation consists in the fact that the ethnos is acknowledged as the primordial characteristic of human society and human culture. The ethnos lies at the basis of social structures, which are its variations and dialectical moments.

This term was introduced in 1957 by the American sociologist Edward Shils (1910–1995).[3] He noticed that in archaic societies ethnic kinship is recognized as a special closeness to a relative not as a person but as the bearer of a special "significant relationship" which can be described as a "primordial relationship" or as the "Primordial."[4] Shils strictly opposes the structure of the "Primordial" to those social structures that are established

---

2   Eriksen, T. H. *Ethnicity and Nationalism: Anthropological Perspectives.* London: Pluto Press, 1993.

3   Shils, E. *Primordial, Personal, Sacred and Civil Ties* / The British Journal of Sociology. 1957. Vol. 8. No. 2. June. pp. 130–145.

4   Ibid. p. 130.

on the basis of interpersonal interactions. Earlier we gave the example of the figure of *Do Kamo*, studied by Maurice Leenhardt.

The ethnos is something original, primordial, unfolded around the figure of the Primordial.

All types of Primordialism come together in this main point. And this assertion is so self-evident and confirmed by historical observations that it is rather difficult to dispute — at least in such a formulation. If we understand by the ethnos that which the majority of ethnosociologists understand and which Shirokogoroff formulated in his definition, then, indeed, language, belief in a common origin, and customs (i.e., the ethnos) characterize human society, beginning from the most ancient (original, primordial) epochs right up to today. And even in societies which we have defined as derivations from the ethnos and in which the ethnos, it would seem, should long ago have ceased to be, it is always possible to discover an ethnic component, which becomes manifest at a glance during a certain confluence of events.

Hardly any opponents to such an approach to the ethnos would be found if primordialism were to be formulated precisely in this manner. But besides recognition of the primordialism of the ethnos, various authors added to this a variety of additional characteristics, which gave cause for criticism.

Different Types of Primordialism

In his work *Myths and Memories of the Nation*, the contemporary English sociologist Anthony Smith (founder of the school of "Ethnosymbolism," about which we shall speak below) summarized the diverse approaches to Primordialism.[5]

Primordialism, according to Smith, is of three kinds:

- *Essentialist*, which proposes that the ethnos is the immutable form of the existence of society from antiquity to contemporary

---

5   Smith, A. D. *Myths and Memories of the Nation*. Oxford: Oxford University Press, 1999; Ibid. *Nationalism: Theory, Ideology, History*. Cambridge: Polity, 2001.

nations and that between contemporary nations and ancient ethnoses there exists an uninterrupted connection (this is an extreme form of primordialism);

- *Kinship,* which insists that all ethnic symbols are directed toward demonstrating an uninterrupted line of kinship among generations;

- The so-called *"Geertz's Primordialism,"* is named after Clifford Geertz (1926–2006), author of the theory of "Symbolic Anthropology," who asserted that despite the fact that it is impossible to prove a direct connection between historical forms of the ethnos, belief in such a connection is such a stable sociological fact that it must be taken account of in the analysis of a society *as though* it were indeed the case.[6]

All of these definitions demand immediate commentaries. In the category of "Essentialist Primordialism," Smith includes theories that do not at all distinguish between the ethnos and the nation and do not assign the narod to a separate category, considering ethnoses as an organic phenomenon, unchanged in the course of all history. This is obviously untrue, since during the transition from simple society, which is an ethnic society, to complex society there occur fundamental changes, affecting all social structures. That is why an ethnos in an ethnic society and an ethnos in a formalized state, religious context, or civilization will be different realities. To an even greater extent this concerns the nation, which is built on an entirely different principle than the ethnos is built on. Thus, "Essentialist Primordialism" should be recognized as excessively naïve and of very limited scientific worth.

Even less adequate is "Kinship Primordialism," which insists on an uninterrupted lineal history, around which, supposedly, the development of a culture occurs. We have already seen that an ethnos necessarily consists

---

6   Geertz, C. J. *The Interpretation of Cultures: Selected Essays.* New York, NY: Basic Book, 1973; Ibid. *Local Knowledge: Further Essays in Interpretive Anthropology.* New York, NY: Basic Book, 1983.

of a few exogamous parts (*lineages*), the relationship between which is built along rather complex sociological scenarios even within the simplest ethnoses. The lineage ties are only one of the elements of the ethnos, and ethnic culture consists of the recognition of plurality of lineages (duality as a minimum) and the rules of marriage relation with it. Thus, the basic culture pattern is much more complex than the lineal in the simplest societies, and in more differentiated ones this complex structure becomes even more complex. That is why "Kinship Primordialism" should also be set aside.

Most adequate of all seems to be "Geertz's Primordialism," which considers the ethnos precisely as a society and as a sociological phenomenon and considers it most important in the complex of factors that form social identity.

We can put in this same category of approaches the school that Smith calls "Perennialism" (from the Latin *perennis*, "long," "constant," "lasting"), and more specifically, one of its varieties, "perpetual Perennialism." The upshot of the perennialist approach to the ethnos is that it considers the ethnos not as an *organic*, but as a *historical* category, changing constantly and connected with extraneous motives: power, dominion, economic interests, the struggle for resources, etc. Perennialists as a whole think that the ethnos is a variable. But "perpetual perennialists," much closer to "Geertz's Primordialism," propose that the ethnos always exists, but is found in constant change. This "perpetual Perennialism" can perfectly well be accepted in that part in which it emphasizes the change of the sociological structure of the ethnos in history. This indeed occurs, but only when the ethnos enters into history, and this we call transition to the stage of the narod. With such a correction, this approach can be acknowledged as helpful, especially in that it proposes to consider various forms of transformation of the ethnos in history.

We now approach another important division of Primordialism. Generally, we can distinguish two primordialist approaches: one considers the ethnos *only* as a society, as a social and cultural phenomenon (the German Sociology of Thurnwald and Mühlmann, the American cultural anthropology of Franz Boas and his followers, the English Functionalism of Malinowski and Radcliffe-Browne, the French Structural Anthropology of Lévi-Strauss, "Geertz's Primordialism," "perpetual perennialism," etc.); the other adds to the ethnos biological, generic and racial factors.

We should recognize only the first approach as fully adequate, but in order to have a complete picture we should survey also the second one.

The Biosocial[7] Approach

The supporters of the biosocial approach to the ethnos are guided by a specific anthropological attitude, according to which man is a dual phenomenon: on one hand, he is a biological organism, pertaining to a variety of animals (mammalia), and on the other hand he is the carrier of a rational, intelligent principle, on the basis of which he develops social structures, the socium. The origin of the understanding of man as a peculiar animal endowed with reason stems from Greek antiquity. Already Aristotle defined man as "an animal endowed with reason" (ζῷον λόγον ἔχον [zóon lógon échon]), which sounds like the Latin animalis rationalis.

This allows one to understand all the actions, creations, reactions, and deeds of in two ways, discovering in them the animal (biological, zoological) element and the properly reasonable, rational nature. The supporters of the Biosocial theory consider the ethnos through such an approach, discovering in the ethnos a biological (animal) and rational component. The ethnos on the whole is seen in this case as the extension of a genus with the addition of the animal component — the members of the genus perceive themselves as a flock, not unlike animal species; they hold one another, help one another, and battle with foreign lineages for loot, food, territory, and other material resources. A reasonable nature restrains these animal impulses and motivations and tries to limit them and to order, censor, crush, and supersede them.

---

7   TN: Or "Sociobiological."

In this theory, the ethnos is a society based on a compromise between the animal and the rational; moreover, the animal principle is manifest here to a greater degree than in other forms of society.

The general logic of social history is seen as a process of strengthening the rational principle in relation to the biological, animal principle. Each following form of society strengthens the rational component, elevating it into a social law. But the biological principle preserves its positions and continues to act as the motivating force of human activity, from the simplest spheres (struggle for survival) to the most complex ones (will to power). For this reason, man even in the most complex and highly differentiated social systems continues to preserve his biosocial nature, and thus, also some ethnic features, as a rudiment of the animal feeling of kin and flock.

Such are the theoretical premises of the biosocial approach. It can be categorized as primordialist on account of its assertion of the primordiality and constancy of the ethnic factor.

If we analyze this approach carefully we will see that the properly ethnic is interpreted here as a manifestation of precisely the biological element, whence the increased attention to the genus. Ethnic (simple) society is seen here as a society in which the animal principle is maximally manifest and the social, reasonable one, minimally. The ethnos is thereby declared to be the biological side of man. And that which is preserved in complex societies is interpreted as a contribution of the animal side of man as such.

We have already spoken repeatedly the insufficiency of such an approach and shall again return to this after considering a few, more concrete forms of its manifestation.

Evolutionary Theory: Herbert Spencer

The classic expression of the biosocial approach is the theory of evolution of species (Charles Darwin), applied to society and its history. The English sociologist and eminent theoretician of liberalism Herbert Spencer

(1820–1903) formulated this theory in a completed form in his ten-volume work *A System of Synthetic Philosophy*.[8]

Spencer's idea consists in the following: the world is a process of constant and irreversible development from simple to complex. This is a common characteristic of matter, living organisms, and societies. The complication of systems is always positive and creative. That is why the transition from simple to complex is considered "progress," a "good," a "value," etc. "Complexity," "complication," and "differentiation" are thought of as ethnical categories, and not simply as neutral constants.

The movement towards the complication of a system occurs in the form of conflicts. In the study of biological species Spencer relies on the theories of Darwin (1809–1882), seeing in them the confirmation of his own ideas of general evolution, formulated under the influence of the romantics, such as the philosopher Friedrich Wilhelm Joseph Schelling (1775–1854) and the poet Samuel Coleridge (1772–1834), a few years before he became acquainted with Darwin's main work *On the Origin of the Species*.[9, 10] As in other animal species, the "struggle for survival," which comprises the main law of evolution, is the same basic vector of human history. In this struggle, "the fittest," capable of complicating their behavioral strategies, always win. Thus, there is a continuity between animals and men, supplied by the unity of the universal law of evolution.

Spencer and his *Social Darwinism* do not so much explain human behavior by the presence in man of an animal principle as they consider the algorithm of both animal and human behavior as particular cases of a general law of complication of systems, which operates even for inanimate matter. Human society becomes a battlefield, as do all other levels of reality. In the animal world, we only see the grand and graphic horizons of evolution, which serve as an example for the explanation of human

8   Spencer, H. *A System of Synthetic Philosophy*. V. 10. London-Edinburgh: Williams and Norgate, 1862–1896.

9   Darwin, C. *On the Origin of Species by Means of Natural Selection, or the Preservation of Favoured Races in the Struggle for Life*. London: John Murray, 1859.

10 Spencer, H. *First Principles of a New System of Philosophy*. London: Williams & Norgate, 1862.

history. Human society, in itself more complex than a herd of animals, moves in the direction of complication along the same trajectory as in the evolution of species: the struggle for resources forces societies to produce ever more effective strategies and to adapt themselves to circumstances. Only "the fittest" societies win on this path.

Spencer distinguishes two fundamental types of society, the militant and *industrial*. In a forceful society, the struggle for survival proceeds with the help of domination, violence, coercion. It is arranged hierarchically: the most "fit" mercilessly exploit the less "fit" and live at their expense. Forceful society is relatively simple.

In industrial society, the social strategies of struggle become more complicated and are moved into the economic and contractual sphere. The essence of the struggle for survival remains the same, but the rules of its conduct become more complicated. Special laws are introduced, strictly determining the forms of struggle and the zones of its legitimate conduct, which are permissible. The war for survival in industrial society is transformed into economic competition, which moves society in the direction of greater complication. According to Spencer, this movement has a goal, consisting in universal equilibrium, when the complications of the social system reach their culmination. Then the state will die off, and each individual will represent a maximally complex autonomous system. This kind of society will gradually leave only "the fittest"; the rest disappear as not conforming to the laws of evolution.

Spencer does not speak directly about the ethnos and begins to build his social typology from forceful society, which in Ethnosociology corresponds to the stage of the narod.

From an ethnosociological point of view, Spencer's Social Darwinism can be accepted in its description of the process of complication of societies, which corresponds to empirical data, at least in the framework of Western-European civilization. But what should be rejected is his biological and Darwinist interpretation of the basic motive of human action (a purely biological approach, considering the main motive impulse of man to be the striving towards physical pleasure, identified in the spirit of English pragmatism with "happiness") and confidence in the irreversibility and uni-directionality of evolution and progress. We know that the majority of societies can move from the point of view of the simplicity or complexity of its systems in both directions.

Spencer's ideas, which give the "struggle for survival" a legitimate status in society, were picked up by two political ideologies of the 20th century: neoliberalism, which considers inequality and the rule of the rich and successful over the poor and unlucky a norm of economic life, and racism, justifying the inequality of races among themselves and the dominance of the White race on a global scale as the results of this struggle, in which the "fittest" (the Whites) were victorious.

Evolutionary ideas affected a whole series of anthropologists, who accumulated significant material concerning simple societies, i.e., ethnoses. Their approach was based on the conviction that they were studying lower types and forms of social life from the position of the higher. Hence their conclusions and methods are very doubtful: in archaic tribes, they tried to find something resembling contemporary or historically fixed complex societies and to interpret antiquity as a crude and primitive form of that which is known to them as complex societies. They ignored everything that would not fit into this conception. Despite "evolutionary racism," substantially lowering the worth of such works, they can be considered as working material for ethnosociologists, after, of course, the corresponding adjustments have been made.

The classic representatives of this line are the American ethnologist Louis Morgan (1818–1881), the English anthropologists Edward Taylor (1832–1917) and James George Frazier (1854–1941), and the French anthropologist Lucien Lévy-Bruhl (1857–1939).

Racial Theories

Racial theories broadly understood are anthropological, sociological, or culturological systems at the basis of which lies the assumption that *phenotypic (appearance), psychological, physiological and other biological characteristics of people indicating their common origin (race) directly and tangibly affect the structure of the societies formed by these people.* Thus, racial theories are based on the assertion of a direct connection between biological and social factors in the understanding of society and the ethnos. Racial theories try to describe and justify this connection.

S. M. Shirokogoroff characterizes the variety of racial theories as follows:

> In modern times the naturalist Carl Linnaeus separated all people into three types:
>
> 1) 'Wild man', '*Homo ferus*', to which were ascribed chiefly cases of the transformation of children left without a human upbringing into a wild, animal condition;
>
> 2) 'Monstrous man', '*Homo monstruosus*', to which were ascribed microcephals and other pathological cases, and
>
> 3) 'Upright man', '*Homo diurnus*', of which there are four races: American, European, Asian, and African, differing by a set of physical peculiarities. Linnaeus specifies also ethnographic markers. In his opinion, Americans are led by *customs*, Europeans by *laws*, Asians by *opinions*, and Africans by *lawlessness*. (…)

At the end of the 18th century Johannes Friedrich Blumenbach (1752–1840) developed a completely independent classification, basing it on hair and skin color and skull shape. Blumenbach counts five races, specifically:

1) The Caucasian race — white, with a round head, lives in North America, Europe and Asia to the Gobi Desert;

2) The Mongolian race — has a square head shape, black hair, a yellow-colored face, and slanting eyes, and lives in Asia, except for the Malaysian archipelago;

3) The Ethiopian race — black, with a flattened head, lives in Africa;

4) The American race — with copper-colored skin and a deformed head;

5)   The Malay race — has chestnut hair and a moderately round head. This clas-
     sification should be considered as purely anthropological and somatic.

Fr. Miller introduced language as a marker in his classification. He proposed that hair color and language are the most stable markers and can
serve as a foundation for the subdivision of people into races; and he
establishes that there exist:

1)   Wooly-haired — Hottentots, Bushmen, Papuans;

2)   Fleecy-haired — Africans, Negroes, Kaffirs;

3)   Straight-haired — Australians, Americans, Mongols, and

4)   Curly-haired — Mediterraneans.

In sum these races give another twelve groups.

Skipping other classifications, as for instance that of Schiller, White,
and Haeckel, which recognized four lineages and thirty-four races, that of
Coleman, which recognized six races and eighteen varieties, and others,
I will also state, as the most original effort, the classification of Deniker,
who established thirteen races and twenty-nine groups, basing himself,
similar to a botanist, as he himself says of his method, on all anthropological markers. Finally, Professor Ivanovski established another forty-one
groups.[11]

Racism

Not always but often enough racial theories spill over into racism, which
is their extreme expression.

Racism is a theory that asserts that a person's individual traits and the
specific character of the social arrangement are determined to a significant (sometimes, decisive) extent by the fact of their racial makeup. The
hierarchy of races built on this foundation subdivides them into higher

---

11   Shirokogoroff, S. M. *Etnos. Issledovanie osnovnyih printsipov izmeneniya etnicheskih
     i etnograficheskih yavleniy.* Shanghai, 1923.

and lower. The thesis of the inequality of races is the fundamental marker of racism.

The French sociologist Joseph Arthur de Gobineau (1816–1882) was the first to try to formulate a racist theory, in his book *Essay on the Inequality of Human Races.*[12] In the four volumes of this lengthy work, Gobineau summarizes a tremendous amount of data, in which are included also his own observations and studies. On this basis, he advanced the hypothesis that three races — the White, Black, and Yellow — display vividly expressed (innate) tendencies, skills, priorities, and social attitudes, each structured differently. The White race is distinguished by its *rationality, tendency towards the ordering of systems, and interest in technology.* The yellow race is *contemplative and unhurried.* The Black race is *chaotic and anarchic, but talented in music, dance, and plastics.*

Despite conventional opinion, Gobineau does not order the races in a hierarchy, but understands inequality as differences predominating in each of their sociological patterns. Claude Lévi-Strauss, one of the most authoritative and fundamental opponents of racism, in his book *Race and History* specifies that one should not confuse the ideas of Gobineau with those conclusions that racists made from his work.[13]

The sociologist and founder of social psychology Gustave Le Bon (1841–1931) notes inequality in the psychology of different narods. In his book *The Psychological Laws of the Evolution of Peoples,* he, in the spirit of Gobineau, remarks that different ethnoses, narods, and races gravitate predominantly to diverse spheres of action and bear in their psychology one set of attitudes and inclinations to the detriment of others.[14] Le Bon notes that left to themselves, Englishmen, for instance, will quickly form a political system of self-government, while the members of the Romantic narods (Spaniards, Portuguese, or Italians) will more likely descend into anarchy and chaos.

---

12   Gobineau, J. A. *Essai sur l'inégalité des Races humaines.* Paris: Pierre Belfond, 1967.

13   Lévi-Strauss, C. *Race et histoire.* Paris: Gonthier, 1961.

14   Le Bon, G. *Lois psychologiques de l'évolution des peuples.* Paris: Felix Lacan, 1894.

The semantic transition from the constant "inequality," understood as difference, to the hierarchization of race occurs with the English sociologist Houston Stewart Chamberlain (1855–1927), who is a key figure in the establishment of racism. In his major work *Foundations of the 19th Century*, Chamberlain describes his version of world history, in which the members of the "White race" ("Aryans") act as the positive force and are opposed by the "lower" ("colored") races. In Chamberlain's opinion, the Semitic narods, chiefly the Jews, bring the greatest harm to the "Aryans." The struggle of the "higher" races ("Aryans") with the "lower" ones comprises the essence of history, both ancient and modern. Chamberlain's theory is not only racial, but racist, since it is based on the recognition of "lower" and "higher" races. This theory was put at the foundation of German National-Socialism and practically became the official version of the exposition of world history in the Third Reich.

The French sociologist Georges Vacher de Lapouge (1854–1936) built his racial theory on the opposition of "dolichocephalics" (people with an elongated, oblong skull) and brachycephalics (people with a round skull-structure).[15] He considered the first "higher" people ("Aryans") and the second "lower" ones. He distinguishes three races in Europe:

- *Homo europeus* — this type is characteristic for Northern European countries, in the first place of German origin);

- *Homo alpinus* — the inhabitants of Central Europe;

- *Homo mediterraneus* — the type most diffused around the Mediterreanean

De Lapouge establishes a hierarchy between them, claiming that *Homo europeus* is the "pure" racial type, and *Homo mediterraneus* a mix with other non-European races and hence lower. *Homo alpinus* represents an "intermediate instance."

In the United States, the anthropologist Madison Grant (1865–1937), a close friend of two American presidents, Theodore Roosevelt and Herbert

---

15   Vacher de Lapouge, G. *L'Aryen et son rôle social*. Paris: Albert Fontemoing, 1899; Ibid. *Race et milieu social: essais d'anthroposociologie*. Paris: M. Rivière, 1909.

Hoover, tried to give racism a "scientific" character. Grant was able to advance a few key legislative initiatives, limiting immigration to the US and even facilitating the "Act Concerning Racial Purity" (1924), formally forbidding interracial marriages.

In his book *Disappearance of the Great Race* Grant celebrates the "Nordic race" (by which he understands the population of Northern Europe), to which, in his opinion, the US owes its world might, and he demands the implementation of "eugenics" — special rules of marriage laws, aimed at the purification of race and its improvement. He glorifies the principle of "racial purity" and proposes to place members of the "lower races" into the ghetto by force, forbidding them to leave its confines.

One of the most influential theoreticians of racism alongside de Lapouge and Madison Grant in the 20th century was Hans Friedrich Karl Günther (1891–1968), who distinguished the following taxonomy of races in Europe:[16, 17]

1. Nordic

2. Dinaric

3. Alpine

4. Mediterranean

5. Western

6. Eastern-Baltic

Günther considered members of the Nordic race — tall, blue-eyed, dolichocephalic — to be the creators of civilization. He considered Africans and Asians defective. The worst lot fell to the Jews, whom Gunter associated with the "representatives of Asia in Europe" and, correspondingly, considered the main "racial enemy."

---

16   To this list Günther occasionally added the "Phalic" race.

17   Günther, H. *Rasse und Stil: Gedanken uber ihre Beziehungen im Leben und in der Gesitesgeschichte der europeischen Volker.* Münich: Lehmann, 1926.

Alfred Rosenberg (1893–1946), who was one of the ideologists of the Third Reich and who was executed in accordance with the judgement of the Nuremberg tribunal, in his writings (in particular, in *The Myth of the 20th Century*), set out the political-dogmatic version of these ideas, aiming at their practical implementation.[18]

Racism became a fundamental part of National-Socialist ideology, and the realization of racial principles carried in its wake the death of millions of innocent people.

The Racist Aspect of the Study of the Human Genome

In our time, scientists working on calculating the structure of the human genome are often subjected to accusations of racism. Fears are especially evoked by attempts to create a centralized genetic bank, where facts about the genes of different ethnic and racial groups would be amassed.

At the vanguard of such research activities the Institute of Population and Resource Studies (Morrison Institute), acting within the framework of Stanford University on the "Human Genome Diversity Project" (HGDP) stands out in particular.[19]

The project's goal is to collect data concerning the blood composition of a great number of inhabitants of the Earth, classified along ethnic and racial markers, in order to trace the genealogy of their distant ancestors. It is offered to anyone who wishes to send a few drops of their blood, collected and packaged in a certain way, to this institution can learn of their origins right up to the first humans. For a separate fee the employees of this institution take it upon themselves to reconstruct the full ethnic genealogy of the ancestors and to send out an attestation of its authenticity.

Besides the fact that the models of genetic reconstruction of the past are based on rather contestable paradigms and cannot be considered scientifically reliable, the use of genetic information in the future provokes serious

---

18   Rosenberg, A. *Der Mythus des 20. Jahrhunderts. Eine Wertung der seelisch-geistigen Gestaltenkämpfe unserer Zeit.* München: Hoheneichen-Verlag, 1934.

19   Online at: http://www.stanford.edu/group/morrinst/hgdp.html (accessed 29.08.2010).

apprehensions. Many fear that this will be used for the development of a genetic weapon, capable of striking the members of some specific ethnos or concrete race. A number of countries — China in particular — prohibit the collection of such information on their territories, with the aim of bolstering state security.

Criticism of Racial and Biological Approaches

Racial and racist approaches are inadmissible in Ethnosociology for a number of reasons. Even if the moral side of the question and the memory of the criminal practice of the introduction of "racial laws" in the Third Reich and the millions of people who became their victims require no further discussion, it is still much more important to explain the scientific unfitness of these theories.

First, the very notion of human races, as Shirokogoroff showed, is exceedingly imprecise, and different systems of classification propose mutually exclusive forms of their definition. Either too few (three or four) or too many races are distinguished. In such an unsettled and imprecise taxonomy, it is simply impossible to make some kind of justified socio-logical conclusions.

Second, there are no clear and well-founded studies scientifically proving a direct connection between the structure of a society and the ra-cial peculiarities of the people who created it. Even if certain observations do attest to different tendencies of this or that racial group, then it still is not completly obvious that genetic and racial, rather than sociological, cultural, and historical factors are specifically responsible for them.

Third, when we are talking about the variation of races and more so of the hierarchy among them, then those characteristics, values or attitudes dominating in the society to which the researcher himself belongs serve as criteria. He implicitly accepts his values as normative, and the values of other groups, different from his own, as lower. There are no racial theorists who would reckon themselves among the "lower race." Consequently, in this case we are dealing not with science, but with ideology.

Fourth, there are no reasons to impart to the quality of greater complexity and differentiation of society a mark of superiority. A more complex society is more complex, period; it does not follow from this that it is *better* than a simple one. We live in a complex society, but this does not at all mean that simple societies are *worse* than ours.

Fifth, nothing proves that the technical and material advancements of a society are the final criteria of its superiority or that they are related to underlying racial factors.

Sixth, all ethnoses existing today and existing previously are products of a repeated and many-sided mixing, including also racial mixing. To separate out a "pure" element is impossible both theoretically and practically. It is curious that in our time the maximum quantity of blonde and blue-eyed people is met with among the Finno-Ugric population, which not a single racial theory relates to the "Aryans."

Seventh, there is not one criterion (phenotype, craniometry, osteometry, the structure of the hair covering, etc.) which might serve as a reliable marker in the study of the genetic continuity of a race.

Eighth, the biological constituent and hypothesis of the "animal" principle in man, which lies at the basis of the biosocial and racial approaches, cannot serve as an explanation of social phenomena, since the properly human in man is precisely not the animal but another principle, separating man from beasts and other creatures and things of the external world. This is the fundamental fact that man does not exist without society.

All of this applies not only to properly racial and racist theories, but also to Social-Darwinism and the theory of evolution, which also carry a veiled racist charge. The more developed and complex society is considered *better* in comparison with less developed and simpler ones; more technologically equipped and materially successful societies as *higher* in comparison with less equipped and successful ones. Such a model of reasoning and system of appealing arguments completely reproduces the logic of racism: the White race is stronger and better equipped (more successful), consequently, it is higher than the "colored" races. Evolutionists and supporters of the theory of progress do not appeal to white and non-white races, but societies are subject to hierarchization: developed societies are strong and better equipped (more successful), consequently they are higher than undeveloped ones. In both cases, the position that the researcher himself occupies is *higher*. And this is racism.

Ethnosociology as a discipline accepts neither the biosocial nor, even more importantly, the racial approach. It is based on the study of societies, the ethnos and its derivatives as a *human* phenomenon, "human society," in which neither the animal nor the material components are dominating and decisive.

Ethnosociology rejects social analysis in which terms such as "lower" and "higher society," "more developed" and "less developed," "more perfect" and "less perfect" are used. We know different types of society and different forms of social processes exist. We can compare the former and clarify the orientation of others, but all of this must be done without moral assessment and without the certainty that that we know the goal towards which social history aims. Social history is reversible.

That Primordialism which can be taken as a basic paradigm of ethno-sociological analysis is exclusively *cultural*.

Cultural Primordialism

Cultural Primordialism is fundamental for Ethnosociology. Cultural Primordialism means that we consider the ethnos as a basic, fundamental category and the primordial basis of society. But Cultural Primordialism does not include a biological component in the concept of the ethnos, while the question of lineage and lineal belonging is considered in the general context of the ethnic structure.

Cultural Primordialism considers the ethnos as the most basic form of an endogamous social group, and, accordingly, as a koineme.

Many arguments over the definition of the term "ethnos" circle around the questions of whether the ethnos is a constant or variable, whether it has a historical dimension and whether ethnicity is preserved in complex societies. We shall examine these questions in detail in the corresponding sections of the book; here we shall state a few basic theses.

Cultural Primordialism thinks that the ethnos is principally *static*, although inside this stasis there constantly run dynamic and sometimes very intensive processes, aimed at preserving this stasis. We can call this "active conservatism"; in order to remain unchanging, the ethnos must constantly undertake a multitude of efforts which are put together in the broad field of intra-ethnic dynamics.

When the structure of the ethnos actually begins to change and the historical factor appears, we are no longer dealing with an ethnos, but with its derivatives. The ethnos as such is invariable, but if changes in the structure of the ethnos acquire an irreversible (historical) character, they transform a purely ethnic society into something else, more complicated and differentiated. The ethnos as such is not historical, but when it proves to be inserted into history, it is transformed into a more complex social structure.

And, finally, the question of the preservation of the ethnic factor in more differentiated societies. Cultural Primordialism answers this in the spirit of "perpetual primordialism" (according to the classification of Anthony Smith). The ethnic dimension, in fact, is present in all types of society available to observation. This dimension is present even where nominally and normatively it is not there (not supposed to be there). This does *not* mean, however, that the ethnos in complex societies is entirely identical with the ethnos in simple societies, where it is by itself. It plays another role and in a different capacity, being a kind of "basement" or "social unconscious."[20]

The conception of Cultural Primordialism as the basic ethnosociological method removes the criticism of Primordialism as a whole, which absolutely justly points to the fact that ancient ethnoses, historical narods, and contemporary nations, and also ethnic phenomena in today's world, are entirely *different phenomena*, which categorically cannot be identified with one another (as the representatives of naïve Primordialism, the sociobiological approach, evolutionists and supporters of racial theories

---

20 See Dugin, A.G. *Sociology of the Imagination. Introduction to Structural Sociology.* Moscow: Academic Project, 2010.

do). Cultural Primordialism agrees with this entirely. We deal with the ethnos in its pure guise only in "primordial" societies. When we register their complication, we are speaking of a derivative of the ethnos. And, accordingly, the criteria, principles, structures, regularities, function sets, etc. of these derivatives of society must also be considered as derivatives. Analogies can usefully be drawn between them, emphasizing meanwhile the qualitative difference of the diverse processes.

We can illustrate this in the following way. In Shirokogoroff's definition of the ethnos we see three main criteria: (1) language, (2) belief in a common origin, (3) common rituals. These are the properties *only* of the ethnos.

In the case of the "first derivative" of the ethnos, the narod-laos, we will have a derivation from language (a common koine and polyglossia), a "derivation" from belief in a common origin (to which is added belief in a common goal, which creates the historical arrow of time) and a "derivation" of shared rituals (which will be differentiated along a caste-estate principle).[21, 22]

In the nation those same three criteria will represent three other "derived" characteristics: (1) instead of language, koine, and polyglossia, the idiom (Ernest Gellner) appears; (2) replacement of the belief in a common origin by the rational foundation of an administrative-territorial arrangement; (3) a secular calendar and the organization of labour and leisure (for instance, the five-day work week) instead of shared rituals.

These criteria will be even more complex at the level of the "fourth derivative" in the context of civil and global society: (1) an artificial world language, (2) the concept of the auto-genesis of the individual, (3) personality sacrality.

---

21   Koine (from the Greek κοινή, "whole,") is the language spoken, due to historical circumstances, by two or more ethnoses.

22   Polyglossia (from the Greek πολύς, "many," and γλῶσσα, "language,") is when in one society many languages coexist.

If we look into futurology, then post-society brings with it: (1) a machine (computer) language, (2) system-network creativity, (3) the cult of effectiveness and optimization.

SECTION TWO
Constructivism

Classical Constructivism: Ernest Gellner, Benedict Anderson, Eric Hobsbawm

Very often in the scientific literature the primordialist approach is contrasted with Constructivism. In its most general features, constructivism insists that the ethnos is not an organic community, but an *artificial social construct*, produced alongside others for the resolution of certain problems during the organization of power and property relations.

Constructivism asserts that the ethnos is an abstraction and the product of a specific, conscious act of the political elite.

Sometimes the constructivist approach in Ethnosociology is equated with "Modernism," which points to the idea, shared by the majority of constructivists, of the strictly modern origin of "nations" as political strategies of the Modern Era.

The philosopher and sociologist Ernest Gellner (1925–1995), the sociologist Benedict Anderson, and the Marxist historian Eric Hobsbawm are considered the most significant representatives of the constructivist approach.

Ernest Gellner is one of the most authoritative researchers on the question of the origin of modern nations. He proposes that nations emerged into a practically "empty space" as a result of the rational demand of modern states to organize, order, mobilize, and unite their population with the aim of their effective management in the process of the attainment of concrete material goals.[23] Gellner shows that nations arise

---

23   Gellner, E. *Nations and Nationalism*. Oxford: Blackwell, 1983.

simultaneously with the bourgeouis state, where the "third-estate," which finds itself before the historical problem of the new political organization of capitalist society, dominates. The concept of the "nation" resolves this problem in the most optimal way and becomes the primary form of the political organization of society in the Modern Era.

Gellner shows that at the basis of the phenomenon of the nation lies not myth, but a conscious *mystification*. In the sociological terms of Ferdinand Tönnies (1855–1936), who distinguished artificially established "*society*" (*Gesellschaft*) and naturally arising "*community*" (*Gemeinschaft*), Gellner interprets the concept of the "nation" as the knowingly false endowment of the former with the characteristics of the latter for the realization of concrete administrative tasks. All "stories" (narratives) met with in the first stage of the formation of the nation in Europe are crude ideological forgeries — and, in the first place, the idea of the continuity of the ethnic and racial belonging of contemporary men and the ethnoses and narods of antiquity.

Another well-known sociologist, Benedict Anderson, developing this kind of approach, calls the "nation" an "imagined community," meaning by "imagination" "illusion," "deception," and a coarse and conscious forgery.[24]

Eric Hobsbawm (a Marxist) goes even further and asserts that "antiquity" and "tradition" were thought up by the bourgeoisie for the justification of their dominance, and for this reason, ethnoses, nations, and religions are reconstructions of the Modern Era, necessary for the resolution of concrete tasks by the capitalist class.[25]

The Limits of Constructivism's Relevance

Among the various constructivist and near-constructivist approaches, two in particular should be distinguished. Both of them deny the

---

24 Anderson, B. *Imagined Communities: Reflections on the Origin and Spread of Nationalism*. London: Verso, 1991.

25 Hobsbawm, E & Ranger T. O. *The Invention of Tradition*. Cambridge: Cambridge University Press, 1983.

primordialist approach, but in that approach itself we saw significant differences and even contradictions (for instance, between cultural and sociobiological Primordialism). Very approximately, the differences between Primordialism and Constructivism can be formulated as follows: if Primordialism asserts that ethnoses are organic and natural phenomena that have always existed and remain to this day, constructivism retorts that ethnoses and everything resembling them (narods, nations, etc.) are products of political manipulation on the part of governing elites, existing only in certain historical circumstances, and are ideological fictions. In such definitions, indeed, we are dealing with two mutually exclusive approaches, between which we must choose according to the principle *either/or*.

But everything changes as soon as we place both of these general approaches into our ethnosociological model "ethnos–narod–nation" and reject biological forms of Primordialism as scientifically irrelevant. Then we get the following picture.

The ethnos in its purest state (the simplest form of society, the koineme, the archaic community), is an organic and primordial phenomenon, in which social stratification, political and economic elites, and the division of labor are absent. Hence, *a fortiori* there is no authority that could construct the ethnos for the realization of its goals. Only and exclusively the primordialist approach is suitable for the study of the ethnos.

But if we take the nation as the "second derivative" from the ethnos, then, on the contrary, Primordialism in its purest state is not applicable to it, and Constructivism or Modernism will be the most effective means for its study. That which constructivists mean by the "imagined," "invented" and "manipulative" quality of the nation is called in Ethnosociology the *derivative*. The nation is an artificial construct that emerged in the Modern Era in the bourgeois states of Europe. In no way can the nation be identified directly with the ethnos since these are two entirely different social forms: the ethnos is a "community" (*Gemeinschaft*), and the nation, a "society" in the sense of *Gesellschaft*. Constructivists are entirely right concerning the nation. And those primordialists who do not distinguish between ethnos and nation, on the contrary, are deeply mistaken. But when constructivists transfer their view of the nation as an "imagined community" to the organic community of the ethnos and assert that this community is artificial, they also prove to be wrong, executing the unauthorized transfer of a modern paradigm onto an archaic society.

The narod (laos) is found between two poles, the ethnos and the nation, and for this reason both organic (ethnic) and artificial (constructed) elements can be found in it. In the narod there is already social stratification, political and economic elites, and problems of the projective organization of society. But the construction of the narod differs qualitatively from the construction of the nation, which must also be accounted for. Hence, for the ethnosociological analysis of the narod it is necessary to use a combination of the primordialist and constructivist approaches.

By such a synthesis, the apparent contradictions between (cultural) Primordialism and correct Constructivism are resolved, and instead of these two approaches being construed as strict alternatives, we can use them simultaneously or by turns, depending on the precisely defined stage of the examined society.

The Ethnosymbolism of Anthony Smith

The contemporary English sociologist Anthony Smith, who, in order to overcome methodological contradictions, proposed the introduction of another approach, which he called "**Ethnosymbolism**," and which holds a similar position.[26]

Smith argued with extreme constructivists, who assert that there are no common traits between the nation and the ethnos, and that they are radically distinct realities. On the whole, while agreeing that the nation is an artificial construction, Smith nevertheless affirms that it is not completely broken off from the ethnos and that the ethnos is present in the nation in *symbolic* form. In this Smith follows the course of the symbolic anthropologist Geertz. In the nation, we are dealing with the symbolic

---

26 Smith, A. D. *Myths and memories of the Nation*. Op. cit.

presence of the ethnos, with a "narrative" about the ethnos, and, hence, the ethnic factor and ethnic identity participate, in a certain way, in the phenomenon of the nation, which, thereby, cannot be reduced entirely to the manipulations of the ruling class.

Smith's Ethnosymbolism is important and operationally useful for the ethnosociological discipline from two perspectives.

First, he establishes a connection between the ethnos and the nation (as the second derivative of the ethnos), which is completely denied by the constructivist approach. In this case, Smith's notion of the "symbolic" corresponds in meaning to the notion "derivative," which we use. The idea of the "symbolic presence of the ethnos in the nation" is identical to our thesis of the "nation as the second derivative of the ethnos."

Second, just as the ethnos is present within national society non-legally, non-normatively, and on the level of the social unconscious, in this case "symbolism" might be understood psychoanalytically, as remembrance of the excluded and censored element of the collective unconscious. In a nation-state of the Modern Era, the ethnos is nominally abolished, but it remains in the form of a collective unconscious and manifests itself in a "symbolic" form: for instance, in nationalism, xenophobia, and chauvinism (which possess numerous irrational characteristics). Smith's Ethnosymbolism successfully supplements Cultural Primordialism and appropriately used Constructivism; hence, it should be used by ethnosociologists as further support.

SECTION THREE
Instrumentalism

The Emergence of Instrumentalism

It remains for us to consider the instrumentalist approach. It is rather similar to Constructivism, only differing from it in that it is not tethered to the Modern Era (as constructivists-modernists like Gellner and

Anderson are) and does not consider the phenomena of the nation and nationalism a priority.

Instrumentalism in the study of ethnic processes took shape in the 1960s and 70s in the United States over the course of the sociological analysis of the integration of the colored population of that country, inter-racial marriages, and the position of the White population.[27] Studies revealed the decisive role of *political elites* in this process. Earlier these elites were interested in supporting the segregationist model of the administration of society, but gradually, owing to the necessity of broadening the middle class and the consumer potential of the population, they came to the technique of racial integration.

To this were added studies of the behavior of minorities in poly-ethnic societies (the USA, contemporary Europe, etc.), which used their ethnic belonging exclusively with the aim of receiving with its help supplementary material and social goods.[28] A picture formed, of the ethnos being nothing more than an instrument for the attainment of social aims.[29] Defining the instrumental approach, the sociologists Steven Cornell and Douglas Hartmann write: "Ethnicity and race are here understood as instrumental entities, organized as a means for the attainment of concrete aims."[30]

These situationally correct conclusions of the instrumentalists were applied to all ethnic processes in principle, without taking into account the historical context or specific social character of the society.

Instrumentalists focused specifically on the study of *ethnic* processes, but as organized artificially and with the goal of strengthening or reorganizing social stratification in the interests of a concrete political group.

27 Smith, A. *Nationalism: Theory, Ideology, History*. Cambridge: Polity, 2001.

28 Portes, A. & Bach R. L. *Latin Journey: Cuban and Mexican Immigrants in the United States*. Berkeley, CA: University of California Press, 1985.

29 Cohen, R. *Ethnicity: Problem and Focus in Anthropology* / Annual Review of Anthropology. 1978. №7. pp. 379–403.

30 Cornell, S. & Hartmann D. *Ethnicity and Race: Making Identities in a Changing World*. Thousand Oaks, CA: Pine Forge, 1998. p. 59.

Ethnicity as a Strategy

In his book *Ethnic Studies: Issues and Approaches*, the sociologist Philip Yang, himself inclined toward a moderate form of Instrumentalism, gives a similar definition of the instrumentalist school in the USA.[31]

The Americans Nathan Glazer and Daniel Moynihan were the first sociologists to advance the concept of the instrumentalist approach. In their book *Ethnicity: Theory and Experience*,[32] they formulated the foundations of such an approach. According to Glazer and Moynihan, ethnicity is not simply a set of sentiments and active feelings, but a form of realization of social strategies, together with nations and classes. From their perspective, the ethnos is a group of common interests, i.e., an artificial organization. Glazer later developed this theme in his book *Ethnic Dilemmas*,[33] where he radicalized his approach even more.

Another sociologist, Orlando Patterson, a native of Jamaica, analyzing the structure of the imperialistic dominance of the "White" nations over the "colored" ones, asserts that "the power, structure, effectiveness, and grounds of the ethnic factor depend entirely on the individual and group interests that use it and which it serves."[34]

Instrumentalists (such as American sociologist Michael Hetcher, for instance) apply rational choice theory to the study of ethnic identity, according to which the behavior of an individual is dictated by his striving to attain certain goals by the shortest and simplest path, which also predetermines the structure of his identification: he identifies with those

---

31 Yang, P. Q. *Ethnic Studies: Issues and Approaches*. Albany, NY: State University of New York Press, 2000.

32 Glazer, N. & Moynihan D. P. (ed.) *Ethnicity: Theory and Experience*. Cambridge, MA: Harvard University Press, 1975.

33 Glazer, N. *Ethnic Dilemmas, 1964–1982*. Cambridge, MA: Harvard University Press, 1985.

34 Patterson, O. *Dependence and Backwardness*. Mona, Jamaica: Institute of Social and Economic Research, 1975. p. 348.

collective forms with which it is advantageous to do so.[35] Thus, ethnicity becomes no more than a means for the attainment of a concrete goal. If his ethnicity helps him to attain that goal, it is accented; if it hinders him, it is ignored.

Instrumental Perennialism

Anthony Smith places the "instrumental perennialists" in a separate category, in order to emphasize their conviction in the permanence of ethnic phenomena.

The sociologist Donald Noel, a member of the instrumentalist school, reduces the factor of ethnic identity to the cases in which one group of people aims to impose its power on another group and has, for this purpose, resorted to the instrumental construction of a specific community (ethnic or religious).[36] The ethnos and ethnic identity are invented by the elite for the consolidation of social stratification. Noel calls such stratification "ethnic" and considers it a particular case of social stratification. Ethnic stratification is most often used when two ethnoses with a sufficiently expressed ethnic identity collide and intermingle with one another.

The English sociologist and supporter of instrumentalism David Mason asserts that "ethnicity is situational. Different people in different situations declare a different ethnic belonging".[37]

Situational Perennialism

"Situational Perennialism," which states that the ethnos and ethnic societies are something whole which emerge in specific historical *situations* and

---

35   Hechter, M. Containing Nationalism. Oxford and New York: Oxford University Press, 2000.

36   Noel, D. L. A *Theory of the Origin of Ethnic Stratification* / Social Problems, 1968. № 16 (2) pp. 157–172.

37   Mason, D. *Race and Ethnicity in Modern Britain*. Oxford: Oxford University Press, 1995.

serve the realization of concrete political or group interests, is another version of instrumentalism. At the same time, supporters of this approach do not distinguish between the ethnos, narod, and nation.

Smith classifies the well-known ethnosociologists Frederick Barth and S. Seidner as situational perennialists.[38]

The main idea of the Norwegian ethnosociologist Frederick Barth consists of the refusal to consider ethnoses and nations as fixed societies and the suggestion to understand ethnic identity as a constantly changing "border" between different social segments.[39] In different contexts, according to Barth, a single individual can act perfectly well as the carrier of different ethnic identities, which are determined not once and for all by a given structure, but by flexibly changing situations.

The difference between constructivists and situational perennialists consists only in the fact that constructivists think that the strategy of political and economic elites concerning the "artificial production of ethnoses" is characteristic for certain stages of social development, and in other stages its demand falls off; whereas the "situational perennialists" are convinced that the ethnos as a constant ("perennial") form of the rearrangement of governing and economic powers in society will always exist.

The Historical Context of the Appearance of the Instrumentalist Approach

In its understanding of the ethnos, instrumentalism, at first glance, so contradicts the primordialist approach that it seems entirely irrelevant for comprehending the essence of ethnic phenomena. It is obvious that ethnoses as simple societies are found outside of such categories as "rational choice," "the use of identity for the realization of individual interests and increase of social status," since in the koineme there exists neither those preconditions nor the space for them. Social stratification and, even

38 Seidner, S. S. *Ethnicity, Language, and Power from a Psycholinguistic Perspective.* Bruxelles: Centre de recherche sur le pluralinguisme, 1982.

39 Barth, F. *Ethnic Groups and Boundaries: The Social Organization of Culture Difference.* Oslo: Universitetsforlaget, 1969.

more so, the principle of individuality, first arises in other stages and types of society. One gets the impression that instrumentalists are speaking of some entirely different phenomenon than the ethnos. And when they do not make a distinction (as the constructivists also sometimes fail to do) between the ethnos and the nation (to say nothing of the even more rarely mentioned but just as important category of the narod), then their conceptions become entirely confused and inadequate.

However, it is worth looking more closely at this approach and trying to understand what instrumentalists have in mind.

Much will become clear if we pay attention to the time and place of the appearance of this approach — the United States of America in the 1860s and 1870s. At this time in America, there was a storm surrounding the abolition of the last remains of racial and ethnic segregation, which was a familiar feature of American politics right up until the 20th century. If we recall the initiatives of Madison Grant to forbid interracial marriages by law in the 1920s, it becomes understandable how fresh and how relevant questions about the ethnos were in that period. At that same time, the foundations of "political correctness" — norms of official, public expression — were laid, which had to take into account some ethnic norms: equality, tolerance, respect for human rights, and the rejection of discrimination on racial, gender, or social grounds.

Instrumentalists argued with those circles in the USA that still held to racist views and which had to be convinced that ethnic identity was nothing other than a social convention. Hence the polemical fervor of the instrumentalists and the explicit signs of their being ideologues. This position can well be understood and supported; however, in the overall body of instrumentalist studies, it is worth distinguishing that which is of actual scientific worth for Ethnosociology from that which should be discarded as excesses and ideological polemics.

The Relevance of Instrumentalism and its Limits

Let us determine the place of American society from the 1950s–1970s until today on the ethnosociological scale of societies. In the US, we find a contemporary national state with a high degree of development of civil society institutions which are found in an active stage of development and which attack the national conscious that has formed from the side of greater openness, tolerance, globalism, and attention to human rights. Instrumentalism is one such theoretical, conceptual weapon in the attack of civil society on all the forms of collective identity that preceded it (hence the mixing of ethnos, race, and nation). For civil society, all forms of collective identity are "hostile" and require dismantling. This attitude lies at the foundation of the instrumentalist approach, the task of which is to analyze society down to the individual and to explain social structures on the basis of the interaction of individuals. This explains much in instrumentalism and allows us to find a corresponding place for it.

At the same time, instrumentalists, despite their constant confusion of concepts (ethnos, nation, race) sometimes stumble across the ethnos and ethnicity in their proper sense. And these moments can be valuable for Ethnosociology as a whole.

From the perspective of a social façade, the ethnos retires into the background during the transition to the narod, and during the development of a nation it is altogether hidden from view (the nation is a simulacrum of the ethnos). In the transition to civil society, it seems, the ethnos simply should not exist. But it is present phenomenologically, and instrumentalist sociologists are called upon to allow this discrepancy. Instrumentalists "stumble across" the ethnos in the process of transitioning to a civil society and try to interpret it from the position of new criteria. Many of the conclusions that instrumentalists draw in the course of the work have worth as a description and analysis of the status of the ethnos in a society transitioning from national state to civil society. And here Instrumentalism is entirely appropriate and adequate.

If we reject the untenable pretensions of the instrumentalists to describing the ethnos as such and the phenomenon of ethnicity as something universally applicable to all types of society in all epochs, then we are left with a fully workable set of sociological analyses of the ethnos and ethnicity in highly differentiated Western capitalist societies. And in this case Instrumentalism will be an altogether adequate approach to use in analogous situations, for instance in the case of Western Europe, where we are dealing with a society in the transitional state from the nation to civil society and where the ethnic factor is also becoming more and more topical.

Thus, Instrumentalism is effective and adequate for the study of ethnic phenomena in highly differentiated societies, where it actually very often serves the realization of concrete social tasks of an entirely rational quality. In such complex societies, the ethnos exists in special circumstances: it is torn away from its natural environment, placed in the milieu of a more complex social structure, and in these conditions, begins to manifest itself according to an entirely new script. In this new ethnic script, an *instrumentalist* exploitation of the ethnic factor both by political and ethnic elites and by members of the middle and lower social strata is entirely plausible.

In a complex society, the ethnos can manifest itself in the form of ethnic lobbying, ethnic crime, the creation of ethnic networks which help its members climb the social ladder predominantly on the basis of their ethnic identity, and even the use of ethnic motifs in political campaigns. In a complex society, the ethnos becomes the object of many-sided manipulations. Instrumentalists focus on this phenomenon and describe it entirely correctly.

Instrumentalism is a means for the study of ethnic phenomena in complex societies that are transitioning from nation-states to civil societies.

With this clarification, the very reason for the argument between primordialists and instrumentalists, as well as between constructivists and instrumentalists, is lost. Each approach has its limits, beyond which it loses its meaning and applicability.

Instrumentalism and the Sociology of the Narod

The instrumentalist method can be applied in another situation: in the study of the narod. The narod is a society that, in contrast with the ethnos, is socially differentiated, contains within it upper and lower classes, and consists of several ethnic groups. In it there are not yet distinctly separated individuals as social actors and distinctly rational scripts of conduct. But a certain distance in relation to the ethnos and its Primordial (Edward Shils) allows it to relate to the ethnic factor pragmatically, on which instrumentalists insist.

One form that this kind of instrumental use can take is the ascription of a certain, distinct ethnic origin to the elites, which helps consolidate their distinction from the masses and legitimize their power. It is another matter to what extent this ascription reflects conscious manipulation, ethnic fact (often, if not always, in ancient states elites did indeed have a different ethnic origin than the masses), and symbolic-religious-magical factors. In certain narods and in certain situations one could well meet with the instrumentalisation of the ethnos and its "politicization," despite the fact that the ethnos itself has neither a political nor a pragmatic dimension in itself.

Conclusion

Completing our overview of the fundamental methods of Ethnosociology, we can separate out the following points:

1. The most productive method is Cultural Primordialism, which states that the ethnos is an organic, primordial, fundamental concept (Primordial, koineme). But at the same time, we must immediately take account of two additional points:

    a) Neither biological, zoological, nor racial elements, nor the factor of kinship (lineage) enter into the basic definition of the ethnos, since the ethnos is above all a social and cultural phenomenon.

    b) Furthermore, the ethnos exists by itself only in simple societies; beginning with the "narod" right up until the "nation" and "civil society," we meet with its derivatives, i.e., not with the ethnos itself, but with its transformations, although in these more complex societies, too, the ethnos can, with a certain amount of effort, be tracked down in the sphere of the "social unconscious."

2. The constructivist method is entirely adequate for considering the phenomenon of the "nation" (as the "second derivative" of the ethnos), since in the "nation" we are dealing with an artificial phenomenon, constructed for pragmatic purposes. At the same time, we should take into consideration the correction of the ethnosymbolists (Anthony Smith, John Breuilly) and turn our attention to the fact that according to their orientation, the ethnos is present in national societies in a "symbolic" form.[40] To apply the constructivist paradigm to the ethnos, however, and to assert that it was produced at some point out of the political aims of a group of elites is absurd.

3. Instrumentalism is suitable for the study of the ethnic factor and ethnic processes in complex societies, especially in the period of transition from a *national state* to *civil society*. Moreover, it can be applied in certain cases to the analysis of social stratification in traditional societies with a prevalence of the "narod," when the issue at hand concerns the coupling of ethnic indices with social status (most often in the religious and governing political elites). But an instrumentalist approach to the analysis of the ethnos as such is entirely fruitless and leads to irresolvable contradictions.

---

40 Breuilly, J. *Nationalism and the State*. New York, NY: St. Martin's Press, 1993.

CHAPTER FOUR

Foreign Ethnosociology

The German School of Ethnosociology, Cultural Circles, Ethnopsychology

The Term "Ethnosociology"

The term "Ethnosociology" was introduced in the earliest stage of the establishment of Sociology as a science by, Ludwig Gumplowicz (1838–1909), one of the first sociologists.[1]

Gumplowicz was born in Poland and later emigrated to Austro-Hungary, and the majority of his texts were published in German. He is also originated the term "Ethnocentrism," which the American anthropologist William Sumner later made popular.

The term "Ethnosociology" was most used in German-speaking circles for precisely these reasons. Therefore, we will begin our consideration of ethnosociological schools with Germany, including here the German-speaking authors from Austria and Switzerland, and will then move to those countries in which this discipline is known by other names: "Cultural Anthropology" in the USA, "Social Anthropology" in England, and "Structural Anthropology" and "Ethnology" in France.

---

1   Gumplowicz, L. *Der Rassenkampf.* Saarbrücken: VDM Verlag Dr. Müller, 2007.

Johannes Gottfried Herder: Narods as the Thoughts of God

The German philosopher Johannes Gottfried Herder (1744–1803), prede-cessor of the Romantics, prominent figure of the German Enlightenment, and one of the first thinkers of modernity, tried to describe the history of mankind as an intelligent and goal-directed process, the main driving forces of which are narods. The concept of the "narod" (*das Volk*) is cen-tral in Herder's philosophy. According to Herder, the diversity of narods arises from a diversity of natural, historical, social, and psychological conditions. All narods are distinct, which is expressed in the diversity of their languages. And in languages, primordial consciousness and freedom manifest themselves. The highest manifestation of humanity is religion.

Herder asserted that the structure of language predetermines the structure of thought (the famous Sapir-Whorf hypothesis, made two hun-dred years later).[2, 3] Herder thought that each narod is completely unique and that diversity is not a limitation but abundance: "In a wonderful way, Providence separated peoples (narods) not only by forests and mountains, seas and deserts, rivers and climatic conditions, but also by languages, inclinations, and characters."[4]

The difference between societies shows to what extent each of them is unique and original, and not to what extent they are "backward" or, on the contrary, "correspond to the times." In this respect, Herder expressed himself very precisely: "The savage who loves himself, his wife, and his child, with quiet joy, and is devoted to the life of his tribe as much as to his

---

2   Herder, J. G. *Ueber die Faehigkeit zu sprechen und zu horen* (1795) / Herder.

3   The theory of the cultural anthropologist Sapir and physicist Whorf's asserts that reliable translation from one language to another is impossible, since each language formulates a unique semantic structure and codifies consciousness and perception in accordance with its own peculiarities.

4   Herder, J. G. *Auch eine Philosophie der Geschichte zur Bildung der Menschheit.* Frankfurt am Mein: Suhrkamp, 1967. p. 559.

own, is in my eyes a truer being than an educated shadow, involved in the endeavors of the fellow-shadows of the whole human race."[5]

We cannot measure one *Volk* (narod) by the yardstick of another, Herder insists, since each one bears within itself the standard of its own perfection, entirely independent of the standard of another. Herder maintains that "each people carries in itself the center of its happiness, as a bullet its center of gravity."[6] For him, *Volks* (narods) are "the thoughts of God," his manifestations. The German poet Heine said of Herder: "According to his thought, peoples are the strings of a harp, on which God plays".[7] In such an understanding, the concept "narod" can be likened to Leibniz's monad, which synthetically absorbs all contradictions into itself.

Although Herder did not hold strictly to one specific terminology, it becomes clear from a substantial analysis of his works that he understood the concept *das Volk* to simultaneously be both the ethnos and the narod (as ethnosociology understands them), but not the nation. The nation as a phenomenon of the epoch of Modernity and a construct of the third estate is a class formation and is inseparably connected with the state. Herder, especially in his early works, harshly criticized the instrumental use of the concept of *das Volk* for political aims, all forms of nationalism (the attack of one narod on another was, according to Herder, an attempt on "a thought of God" and the "plan of Providence") and attempts to hierarchize peoples (narods) on any scale — racial or evolutionary. The idea of the hierarchization of ethnoses seemed as absurd to him as the attempt to figure out whether the note "do" is better than the note "re." Moreover, Herder strictly opposed the class stratification within the narod. "There must be only one class in the state," he wrote, "*das Volk* [the narod], but not the crowd; and to this class both the king and the simple peasant must

---

5   Ibid. p. 511.

6   Ibid. p. 509.

7   Quoted in Bollenbeck ,G. *Eine Geschichte der Kulturkritik: Von Rousseau bis Günther Anders*. München: C.H. Beck Verlag, 2007.

belong."[8] Herder recognized a hierarchization within the narod (the presence of stratification is a sign of the narod as laos), but he denies "class differentiation," rejecting thereby the nation as an artificial construct. His understanding of the "narod" is holistic and integral and gravitates to the "ethnic." Sympathy to ethnicity (although without the use of this term) is also displayed by Herder in that he emphasizes the adequacy of the simplest societies ("savages") and calls for a *"living into"* (*einfuhlen*) them in order to understand them and to establish for oneself a picture of how they understood the world from their position. This anticipates the method of "psychological empathy," "sociology of participation," "Sociometry" (G. Moreno), as well as the techniques of contemporary ethnosociologists and anthropologists.

Herder asserts that at the basis of the narod lies its spirit, which he called *der Volksgeist* (narodni spirit) and identified with "culture." Herder was one of the first in Europe to use the term "culture" with its current meaning, as the totality of customs, rites, beliefs, attitudes, and value-systems, defining the mode and identity of a society.

Herder is famous for his polemics against Kant, who in those same years advanced the concept of "civil society," based on universal values and the domination of reason, which completely contradicted Herder's pluralist notions of a multiplicity of cultures and their independent value.

Johannes Gottlieb Fichte

The first-rate German philosopher Johannes Gottlieb Fichte (1762–1814) together with Herder is considered a herald of the *theory of the ethnos*. Fichte's ideas about the narod (he, like Herder, did not distinguish between the narod and the ethnos) were developed in the spirit of his philosophical theory about the "absolute subject." He considered the narod the expression of such a subject and a historical-cultural unit, preceding the division into "individuals."

---

8   Herder, J. G. "Briefe zu Beforderung der Humanitat (1793–1797)" / Herder, J. G. *Samtliche Werke*. Bd. 18. Berlin: B. Suphan, 1877–1913. p. 308.

In his political texts, Fichte formulates the principle of the primacy of
the narod over the state and calls the Germans to a narodni rebirth on the
basis of a cultural and ethnic unity.[9]

Fichte thought that between the Germans contemporary to him and
ancient Germans there existed a direct, immediate, ethnic connection, expressing itself in the continuity of language. On this basis, he analyzed the
German character as a direct trace of the behavior of ancient Germans,
described by Tacitus.

In contrast to Herder, Fichte was a follower of Kant and paid attention
mainly to the rational side of culture.

We can define Fichte's views in the sphere of Ethnosociology as "naïve
Primordialism," and to correlate his function in the self-awareness of the
German society of his historical situation with the transition from a con-
dition of the narod (laos) to a condition of the nation.

Johann Jakob Bachofen

The Swiss German author, historian, and jurist, Johann Bachofen
(1815–1877), formulated exceptionally important anthropological theories
concerning the structure of simple societies and the stages of their development. According to Bachofen, simple (ethnic) societies were organized
according to the principle of "maternal right" and were egalitarian communities, in which a matriarchy dominated. He summarized these ideas
in his main work *Mother Right: Studies of Gynaecocracy in the Ancient
World in its Religious and Juridical Nature.*[10]

From Bachofen's perspective, the historical stratification of societies
was directly connected with the establishment of a patriarchal order. This
order was not established in an empty space, however, but on the basis of
more archaic institutions, which were formed along the principle of the
domination of the mother. Bachofen studied a broad range of archeologi-
cal, historical and linguistic data concerning the Mediterranean area, and

---

9   Fichte, J.G. *Address to the German Nation.* New York, NY: Harper & Row, 1968.

10   Bachofen, J.J. *Mutterrecht. Eine Untersuchung über Gynaikokratie der alten Welt nach
     ihren religiösen und rectlichen Natur.* Stuttgart: Krais & Hoffmann, 1861.

everywhere he found traces of an ancient "gynocratic" (from the Greek *gyné,* "woman," and *krátos,* "rule") culture, preserved in rites, myths, traditions, and a series of legal guidelines.

Despite the many-sided criticism of Bachofen's theory, it gave an important impulse to anthropological studies and drew attention to the social role of gender, which subsequently became one of the most important themes of sociology as a whole and ethnosociology in particular.

Adolf Bastian: Elementary Thought and Narodni Thought

Adolf Bastian (1826–1905), founder of the Berlin Museum for Ethnography (*Berliner Museum für Völkerkunde*) was an eminent figure in German ethnology and anthropology. Bastian adhered to the theory of evolution and of the single origin of humanity (he called this the "psychic unity of mankind"). But in contrast with many other supporters of evolution, he did not consider it as a linear, but as a helical process, developing in history by ascending cycles. Bastian shared the positivist approach of the French philosopher Auguste Comte (1798–1857) and strove to elaborate a consist teaching about society (thereby acting as a forerunner of sociology). At the same time, Bastian accented the psychological side of culture and studied diverse social phenomena — myths, dances, mystical states and other forms — from the perspective of their psychological content.

Bastian laid out his basic theoretical conclusions in his work *Man in History. Towards the Justification of a Psychological Worldview.*[11]

According to Bastian, on the Earth's territory one can mark out several "geographical provinces," where the parallel development of diverse types of human society occurred. All these societies followed the same trajectory and the same logic, despite never intersecting or interacting with one another. Unity was founded on the fact that the consciousness of all people is a qualitatively homogeneous phenomenon, which he called "elementary thought" (*Elementargedanken*). Differences in

11   Bastian, A. *Der Mensch in der Geschichte: Zur Begrundung einer psychologischen Weltanschauung.* 3 Bände. Leipzig: Wigand, 1860.

culture are due to the influence of a geographical environment, which affected the process of evolution of societies, arrested or on the contrary pushed it or developed some or other psychological qualities and social practices as a priority. Thus, according to Bastian, from the "elementary thought" common to all mankind, various social and cultural forms took shape with each narod. Bastian called these secondary forms "narodni thought" (*Volkergedanken*). Bastian also used the term "social thought" (*Gesellschaftgedanken*), anticipating Durkheim's "collective consciousness." "Social thought" is not composed of the mathematical summation of the thoughts of separate persons, but more often represents a unique intellectual breakthrough of the spiritual and political elite, imprinted in the form of general culture, which gradually becomes part of a society's heritage in the aspect of "narodni thought."

On this theoretical foundation, Bastian grounded his method of study of ethnic cultures. At its basis lies "cross-cultural" comparative analysis, i.e., the juxtaposition of distinct cultural forms of diverse ethnoses and narods with the aim of separating out the structures of "elementary thought" (as universal) and the empirical description of "narodni thought" as a specific.

Friedrich Ratzel: Anthropogeography and Ethnology

Friedrich Ratzel (1844–1904), a German geographer, undertook one of the first attempts to provide a general overview of ethnoses in their geographic dimension.[12] From Ratzel's perspective, man, being one of the most mobile living organisms, is nevertheless tied to the Earth and depends on that natural environment in which he dwells and is formed. In this way, the differentiation of societies and narods occurs.

In the spirit of evolutionism, Ratzel divides ethnoses into "savage" and "cultured," considering the main criterion the degree and quality of dependence on nature. Nature looms over "savage" narods. Cultured narods liberate themselves from it and enter into a more equitable and

---

12   Ratzel, F. Narodovedenie. Tom 2SPb: "Prosveshcheniye, 1902–1903."

mutually beneficial dialogue with it. On the basis of such an approach Ratzel elaborates his system of "Anthropogeography," i.e., a study of the maps of the historical dynamics of the interaction of narods in concrete geographical conditions.

Ratzel laid the foundations simultaneously for a few approaches that received further development in the 20th century. Thus, in particular, he:

- Worked out the preconditions for geopolitics (this term was first introduced into scientific use by his disciple, the Swede Rudolph Kjellén and formulated its main postulates ("the law of the spatial growth of states," the idea of a "living space," etc.);[13, 14]

- Drew the attention of sociologists to the significance of the factor of space, with the help of which he explained the differences in cultures of various ethnoses;[15]

- Introduced the very important concept of "spatial sense" (*Raumsinn*), which served as a prototype for the concept of "place of development" as advanced by Eurasian philosophers such as P. Savitskii;[16]

- Laid down the premises of the theory of "cultural circles," which affirms that all material, technical, and cultural discoveries in history were made only in one place and by one narod, and were further spread among other narods by the method of their transmission;[17]

---

13   Ratzel, F. *Politische Geographie*. Munich: Oldenburg, 1897.

14   Dugin, A. G. *Foundations of Geopolitics*. Moscow: Aktogeia-Center, 2000.

15   Dugin, A. G. *Sociology of the Imagination. Introduction to Structural Sociology*. Moscow: Academic Project, 2010; Ibid. *Sociology of Russian Society*. Moscow: Academic Project, 2010.

16   Dugin, A. G. *Foundations of Eurasianism*. Moscow: Arktogeia-Center, 2002.

17   Ratzel, F. *Anthropogeographie*. Stuttgart: J. Engelhorn, 1899.

- Proposed for Archeology the model of the criterion of the form of an object, and not its function, for the clarification of the area of its primary contrivance;

- Advanced the hypothesis of the origin of the state out of the subordination of one ethnos to another, more aggressive, ethnos-conqueror, which was the basic for Ethnosociology.

Robert Graebner: The Methods of Ethnology

At the same time as Ratzel, the German anthropologist and ethnologist Robert Graebner (1877–1934), who became a crucial figure in the "diffusionist school," developed and systematized a theory of cultural circles. *Methods of Ethnology* is considered to be his most important work.[18]

Supporters of Diffusionism made Ratzel's intuition about the uniqueness of all historical inventions and discoveries the main principle of their studies and on this foundation built a reconstruction of the phases of the historical establishment of ethnoses and cultures.

The basic idea of the diffusionists consisted in their criticism of Adolf Bastian's evolutionary theory of "elementary thought," which dominated in German-speaking circles of that time. Bastian asserted that all members of the human species are mentally identical, while Graebner and the supporters of the idea of "cultural circles" rejected such an approach.

According to Graebner, during a weak occupation of territory, a society has no stimulus to technical and cultural innovations, since relations with the surrounding natural world are sufficient for the maintenance of the status-quo. Hence all discoveries — metal working, the taming of diverse livestock, the manufacture of instruments of labor, vehicles, as well cultural rites and customs — were made either accidentally or in strictly specific geographical places, where there were entirely unique natural or ethnic conditions. Graebner likened invention to a stone thrown into water: the point of contact is strictly singular, but circles spread in all

---

18   Graebner, F. *Methode der Ethnologie*. Heidelberg: Winter, 1911.

directions. Robert Graebner was the one to introduce the concept of the "*culture circle*" (*Kulturkreise*).

Following Graebner, this approach received the name "the Cultural-Historical School of Vienna."

Wilhelm Schmidt: Primitive Monotheism

Graebner's ideas were picked up by the Catholic priest and ethnologist Wilhelm Schmidt (1868–1954), who used the method of "cultural circles" as a justification for his own hypothesis about the origin of religion. Schmidt advanced the idea of "**Primitive Monotheism**," according to which the most ancient beliefs in ethnic societies were not "Animism," "Totemism," "magic," or "Polytheism," as classical evolutionists thought, but a primordial form of "Monotheism."

Schmidt summarized his ethnological and ethnosociological theories in a monograph, written by him jointly with another Catholic priest and minister Wilhelm Koppers (1886–1961), *Handbook of the Methods of Cultural-Historical Ethnology.*[19]

One of Schmidt's goals in using the cultural-historical method was to criticize the theories of evolution and Marxism as contrary to the Christian view of history. Schmidt separates all societies into "primitive," "initial," "secondary," and "tertiary," thinking that "primitive" societies stand closest of all to the moment of the creation of the world and bear the mark of the most ancient forms of "Monotheism."

In this instance, ethnology and sociology cross with a theological approach of a clearly expressed confessional color.

Leo Frobenius: Tellurism, Chtonism, and Paideuma

The German ethnologist Leo Frobenius (1873–1938) was one of the brightest and best known representatives of the theory of "cultural circles."

---

19 Koppers, W. & Schmidt W. *Handbuch der Methode der kulturhistorischen Ethnologie.* Münster, Westfalen: Aschendorff, 1937.

He put forward an entire array of conceptions in use in contemporary Ethnology and Ethnosociology.

Thus, the idea of the division of all types of cultures (above all, archaic ones) into two basic, fundamental kinds, *telluric and chthonic* belongs to him. In his works, Frobenius painstakingly observes how these types are dispersed along diverse geographical regions (chiefly, on the continent of Africa, about which Frobenius was a world-class specialist),[20] intersect, mix, and separate anew.

The *telluric* type (from the Latin *tellus*, meaning "earth," often with the added connotations of "earthen knoll" or "embankment") differentiated itself by the steady creation of projecting, bulging structures, pillars, ritual hills, burial mounds, menhirs, stones for burial, housing, and the performance of rituals. This type is active, aggressive, inclined to the complication of societies and patriarchal attitudes.

The *chthonic* type (from Greek χθών [chthón], "earth," in the sense of a plane or a hollow in it) of cultures, on the other hand, is characterized by constructions in the form of pits, dugouts, burrows, caverns, hollows, which influences lodgings, burial forms, and ritual complexes.

Frobenius also introduces the concept of the *"paideuma"* (from the Greek παίδευμα (*paídeuma*), literally "education" or "self-education"), which he defines as a "figure (in German, *Gestalt*), a manner of producing meanings (*Sinnstiftung*)."[21] The paideuma is that radical beginning of culture which remains unchanged in the process of social and ethnic transformations. It secures the connection and very possibility of communication for those who belong to one and the same culture, a kind of ethnic and cultural code of society. It is precisely this paideuma — as the indissoluble wholeness of the spiritual and material beginnings — that comprises the basis of that content which is transmitted in cultural circles. The explication of the paideuma gives meaning to social phenomenon.

---

20 Frobenius, L. *Der Ursprung der afrikanischen Kulturen.* Berlin: Verlag von Gebrtider Borntraeger, 1898; Ibid. *Kulturgeschichte Afrikas.* Zürich: Phaidon, 1933.

21 Frobenius, Leo. *Paideuma: Umrisse einer Kultur und Seelenlehre.* München: Beck, 1921–1928.

Different ethnic groups possess their own paideumæ, which ensures their cohesion.

Leo Frobenius applied his ethnosociological methods to contemporaneity and on the basis of the pluralism of ethnosociological forms, which he defended, he came out against all forms of colonialism.

Ludwig Gumplowicz: Struggle of Ethnoses

The Polish-Austrian sociologist Ludwig Gumplowicz (1838–1909) is a key figure in the field Ethnosociology for many reasons.

1. He introduced the term "Ethnosociology" and laid the foundation for the development of this discipline.

2. He suggested considering ethnoses as the main motivating force of the historical process and the basis of sociality as such, thereby combining the ethnological approach with the sociological. Gumplowicz proposed an ethnic interpretation of human history.

3. He developed and substantiated the idea of the origin of the state arising out of the conquest of one ethnos (predominantly settlers or hunters) by another (predominantly nomadic), creating the "*theory of superposition*" (Überlagerung). At the same time, Gumplowicz proceeds from the principle of the primordial plurality of archaic ethnoses (primitive hordes), which are located a certain distance from one another, and when this distance is shortened, they come into contact and lay thereby the ground of social differentiation. Most often this is expressed in the creation of a state and a hierarchized society, in which elites and masses are distinguished.

4. Government, according to Gumplowicz, is a product of ethnic processes and represents the primordial form of organization of the domination of an ethnic minority over an ethnic majority. He sees here the origins of the family, law, property, etc.

Gumplowicz shows that private law and state law have a different nature: private law limits the masses, while public law is a fact of the forceful presence of government.[22] And even in these purely political and legal models it is possible to discover the roots of their ethnic origin.

5. Gumplowicz anticipated E. Gellner in that he considers the nation (in the political sense) an artificial construction of the state, not connected with an ethnic origin, or by language.

These and other aspects of Gumplowicz's theory make him a crucial figure in Ethnosociology.

We should make one important correction in Gumplowicz's terminology. In his writings he persistently employs the term "race" (*die Rasse*), but means by it not a biological, but a cultural and social concept i.e. the ethnos. He contrasts race (in the sense of ethnos) with the state as a form of political organization in which the conflict of the ethnoses changes into the confrontation of elites and masses, i.e., it becomes an inner contradiction, and to the nation as one of the artificial creations of the state. Hence, Gumplowicz's basic thesis about a "racial struggle" (*Rassenkampf*), as his best-known work is called, should be translated and understood as "struggle of ethnoses."[23] He does not mean "race" in any of the meanings that are implied in "racial theory." By the conflict of "races," Gumplowicz understands not the struggle of the "White race" with the "Black race," the "Nordic" with the "Mediterranean," etc., but the conflict of different ethnoses and nothing more. With this terminological correction, everything falls into place.

Karl Marx saw society's main motivating force in "class struggle," and it served him as a key for the explanation of all social processes. Ludwig Gumplowicz sees society's motive force in the "struggle of the ethnoses," which passes over at a certain stage from the external domain (conflict of

22 Gumplowich, L. *Sotsiologia i Politika*. Moscow: Bonch-Bruyevicha, 1895.

23 Gumplowich, L. *Der Rassenkampf. Soziologische Untersuchunge*. Innsbruck: Wagner, 1883.

two tribes as two societies) into the inner domain (antagonisms between the ruling class and the underlying population).

Gumplowicz's views about the origin of the state and the theory of superposition are similar to Ratzel's theories of "Political Geography" and "Ethnography."

Gumplowicz's ideas about the origin of government became a standard for German ethnosociologists (in particular, for Richard Thurnwald, although his disciple, Mühlmann, criticized some of its aspects).

Franz Oppenheimer: The State as a Result of Ethnic Conflict

The sociologist Franz Oppenheimer (1864–1943) definitively formulated the theory of the superposition of two ethnic groups onto one another during the establishment of the state in his classic work *The State: Its History and Development Viewed Sociologically*.[24] Oppenheimer relied primarily on the work of Ratzel[25] and Schmidt,[26] and proposed the search at the origins of any type of statehood whatsoever — whether archaic and ephemeral or highly developed and settled — the primordial fact of "ethnic conquest" (*Eroberung*). Oppenheimer showed that "ethnic conquest" is most often (practically always) carried out through the invasion of settled and agrarian ethnoses by nomadic pastoral ethnoses. He referred to Ratzel's widely documented observation: "Nomad-shepherds are not only born wanderers, but also born conquerors. As far as the steppes span in the Old World, so far span the states created by them."[27]

In those historical regions in which the cultivation of large livestock was unknown, some types of belligerent hunting tribes (North America) could fulfill the function of the ethnos-conqueror, according

---

24 Oppenheimer, F. *The State: Its History and Development viewed Sociologically*. New York: Free Life Editions, 1975.

25 Ratzel, F. *Anthropogeographie*. Stuttgart: J. Engelhorn, 1921.

26 Schmidt, W. & Koppers, W. *Volker and Kulturen*. Regensburg: Habbel, 1924.

27 Ratzel, F. *Anthropogeographie. Teil. 1 Grundzuge der Anwendung der Erdkunde auf die Geschichte*. Stuttgart: J. Engelhorn, 1921. p. 99.

to Oppenheimer. Oppenheimer classified the Vikings as "nomads of the sea," who "left their herds on the shore," but preserved the nomadic and warlike structure of the "conquering ethnos."

Oppenheimer adduced many historical examples that support the "conqueror" theory of the state: the Babylonians, the Amorites, the Assyrians, the Medes, the Persians, the Macedonians, the Parthians, the Mongols, the Seljuk Turks, the Tatars, the Turks, the Hyksos, Greeks, Romans, Arabs, and other narods which have demonstrated in their history multiple occasions of conquest, producing strong and developed statehood.[28]

Oppenheimer traced this line right to the Modern Era, looking at capitalism as a continuation of this ethnosociological dualism, in which the aggressive, active, and dynamic trader-townsmen (bourgeoisie), mobile and inclined to relocate, impose their dominion onto the predominantly rural masses (peace-loving and conservative), bringing the entire society into movement and creating national states.

Alexander Rüstow: Nomads and Peasants as Fundamental Types

The well-known theoretician of neo-liberalism, Alexander Rüstow (1885–1963), developed these ethnosociological ideas of Ratzel, Gumplowicz, Schmidt, Coppers, and Oppenheimer further.[29]

Rüstow traced the history of conquering invasions in Eurasia and distinguished a few waves in it:

- In the Fourth Millennium BCE, it was a torrent of tribes, engaged in breeding large horned cattle.

- Starting in the Second Millennium BCE the previous sociological type was replaced by tribes breeding horses and moving on chariots.

---

28 Oppenheimer, F. *Der Staat: System der Sociologie*. Jena: Gustav Fischer, 1926. p. 277.

29 Rüstow, A. *Ortbestimmung der Gegenwart: Eine universalgeschichtliche Kulturkritik.* 3 Bde. Zurich: Ehrlenbach, 1949–1957.

- Around 1200 BCE a wave of horsemen ethnoses arise in Asia, attacking Europe and the Near East continuously, the last echo of which is the invasion of the Huns in 375 CE.

All these movements of narods led to the "superposition" of ethnic cultures and the emergence of states and complex, highly-differentiated societies.

Rüstow constructed two figures — the *"shepherd-nomad"* and *"settled farmer"* — as the two basic social and psychological types, explaining with their help the structure of social stratification. The will to power, domination, the repression of others, and, in particular, material accumulation, as well as technical development, is directed towards increasing the speed of movement (including information), psychological sadism, and, in the pathological stage, forms of paranoid disorders, signs of the shepherd-nomad (in the consciousness of contemporary people, too), while meditativeness, conservatism, unhurriedness, adaptability, peace-lovingness, equilibrium, satisfaction with the existing state of affairs, striving towards harmony with one's surroundings, and a readiness to submit — right up to masochism and schizophrenia in pathological cases — are signs of "the settled farmer" (in the structure of the human psyche, too).

Rüstow's conceptions show how ethnosociological observation can be unfolded to the scale of a universal sociological theory, applicable even there, where the ethnic dimension as such no longer remains: in complex political systems and in the human psyche.

Max Weber: The Definition of Ethnicity

The theories of the three brightest German sociologists, Max Weber, Ferdinand Tönnies, and Werner Sombart, who stand at the origins of the field, exerted a significant influence on Ethnosociology.

Max Weber (1864–1920) is considered the father of European Sociology, alongside Emile Durkheim, since these two scholars did more than others for the institutionalization of Sociology as an authoritative academic science. Weber's legacy is tremendous and well-known. We will single out only those aspects of his theory that have a relation to Ethnosociology.

Weber, as we know, gave a definition of *ethnicity* (*Ethnizität*), which is considered foundational:

> Ethnicity is those human groups that entertain a subjective belief in their common descent because of similarities of physical type or of customs or both, or because of memories of colonization and migration; this belief must be important for the propagation of group formation; at that same time, it does not matter whether or not an objective blood relationship exists.[30]

This definition is extremely important, since it moves the ethnos into a sociological category, grounded on "belief," i.e. on a fundamental characteristic of the social system, and not on a direct mark of generic belonging, which could be interpreted in a biological, evolutionary, or racial manner.

This definition should be adopted without reservation, since only such an approach creates the possibility of a full-fledged and adequate study of the ethnos as the *elementary form of society*, as the basic instance of Sociology (koineme).

Weber himself, however, did not give much attention to the concept of ethnicity in his system, thinking that an ethnic group is just one of various kinds of social groups, established more or less similarly, and, consequently, adding nothing of value to Sociology. In order to understand the nature of such an attitude, we should place Weber's sociology and the specific character of his approach in its proper historical context.

The foundation of Weber's approach to Sociology was built on the identification of the individual, the person, as the major building block of society, from which Weber's entire theoretical orientation followed, which he called "*understanding*." Understanding means penetrating into the structure of a person's inner world and correctly deciphering the algorithm of his decisions, aims, thoughts, and actions in society. The same approach, at the basis of which lies *methodological individualism*, is characteristic of the majority of American sociologists, first and foremost those of the Chicago school (Small, Vincent, Thomas, Znaniecki, etc.)

---

30   Weber, Max. *Economy and Society* (1922) vol. 2. Berkeley, CA: University of California Press, 1978, p. 389.

and also of Mead, who is similar to them.[31] Weber strove to comprehend society as the result of the rational, goal-oriented actions of a multitude of individuals.

If we compare Weber's studies with the scale of ethnosociological types of society, then they will occupy precisely the place that lies between "nation" and "civil society," leaning more so towards the latter, in which individual identity dominates as the basis of the whole society. This is a phenomenon of the Modern Era, the traditions of which date from the Enlightenment and Kant. Weber took as normative the European bourgeois, democratic, liberal, capitalistic society known to him, the origins of which he painstakingly studies in both the epochs immediately preceding its appearance (the Reformation, the Protestant world-view) and in more remote ones (Antiquity), where Weber also tried to find its premises.

Like Marx and Engels, who projected the economic parameters of the European capitalism of their time backwards into ages past and who wanted to see in them the origins of classes and exploitation, Weber retrojected the parameters of liberal-capitalism and individualism, characteristic of "civil society," into the most ancient epochs, trying to see in them the rudiments of "individualism" and "rationality." For this reason, Weber sees social differentiation in all social groups (not in the Marxist sense, but in the sociological understanding of classes as strata), or its preliminary phase. Weber did not occupy himself particularly deeply with archaic societies (in contrast to the later Durkheim and, especially, Marcel Mauss), and therefore his extrapolations (rather rare) in this direction do not carry serious weight.

At the same time, Weber describes very delicately the meaning of the epoch of Modernity and of "modern societies" and the way they differ from traditional ones. Weber introduces the concept of the "*disenchanted world*" (*entzauberte Welt*), the Weltanschauung of a society which loses the dimension of the "holy" and "sacred," and which stops believing in

---

31   Dugin, A. G. *Sociology of the Imagination*, pp. 33–34.

myths and religion, replacing them with rational philosophy and science.[32] Indeed, Weber occupied himself chiefly with studying the process of the "disenchantment" of the world. The concept of *"disenchantment"* is as fundamental for Weber's sociology as the concept of "alienation" is for Marxism.

If we apply Weber's terminology to the description of the ethnos as a society, then we can say that the ethnos is an *"enchanted society"* (*bezauberte Gesellschaft*). French Sociology (Durkheim, Mauss, Halbwachs, etc.) studies the theme of the meaning of the "sacred" in detail.

In the general context of Ethnosociology, Weber's theories are entirely relevant to describing the society of Modernity, the establishment of civil society and the depths of the sociological processes that occur during this. The revealed role of the Protestant Work Ethic in the establishment of capitalism is a classic model of Weber's insight into the heart of the sociological processes of Modernity.

Ferdinand Tönnies: Gemeinschaft and Gesellschaft

The German philosopher Ferdinand Tönnies (1855–1936) is another key figurehead of German Sociology.

To Tönnies belongs the well-known dichotomy between *Gemeinschaft* (community) and *Gesellschaft* (society), which is firmly associated with his name and has entered into the arsenal of fundamental sociological methods. Tönnies set forth his concept in the classic 1888 work *Community and Society: The Basic Concepts of Pure Sociology.*[33]

According to Tönnies' ideas, societies can be built in accordance with two distinct paradigms. In one case, they are built as small groups of a family type, connected by the bonds of real or symbolic kinship, united by emotional ties, empathy, care for all its members, unity of reactions,

---

32 Weber, M. *Rationalisierung und entzauberte Welt: Schriften zu Geschichte und Soziologie.* Leipzig: Reclam Verlag, 1989; Ibid. *Wissenschaft als Beruf.* München-Leipzig: Duncker & Humblot, 1919.

33 Tönnies, F. *Community & Society (Gemeinschaft und Gesellschaft).* East Lansing: Michigan State University Press, 1957.

sociological "holism," and the recognition of the community as a single being, which characterize a *Gemeinschaft*. In the second case, societies are created on the basis of agreement, contracts, calculation, rational advantages, and the advancement of group interests, with a distinct stratification and hierarchization, united by common interests, goals, and the pragmatic pursuit of individual profit, achieved with the help of rational social actions, in which case, we are dealing with a *Gesellschaft*.

In German both words derive from different roots and have different meanings (which is why they are left untranslated as sociological terms). *Gemein* means "common," "belonging to all." *Gesell* means "connection" (by assumption, of something separate, uncoordinated, or artificially united). In the Russian words *obshchina* (community) and *obshchestvo* (society) this important nuance (which comprises the essence of Tönnies' distinction) is entirely lost, because of the identity of roots. In Latin, there are two terms that impart the semantic dichotomy precisely enough, *communitas* and *societas*.

The "common" (*gemein*) is a whole and precedes separation and differentiation. The "united" (*gesell*) presupposes the prior existence of the separate, distinct, fragmentary.

Community is thought of organically, as a living being, which is not able to be broken up into parts without detriment to its life; society is thought of mechanically, as an apparatus, which can be taken apart and put back together again (with replaced parts or an updated design, even).

In these terms, the ethnos is unambiguously and exclusively a *Gemeinschaft*, i.e., a community, *communitas*. Ethnosociology takes the community as an ethnic community for its initial instance, the koineme. Derivatives of the ethnos are stages in the transition from community (*Gemeinschaft*) to society (*Gesellschaft*). Civil society is the theoretical model of a pure society, in which nothing remains of community. The narod and the nation are intermediate phases, where the simplicity of community becomes complicated and we meet with elements of both community (preserved from previous phases) and society. In the narod, there is more community than in the nation; and in both cases, they are qualitatively different.

Thanks to such a classification, universally accepted today, we can distinguish two approaches in sociology itself.

One approach interprets community as an *embryo* of society, where society acts as the historic *aim,* towards which community tends (evolutionism, progressivism, methodological individualism). The other, on the contrary, considers society *a consequence of the transformation of community,* the structure and characteristics of which affect all the more complex kinds of social system. *Ethnosociology is built on the second sociological paradigm.* Hence the fundamental ethnosociological thesis of the reversibility of social dimensions, i.e., of the constant open possibility of transition not only from the simple to the complex, from community to society, but also from the complex to the simple, from society to community.

Werner Sombart: Heroes and Merchants

The hypothesis of the reversibility of social transformations or, at least, the absence of enthusiasm in the course of observing the establishment of modern society (*Gesellschaft*) and the search for alternative social paths is characteristic of another major German sociologist, Werner Sombart (1863–1941). If Weber, who was a personal friend of Sombart, welcomed the bourgeois order and liberal democracy, Sombart criticized them harshly, considering them negative social phenomena.

The sociology of the later Sombart is built on the isolation of two basic social types, "heroes" (*Helden*) and "merchants" (*Händler*), who, accordingly, produce two types of society, the *"heroic"* — religious, chivalrous (for instance, like the European Middle Ages) — and *"mercantile"* — mercenary, contractual, individualistic, and bourgeois (Modernity).[34] The domination of one or another type predetermines the value system of a society, its sociocultural profile, and political and economic structure.

---

34 Sombart, W. *Heroes and Merchants* / Sombart, W. *Collected Works.* Sobraniye sochineniy: V. 3. T. 2. SPb: "Vladimir Dal," 2005.

Bourgeois society and its ideological premises, traced by Sombart not only to the Protestant Work Ethic, but also to Catholic scholasticism and to the individualism implicit in it, are examples of the "society of merchants," in which the idea of exchange, a universal material equivalent (money), moral flexibility, social adaptivity, technical development, etc., acquire a right of primacy over alternative family values. A society of a "heroic" type, on the other hand, places honor higher than material success, sees morality as rigid and immutable, extols lofty ideals over material interests, proclaims sacrifice, courage, service, and honor more important than profits and technical inventions, and ascribes less importance to money than to power and prestige.

Sombart, in contrast to Weber, thought that Europe must return to the heroic type. He saw a positive alternative to Modernity in the "normal type" (Sombart's term, analogous to Weber's "ideal type") of *organic socialism*. Sombart rejected Marx's proletarian socialism and insisted on "German socialism," which selected as a socio-political subject not the "class," but rather the *ethnocultural group,* united by a common collective value system.[35] In such socialism, Sombart thought it expedient to deprive separate individuals of any special rights and to regulate the relations of the state only with concrete social groups. At the same time, Sombart, as a consistent sociologist, was a stranger to biological racism and understood belongingness to a narod not as racial belonging, but as a matter of free spiritual and cultural choice.

Sombart does not reject hierarchy or the social stratification of society, but proposes to build them not on an economic (class) basis, nor on an individual (liberal) basis, but on the principle of effective, the "heroic," and in service to the "common good."

On the ethnosociological scale of societies, the type of society which Sombart championed corresponds strictly to the level of narod (laos), which brings him closer to Herder, who lived a hundred years earlier and stood historically on the border between the closing heroic epoch of the narod — the European Middle Ages, so dear to him and the

---

35   Sombart, W. *Deutscher Sozialismus*. Charlottenburg: Buchholz & Weisswange, 1934.

Romantics — and the beginning of the century of classes, nations, and the domination of "merchants." Ethnosociology borrows from Sombart the dichotomy hero/merchant, which corresponds strictly to the first derivative of the ethnos (narod/laos) and the second and third derivatives of the ethnos (nation, civil society).

Moritz Lazarus: Der Volksgeist

Moritz Lazarus, Wilhelm Wundt, and Alfred Vierkandt, representatives of German ethnopsychology, made a major contribution to the development of the discipline of ethnosociology.

The initiator of this orientation was the German philosopher and psychologist Moritz Lazarus (1824–1903), one of the founders of the *Journal of Volk-Psychology and Linguistics* (*Zeitschrift für Völkerpsychologie und Sprachwissenschaft*).

Lazarus further developed Herder's theory of the existence of a Volksgeist (narodni spirit), but he described it in his scientific formulations as the total unification of individual spirits, which forms a common psycho-cultural field.[36] The *Volksgeist* manifests itself in language, mores, customs, institutions, games, folklore, etc. The study of this phenomenon, according to Lazarus, is the psychologist's task.

The concept of a *Volksgeist*, developed by Lazarus, assumed the subordination of the individual, rational, and pragmatic principles of action to the stronger and more effective collective paradigm, which is a total phenomenon and shapes the structure of individual psychology.

The classical sociology of Durkheim and Mauss regards precisely this collective and strictly supra-individual instance as being of principal importance, but it defines it as a "society," whereas Lazarus operates with the concept of the *das Volk* (the narod). For ethnosociology, the very possibility of a methodological identification of the narod (for Lazarus) and society (for Durkheim) is extremely significant, since with certain

---

36 Lazarus, M. *Grundzüge der Völkerpsychologie und Kulturwissenschaft*. Hamburg: Meiner, 2003.

refinements it brings us to the conception of the ethnos as koineme, i.e., as the simplest and primordial form of society.

Wilhelm Wundt: Völkerpsychologie

Lazarus' ideas exerted a massive influence on his contemporary, the philosopher and founder of classical experimental psychology, Wilhelm Wundt (1832–1920). In the early stages of his scientific career, Wundt proceeded from a belief in the universality of psychological experience and in his experiments (he was the organizer of the first psychological laboratory in history) he strove to study the structure of the emergence of religious opinions, the mechanism of emotions, voluntary actions, associations, etc. Wundt's orientation is called "Structuralist" or "holistic," since Wundt thought of the human psyche as an integral whole — a claim that the behaviorist school later opposed actively.

In a later period, Wundt focused on studying the "psychology of narods" (*Völkerpsychologie*), supposing, following Lazarus, that different ethnic societies have entirely unique collective specifics of mind, which Wundt tried to systematize in his hefty ten-volume work *The Psychology of Peoples,* which laid the foundations of Ethnopsychology.[37]

To a large extent, Wundt influenced such eminent anthropologists and ethnosociologists as Boas and Malinowski.

For Ethnosociology, the works of Wundt reveal the prospect of a psychological approach to the study of the ethnos and its derivatives, which proposes to apply the methods and conceptions of modern psychology to the study of ethnic structures and processes.

Alfred Vierkandt: Phenomenology of the Ethnos

Wundt's Ethnopsychology was actively developed even further by his discipline, the psychologist and sociologist Alfred Vierkandt (1867–1953). Vierkandt adhered to the phenomenological view of society, thinking that it was not worth approaching the investigation of social phenomena with

---

37   Wundt, W. *Völkerpsychologie.* 10 Bd. Leipzig: Engelmann, 1900–1920.

ready, rigid conceptions and to trying to find a correspondence for each of them. On the contrary, societies, and especially ethnic societies ("small societies"), are so diverse, that they demand an attentive living-into their structures, which can prove to be entirely unlike what would be expected on the basis of *a priori* sociological approaches. Society is a phenomenon (in the sense of Husserl's Phenomenology) and must be comprehended precisely as such. And the structure of a phenomenon is complex and multiform and has an innumerable plurality not only of variations, but also of paradigms.[38]

Vierkandt dedicated a separate work to the study of the origin of the family, narod, and state from a sociological point of view, where the ethnosociological side of this processes is accented.[39]

In his last period, Vierkandt moved away from Wundt's ideas of the domination of collective psychology in the framework of the ethnic community and started to pay more attention to the psychology of the individual.

Sigmund Freud: Patricide in the Primordial Order

Sigmund Freud (1856–1939), the founder of Psychoanalysis, was such an influential author on the development of the culture and science of the 20th Century in the fields of Psychology, Philosophy, and Sociology, that to evaluate his many works is exceedingly difficult. We will therefore isolate only that which can be related to ethnosociology.

Freud's major discovery was the sphere of the *unconscious* (the *Id* [in Latin, the "It"], *Es* in German), the structure of which, as became clear, exerts a tremendous influence on psychic processes and even on that sphere of human activity which classical psychology attributed to manifestations of rationality and consciousness.[40] Freud showed the immense power of

38 Vierkandt, A. *Gesellschaftslehre: Hauptprobleme der philosophischen Soziologie.* Stuttgart: Enke, 1923.

39 Vierkandt, A. *Familie, Volk und Staat in ihren gesellschaftlichen Lebensvorgängen: Eine Einführung in die Gesellschaftslehre.* Stuttgart: Enke, 1936.

40 Freud, S., Strachey, J. *The ego and the id.* New York: Norton, 1962.

the work of the unconscious, which influences literally all aspects of the personality. Thereby, Freud created the preconditions for a dual hermeneutic (interpretation) of cultural and social phenomena, in the course of which both the rational-logical and the psychic-unconscious sides are studied.[41]

We can refer to sociology and *ethnosociology* in Freud's later works, in which he tried, with the help of the psychoanalytic method, to explain the historical appearance of certain social and religious institutions (such as the totem, cult, monogamy, etc.). Freud gave a summary of his sociological views in the book *Totem and Taboo*.[42]

Freud saw at the start of history a "primordial horde," ruled over by a strict patriarch, founded on the strength of being the oldest man in the lineage. To him belong all material wealth and all the women of the tribe indiscriminately. Then it falls into a universal scenario: the young men of the tribe (brothers amongst themselves and the sons of the one all-powerful father) conspire to kill him and to divide up the resources and women of the tribe with one another. They kill the father and ritually eat him, after which they implement their revolutionary program. From this primordial scenario, all social institutions arise: right, property, power, religion, and rites. Instead of the right of the stronger and older brother, *deconcentrated power* is introduced (as each brother receives a part of the authority). Property, obtained at such a cost (blood and crime), becomes holy. Power in the horde is differentiated and reproduces in part the (pre-murder) patriarchal scenario, but is limited in part by the rights of the brother-killers. Ritual repeats in different modes the first sacrifice. Religion embodies the fear of retribution, repentance for what has been done and the expectation of vengeance.

This work of Freud's was repeatedly subjected to harsh criticism since it contradicted scientific knowledge of the structure of archaic societies.

---

41   Dugin, A.G. *Sociology of the Imagination*, pp. 51–52.

42   Freud, S. *Totem and Taboo: Resemblances Between the Psychic Lives of Savages and Neurotics*. Harmondsworth, Middlesex: Penguin Books, 1938.

Despite this, however, it illustrated the possibility of applying the psychoanalytic approach to the investigation of simple societies (ethnoses).

Ethnosociology can borrow from Freud's psychoanalysis a whole series of extremely important methodological conclusions. We shall list the most fundamental of them.

1. The ethnos and its derivatives can be studied in parallel on two levels: on the level of consciousness and on the level of the unconscious, as with the separate individual.

2. In simple societies the unconscious will be manifested more immediately and openly than in complex ones. At the limit, we can identify the simple society with the unconscious (as, essentially, Freud himself does, when he describes the scenario of the primordial drama of patricide).

3. In complex societies the ethnos (as koineme) will take its place in the zone of the unconscious, acting as a sociological analogue of the instance that Freud calls the "Id."

Carl Gustav Jung: The Collective Unconscious

Although for Freud the psyche was only individual and sub-individual, it is theoretically possible to apply the Freudian method not only to the individual, but also to the group and society. This was partly done by Freud's student, the Austrian psychoanalyst Carl Gustav Jung (1875–1961), who introduced the concept of the "**collective unconscious**." Jung wrote:

> My thesis, then, is as follows: In addition to our immediate consciousness, which is of a thoroughly personal nature and which we believe to be the only empirical psyche (even if we tack on the personal unconscious as an appendix), there exists a second psychic system of a collective, universal, and impersonal nature which is identical in all individuals. This collective unconscious does not develop individually but is inherited. It consists of pre-existent forms, the archetypes, which

can only become conscious secondarily and which give definite form to certain psychic contents.[43]

Jung developed the concept of the "collective unconscious" under the influence of both Freud and his theory of the "unconscious" as well as his own familiarity with a number of ethnosociological and sociological works. Thus, Jung himself often mentions the writings of Lucien Lévy-Bruhl, who described archaic societies as built on "prelogic," "mystical participation," and "collective representations."[44] Jung was also familiar with the notions of the "categories of the imagination," offered by the sociologists Mauss and Hubert.[45] He also referred to Bastian's notion of "elementary thinking."

With the aim of testing the hypothesis of the "collective unconscious," Jung conducted special experiments analyzing the dreams of black Americans at St. Elizabeth Hospital in Washington in 1912. He wanted to make sure that the "collective unconscious" is an innate characteristic, and not the result of cultural attitudes. Experiments confirmed the universality of archetypes and their independence from the racial factor.

But at the same time, Jung spoke in his texts more than once of the specific forms of "collective unconscious" of different narods. Thus, in 1930, he warned Europe about Germany, indicating that the "collective unconscious" of the Germans was possessed by the militant archetype of Wotan and that if this destructive energy were not directed outside (he proposed the Soviet Union as a target), then it could result in horrific catastrophe for Europeans.[46]

Neither Jung himself nor his followers tried applying the concept of the "collective unconscious" concretely to the ethnic group. But ethnosociology can very well take the decisive step and affirm the instance of

---

43 Jung, C. *Archetypes and the Collective Unconscious*. New York, NY: Pantheon Books, 1959, p. 43.

44 Lévy-Bruhl, L. *La Mentalite Primitive*. Paris: Alcan, 1922.

45 Hubert, H. & Mauss M. *Mélanges d'histoire des religions*. Paris: Alcan, 1909.

46 Jung, C. *Wotan* / Neue Schweizer Rundschau. 1936. Zurich. № III. March, p. 657–669; Ibid. *Aufsatze zur Zeitgeschichte*. Zurich: Rascher, 1946.

an "ethnic unconscious" as the intermediate layer between the "collective unconscious" (according to Jung, it is universal and identical for all humanity) and the "personal unconscious."

Richard Thurnwald: The Systematization of Ethnosociological Knowledge

The key figure in the elaboration of the scientific school of German Ethnosociology was the Austrian scholar Richard Thurnwald (1869–1954). Thurnwald was the founder of the Institute of Social and Cultural Anthropology in the Free University of Berlin in 1951, to which he bequeathed his extensive library after his death. In the course of his life, Thurnwald wrote and published many books and scientific articles dedicated to ethnosociology, ethnology, and anthropology, and he also published the journal *Sociologus*, which focused on ethnosociological problems.

His main work, *Human Society in its Ethnosociological Foundations*, is not only a scientific study, but also an encyclopedia of ethnosociological knowledge and can be considered a basic work of ethnosociology, familiarity with which is necessary for any professional in this domain.[47]

If Gumplowicz coined the term "Ethnosociology," then Thurnwald was the one who filled it with concrete scientific content and created the first general system of ethnosociological knowledge.

We should regard the history of Ethnosociology proper as starting precisely with Thurnwald, since the scientific orientations preceding him can only partially be ascribed to Ethnosociology. Thurnwald was the first to start calling himself an "ethnosociologist," and Ethnosociology was the primary orientation with which he occupied himself.

Thurnwald himself personally participated frequently in ethnographic expeditions, and his books are replete with field material, collected and worked over by him in the course of his field work. What is more, they are often accompanied by unique photographs, also taken by Thurnwald

---

47 Thurnwald, R. *Die Menschliche Gesellschaft in ihren ethnosoziologische Grundlagen.* Berlin & Leipzig: Walter de Gruyter & Co, 1931–1935.

himself. In his case, we are dealing not only with an outstanding theoretician, but also with an ethnologist-practitioner.

The "Life-Images" of Natural Narods: Typology of Ethnoses

The first volume of Thurnwald's major work is called *Representative Life-Images of Natural Peoples* and is dedicated to the simplest type of society, which Thurnwald calls "natural" peoples, *Volks*, or narods (*Naturvölkern*), in order to emphasize their harmonious relationship to the surrounding environment and the relative simplicity of their culture.[48]

The natural narod is the ethnos or ethnic society proper, the koineme. Indeed, the volume is dedicated to the study of the sociological structure of the ethnos.

Within the limits of the simple society (natural narods), Thurnwald isolates three types:

1. *Hunter-Gatherers (Wildbeuter)*

2. *Peasants and breeders of small beasts*

3. *Herdsmen and breeders of large beasts*

Each type has its subtypes.

Hunter-gatherers are separated into the inhabitants of icy zones, steppes, forests, and waters; peasants and breeders of small animals, into a pure form (minimal social stratification), a mixed form (average social stratification), and a complex form (developed social stratification); herdsmen and breeders of large beasts, into egalitarian nomadic tribes, stratified nomadic tribes, and mixed nomadic/settler societies.

Thurnwald described thoroughly how archaic tribes extant in his day belonged to one subtype or another, making periodic digressions into the history of more highly developed narods, the cultural monuments

---

48   Turnwald, R. *Die Menschliche Gesellschaft in ihren ethnosoziologische Grundlagen.* Bd. 1 *Represantative Lebensbilder von Natur Volkern.* Berlin & Leipzig: Walter de Gruyter & Co, 1931.

of which preserved evidence of a more ancient stage of development (chronicles, myths, folklore, narodni art, rites, etc.).

The basic division of the ethnos into three types establishes a direct relation between the prioritized economic orientation of a society and its sociological structure. An ethnos can be of three types (in degree of increasing complexity):

1. *Simplest* (hunters and gatherers);

2. *Normal* (peasants and the breeders of small beasts);

3. *Complex* (nomads and the breeders of large beasts).

All three types relate to the ethnos and, in comparison with the derivatives of the ethnos (narods, nations, etc.), can be thought of as simple and undifferentiated. But in the course of a more steadfast focus of attention, it is possible to see even in these ethnoses substantial qualitative differences. Social stratification is practically absent among hunters and gatherers. It begins to take shape on a lineal basis (the elders of the lineage) in settlements of a fixed rural type, where the population works the land and breeds small cattle, and it arises separately in stratified nomadic tribes and mixed nomadic/settler cultures.

The most complex of ethnic societies — the mixed nomadic/settler culture — already leaves the limits of the ethnos somewhat and can be considered as the first phase of appearance of the narod (laos) and its works (most often, a state).

The first volume of Thurnwald's work gives an idea of the ethnic society and its basic "ways of life," by which Thurnwald understands the totality of economic, symbolic, gender-related, ritual, mythological, and social practices, as well as complexes, united into a single paradigm (analogous to Frobenius' "paideuma" or Mauss and Hubert's "categories of the imagination").

The Family and Economy in Simple Societies

The second volume of Thurnwald's major work is called *The Establishment, Change, and Formation of the Family, Kinship and Ties in the Light of Volk-Study.*[49]

Here Thurnwald considers the social forms of the family, which correspond to the three types of ethnic society described in the first volume. Thurnwald considers the forms of the family and family right (monogamous, polygamous, polyandrous), the position of women, sexual taboos, the status of the lineage and clan, male and female unions, forms and types of kinship, the structures of "maternal right" and patriarchy, the role of secret societies in their relation to the family, the social status of ages, and the rites and rituals of "artificial kinship" (adoption, "blood brotherhood").

The structure of kinship, gender functions, and systems of power and right in the ethnoses considered by Thurnwald are arranged in a rather rigorous schema.

The "simplest" societies (hunters and gatherers) have predominantly monogamous nuclear families, based on a relative parity of the genders in a gender-based division of labor (more men are hunters, more women are gatherers).

"Normal" societies (peasants and the breeders of small cattle) present a broad spectrum of family ways: polygamy, polyandry, rudimentary patriarchy, matriarchy with the preservation of gender-based division of labor and thus an increase of the economic role (and, correspondingly, the social status) of women. Thurnwald derives both polygamous patriarchy and matriarchy from one and the same fact: the growth of the social value of women in peasant societies (which can lead to the striving to possess several women at once or, on the other hand, to the raising of the significance of women right up to the creation of matriarchal structures).

---

49 Thurnwald, R. *Die Menschliche Gesellschaft in ihren ethnosoziologische Grundlagen.* Bd. 2 *Werden, Wandel and Gestaltung von Familie, Verwandschaft und Bunden im Lichte der Völkerforschung.* Berlin & Leipzig: Walter de Gruyter & Co, 1932.

In complicated nomadic, pastoral societies, as a rule, strict patriarchy and polygamy dominate, and paternal rule is asserted.

The third volume of the study *The Establishment, Change, and Formation of Economics in the Light of the Volk-Study* again proposes the model of three ethnic societies, but from the perspective of their specific economic character.[50] Thurnwald examines the basic economic techniques of simple, normal, and complex ethnic societies and gives a functional analysis of the instruments of labor and their connection with rites, myths, and symbols, and also with social attitudes.

The theme of the exchange of objects among ethnoses, including those relating to the different categories, is considered separately, which gives rise to a number of symbiotic economic ties. The archaic and embryonic forms of capital, the market, expenditures, accumulation, the division of labor, and the use of instruments of labor (in complex ethnoses) is also examined.

The State, Culture, and Right in Different Forms of Differentiated Societies

The fourth volume of the work, *The Establishment, Change, and Formation of the State and Culture in the Light of the Volk-Study* is dedicated to the social paradigm, derived from the ethnos, which we call the narod (laos, Volk). Thurnwald uses the formula "natural narod" — "cultural narod" (by "cultural narod" he means a concrete narod having a state, rationally formalized religion, or civilization).[51] Thurnwald's "natural narod" is the ethnos. The "cultural narod" (*Kulturvolk*) is the laos.

In this volume, Thurnwald presents a model of all known forms of the division of the ethnos (horde, clan, tribe, lineage, phratry, etc.) and

---

50 Thurnwald, R. *Die Menschliche Gesellschaft in ihren ethnosoziologische Grundlagen.* Bd. 3 *Werden, Wandel und Gestaltung der Wirtschaft im Lichte der Völkerforschung.* Berlin & Leipzig: Walter de Gruyter & Co, 1932.

51 Turnwald, R. *Die Menschliche Gesellschaft in ihren ethnosoziologische Grundlagen.* Bd. 3 *Werden, Wandel and Gestaltung der Wirtschaft im Lichte der Volkerforschung.* Berlin&Leipzig:Walter de Gruyter & Co, 1932.

analyses their political and legal structures, forms of organization of power, and connection with the way of life of ethnoses.

The main theme of this volume is a thorough analysis of the process of stratification, the construction of social hierarchies and the analysis of those historical forms in which these tendencies are expressed: state, religion, and civilization. Thurnwald's task in this part of his work is to describe precisely the "phase transition" between the ethnic society (simple society) and its derivatives (complex, differentiated, hierarchized, organized politically or civilizationally).

Thurnwald traces the history of the emergence of the first political and economic institutions, and also their connection with those phenomena that immediately precede them in simple, undifferentiated societies (koinemes).

Thurnwald, following Ratzel and Gumplowicz, puts at the foundation of the state the imposition of one ethnic group onto a rather different one. Moreover, the more solid and fixed forms of state and civilization take shape where nomadic pastoral tribes establish control over settled peasant communities. Thurnwald's thoroughly documented analysis, based on innumerable examples, many of which are drawn from the experience of contemporary archaic tribes or on the material of recent history, substantially corroborates the theory of "superimposition" (Überlagerung).

In the fifth and last volume of his work, *The Establishment, Change, and Formation of Right in the Light of Volk-Study*, Thurnwald traces the genesis of early legal institutions, the sources of which he sees in the way of life of the simple society (ethnos). All legal procedures and institutions, according to his reconstruction, have their meaning and origin in the social structures of the ethnos, but gradually they are uprooted from their primordial matrix and are transformed into new forms.

The Significance of Thurnwald's Work for Ethnosociology

The work *Human Society* ends at the stage in which the study of properly ethnic processes ceases to be unambiguous and evident and where

Thurnwald closely approaches historical states and literate cultures. But this does not mean that at the border, where we are dealing with highly developed forms of society (starting from the narod as laos), the competence of ethnosociology comes to an end, and its relevance as a scientific method is exhausted. Those tools that Thurnwald systematized and regularized are fully suitable for the consideration of other derivatives of the ethnos, right up to global society and even post-society, especially as Thurnwald carried out the most difficult task: describing with great nuance and gradation (i.e., taking into account semi-tones and details) the ethnosociological structure of the first phase of transition, from simple society to complex (from ethnos to laos), and revealing the essence and meaning of the ethnic processes occurring in this transition.

Thanks to his fundamental work, Ethnosociology has received the following:

1. A thorough description of simple society (the ethnos as koineme);

2. A strict isolation within simple society of three social types and their corresponding subtypes;

3. An explanation of the algorithm of the "phase transition" from the ethnos to its first derivative (the narod), i.e., from an undifferentiated (or weakly differentiated, in the case of complex ethnoses) society to a society with clearly expressed differentiation;

4. Systematization of a mass of ethnographical and anthropological material, distinctly assessed along a sociological marker.

These four points comprise the foundations of the scientific program of Ethnosociology as a discipline. The task of the ethnosociologist is to work in one or more of these orientations at once:

1. Deepening the comprehension of the structure of simple societies;

2. Clarifying the details and variants of the typologization of simple societies;

3. Studying further the structure of the first phase transition (from the ethnos to the narod, laos) and applying its algorithms, made more accurate as one goes along, to other phase transitions (from the narod to the nation, from the nation to civil society, from global society to post-society);

4. Gathering new ethnographic material and sorting it according to basic ethnosociological criteria.

Wilhelm Mühlmann: Ethnos, Narod, Ethnocentrism

Another key figure in contemporary Ethnosociology is Thurnwald's disciple and colleague, the ethnosociologist, sociologist and philosopher Wilhelm Mühlmann (1904–1988).

Mühlmann considered himself to be continuing the business of the Russian ethnologist Shirokogoroff and admitted that he borrowed the ethnos as a sociological category from him. Shirokogoroff's field studies among the Evenki (a Tungusic people) left a big impression on Mühlmann, since the myths, rites, social institutions and economic practices of this small Siberian ethnos allow one to see in miniature the paradigm of the ethnos as such, and through it also the structure of more complex societies.

On the whole, in his books and studies Mühlmann followed the tradition established by Thurnwald, developing his methods, specifying the nuances of sociological and ethnic classifications, and supplementing the fallow or weakly worked cells in the general models of ethnosociological knowledge. But there are a number of directions in which Mühlmann attained serious results, substantially enriching the structure of ethnosociological knowledge.

Mühlmann was the first to propose introducing the concept of the ethnos in a strict sense, following Shirokogoroff and defining thereby the simplest of the possible forms of organization of a society (koineme).

Neither Gumplowicz (who, as we saw, used the term "race," despite the fact that he himself introduced such concepts as "Ethnosociology" and "Ethnocentrism"), nor Thurnwald, who used the term ethnos (*Ethnie*, Ethnos) and *Volk* by turns without any semantic nuance, had such a strict definition.

Mühlmann clearly distinguished four concepts: "ethnos," *Volk*, "nation," and "race" as independent concepts, loaded completely with determinate and non-intersecting sociological meaning.

The ethnos is the simplest society.

The *Volk* (narod) according to Mühlmann, is, on the contrary, the highest form of cultural and spiritual development, the peak of a society's sociological possibilities. In the 1930s and 1940s, Mühlmann separated narods into "genuine narods" (*echte Völkern*), "floating narods" (*schwebende Völkern*) and "imaginary narods" (*Scheinvölkern*), but later he repudiated such a classification. But it is important that the concept of the "narod" (*Volk*) first acquired the status of a scientific sociological concept (in Mühlmann's work).[52]

The nation, according to Mühlmann, corresponded to the contemporary state-political and legal form of citizenship, and he did not pay much attention to it.

In relation to the term "race," Mühlmann proposed to separate *biological* (*a-race*) and *sociological* (*b-race*) racism. Belongingness to a biological a-race can be proved by the method of genetic and anthropometric studies, as in the case of animal species, plants and minerals.

In itself, sociological knowledge does not bear an a-race. But b-race is the *notion* that people have of their belonging to one or another kinship line of the belongingness of others. The sociological b-race, on the other hand, has a big significance in certain life, cultural, historical and political situations and can act as a *sociological* category.

From a philosophical point of view, Mühlmann was a follower of Edmund Husserl and considered the ethnos as a phenomenological datum, which is fundamental for the constitution of both the object

52   Mühlmann, W. E. *Methodik der Völkerkunde*. Stuttgart: Ferdinand Enke, 1938.

(environment) and subject (the human) and precedes all individualization. For this reason, he refused to set "nature" and "culture" at odds with one another: the *ethnic phenomenon* does not know such a duality, and in order to understand the ethnos and its nature deeply, it is necessary to knowingly reject the dual model, customary for Western European man, of the division of everything into subject and object, subjective and objective.

Mühlmann's introduction of the term "*Ethnocentrism*" as the basic structure of ethnic phenomenon is extremely important.[53] *Ethnocentrism is the format of the world in the ethnic consciousness,* where society, nature, myths, right, the economy, religion, and magic are placed into a unified model, at the core of which is the ethnos itself, and everything else is unfolded around it in concentric circles — what is more, the pattern of small circles and the distant periphery of ethnocentrism are preserved as a constant. In the structure of ethnosociological knowledge, the concept of "Ethnocentrism," its transformation, and its derivatives sometimes play a decisive role.

Mühlmann paid a great deal of attention to interethnic ties, studying the processes which unfold at the border of two or more of ethnoses. His book *Assimilation, The Surroundings of a Narod, the Establishment of Narods* is dedicated to an examination of the processes of ethnic assimilation, the inclusion of ethnoses in a narod, and analogous processes of interethnic interaction.[54]

To Mühlmann was also the author of the classic German-language work *History of Anthropology.*[55]

53   Mühlmann, W. E. 'Erfahrung und Denken in der Sicht des Kulturanthropologen' / Mühlmann Wilhelm E., Muller Ernst W. (eds.) *Kulturanthropologie.* Köln/Berlin: Kiepenheuer & Witsch, 1966, p. 157.

54   Mühlmann, W. E. *Assimilation, Umvolkung, Volkwerdung: Ein globaler Überblick und ein Programm.* Stuttgart, 1944.

55   Mühlmann, W. E. *Geschichte der Anthropologie.* Wisbaden: Aula Verlag, 1986.

Georg Elwert: Ethnic Conflicts and "Markets of Violence"

The German scholar Georg Elwert (1947–2005), a specialist on the ethnoses of Africa and Central Asia and professor of ethnology and sociology, was a bright member of the next generation of ethnosociologists. Elwert was the main editor of the journal *Sociologus,* founded by Thurnwald and led by Mühlmann. Elwert continued and further developed the traditions of his predecessors, working in the Institute of Ethnology, founded by Thurnwald, in the Free Berlin University.

Elwert applied the ethnosociological principle to the analysis of the condition of contemporary African countries, describing in ethnosociological categories the processes of development and modernization.[56] Elwert paid special attention to the problems of contemporary forms of imperialism, including *"market imperialism,"* showing how the penetration of contemporary Western economic technologies in certain cases worsens the social picture in developing countries and carries in itself destructive consequences.[57]

Elwert is a recognized authority in the sphere of ethnic conflicts and international terrorism. In particular, he coined the popular term *"market violence,"* which describes the international criminal structure, connected with the service of terrorist networks and sometimes influencing the ethnic balance in the countries of the Third World, including the artificial provocation of interethnic conflict.[58]

56 Elwert, G. *Bauern und Staat in Westafrika: Die Verflechtung sozioökonomischer Sektoren am Beispiel Benin.* Frankfurt: Campus, 1983.

57 Bierschenk, T. & Elwert, G. *Entwicklungshilfe und ihre Folgen.* Frankfurt / New York: Campus, 1993; Elwert G. & Fett R. (eds.) *Afrika zwischen Subsistenzökonomie und Imperialismus.* Frankfurt: Campus Verlag, 1982.

58 Elwert, G. *Gewaltmärkte: Beobachtungen zur Zweckrationalität der Gewalt* / Kölner Zeitschrift für Soziologie und Sozialpsychologie, 1997.

SECTION TWO

The American School of Ethnosociology, Cultural Anthropology, The History of Religions, & Ethnomethodology

Terminological Clarification

In familiarizing ourselves with the American school of Ethnosociology, we should take note of the previously mentioned circumstances connected with its name. The discipline that in Germany (especially after Thurnwald and Mühlmann) and in Russia is persistently called "Ethnosociology," historically has been known in the United States as "**Cultural Anthropology**." This discipline predominantly studies "simple societies" (i.e., ethnoses), and on that basis builds systems and classifications of more generalized cultural and social phenomena; i.e., methodologically and conceptually it does exactly what Ethnosociology does.

Before we move to an overview of the principal authors of this school, we should mention the first American anthropologists and sociologists, who maintained evolutionary and individualistic conceptions, for the overcoming and refutation of which "Cultural Anthropology" was established.

Louis Morgan: Ancient Society

The American historian and ethnologist Louis Morgan (1818–1881) was the founder of contemporary anthropological studies in the USA and laid the foundations for the work of the following generation of anthropologists. He studied the structure of Iroquois tribes and on the basis of his observations of archaic societies he formulated his basic theories. The gist of what he observed is laid out in the summarizing work *Ancient Society*, which compares the level of a society's technical development with the its structure of kinship and attitudes toward property. In an evolutionary spirit, Morgan separates the history of human societies into three phases: savagery, barbarism, and civilization.[59]

He juxtaposes each phase with a level of technological and legal progress and arranges between them a self-evident hierarchy, which is apparent from the names themselves. If we do not pay attention to the offensive sound of the first two terms and try to find an analogue to them in ethnosociology, we can correlate "savagery" with the ethnos, "barbarity" with the narod, and "civilization" with the nation. Morgan's ideas influenced Karl Marx (1818–1883) and Friedrich Engels (1820–1895) and predetermined in many respects the structure of "historical materialism," which was also maintained in the spirit of "evolutionary racism."

Morgan authored some of the first serious studies of the structure of kinship in archaic societies, which subsequently became the central theme of anthropology.

William Sumner: Folkways and Mores

William Graham Sumner (1840–1910) was the founder of the American sociological tradition and an indisputable giant in the field. Moreover, his key work, *Folkways*, pays great attention to archaic simple societies and can be considered a properly ethnosociological study.[60]

Sumner is located in the framework of an evolutionary paradigm under the decisive influence of Spencer. He had no doubts about the ideas of evolution and progress of human societies, nor about the claim that man is driven by animal instincts — hunger, sex, fear, etc. Thus, Sumner belongs entirely to the tradition of Social Darwinism.

At the same time, his works, especially his best-known one, *Folkways*, contain extremely important elements of ethnosociological knowledge, developed by the next generation of sociologists and anthropologists.

---

59 Morgan, L. H. *Ancient Society*. Tucson, AZ: The University of Arizona Press, 1995.

60 Sumner, W. *Folkways: A Study of the Sociological Importance of Usages, Manners, Customs, Mores, and Morals*. New York, NY: New American Library, 1960.

Sumner was the first to introduce the dual concepts of *"in-group"* and the *"out-group"* (or "we-group" and "they-group" respectively) into sociology, which thereafter became a classic instrument of any sociological analysis of group behavior and group identity. In particular, on this fundamental division are based *autostereotypes* and *heterostereotypes*, which predetermine the basic structure of interaction between diverse segments of society. The stereotypes and structure of the in-group and the out-group are found in an especially vivid form, precisely in the sphere of the ethnos, and Sumner introduces this concept, based on the material of archaic collectives or ethnoses. This is already apparent in the fact that he describes the phenomenon of the in-group as "Ethnocentrism," borrowing this term from Gumplowicz, with whose works he was familiar. The processes occurring inside the "we-group" Sumner calls "in-group," distinguishing them from those processes occurring outside the group, "out-group."

Sumner dedicates his foundational study to "folk [narodni] customs," though he himself uses the specific term *"folkways."* He considers this phenomenon entirely unconscious and primordial, built not on philosophy and science, but on the direct process of *life*. One can say that folkways are a basic social phenomenon, characteristic of simple and archaic societies, in which social institutions, classes, legal systems, etc. are absent. Folkways differ among different ethnoses and can vary even in the small social groups of one ethnos, but it is precisely these folkways, the fact of whose presence and whose automatic (unconscious) is recognised by all, which form society as a unity.

The first form of a more determinate structuring of unconscious folkways is that which Sumner calls by the Latin term *mores*, from which is formed the adjective *moralis*, and from that the word "morals." Sumner dedicates the central place in his work to this phenomenon, giving an extensive panorama of the "mores" of the most diverse societies and narods, from archaic to contemporary. *"Mores"* grow out of folkways — their nature is unconscious and is not given to rational explanation, but they themselves are connected with historical, material, climatic, social, and other conditions, which gradually give them an increasingly rational form. The rationalization of mores, according to Sumner, is progress.

Even more formalized constructions are built over mores: social institutions, political and legal systems, religious and economic structures. As a rule, they are rational and pragmatic — they serve concrete aims and express the conscious interests of some social group. But the roots of these rational structures should be sought in the half-rational or weakly rational mores, and those, in turn, take shape on the basis of already irrational folkways, which reflect the archaic structures of an ethnic "we-group."

Sumner made one very serious observation, which influenced the philosophy of the following generations of anthropologists and become the center of passionate arguments about the essence of man and society. He titles one of his chapters in the form of an aphorism: "Mores can make anything right and prevent the condemnation of anything."[61] If we separate this assertion from the context of Social Darwinism and evolutionism, we get a ready-made law of the plurality of human societies: the culture and morals of one society will prove to be incomparable with that of another, and any form of evaluation of one society by another will be nothing other than that same "ethnocentrism" and a knowingly incorrect heterostereotype, the we-group's biased (and therefore false) opinion of the they-group.

If we correlate Sumner's model with the ethnosociological series of societies, then we can relate folkways to the ethnos, and social institutions, legal systems, and political structures to the narod (and further, to the nation and civil society). Mores represent something intermediate. In the ethnos, there are only folkways and the rudiments of mores. In the narod mores reside at the bottom (in the masses), while social institutions are above them (in the elites); folkways here recede into the unconscious. In the nation, mores are abolished (i.e., they also recede into the unconscious, to the folkways) and only institutions and structures remain. Having acknowledged the reversibility of historical progress, it becomes possible through such a correspondence to resolve a multitude of sociological and

---

61   Ibid.

ethnosociological problems — for instance, to clarify the correspondence between rights and morality, laws and customs, etc.

William Thomas: The Ethnography of Civilizational Societies with a Developed Culture

Two major figures in American sociology, William Thomas (1863–1947) and his co-author, the ethnic Pole Florian Znaniecki (1882–1958), also made the majority of their methodological and conceptual discoveries on the basis of the study of ethnic phenomena. Their fundamental five-volume work, *The Polish Peasant in Europe and America*, in which they elaborated the majority of their sociological conceptions (including the famous theory of "social attitudes"), is devoted to an analysis of the behavior of immigrants in different social and ethnic environments.[62] With good reason, this book is considered by many to be the best sociological work written in the USA in the course of the history of American Sociology. William Thomas, for his part, is the author of a fundamental law of sociology as such: "It is not important whether some interpretation or other is right or not: if people define their situations as real, they are real in their consequences."[63]

Thomas, after receiving a grant to study the problem of immigration into the US, left for Europe to study those societies from which the majority of immigrants to America hailed. At this time, according to his own admission, he surprisingly (at least, by the norms of highly differentiated and civilized European societies) decided to apply to them the same method used by ethnographers for the study of the culture of nonliterate, archaic narods. It happened that he focused on the Polish segment, both in Europe and in the US, having previously learnt Polish, and undertook a detailed analysis of the social particularities of the behavior of Polish peasants in their homeland, as well as those who had immigrated to the

---

62 Znaniecki, F. & Thomas W. *The Polish Peasant in Europe and America*. New York, NY: A. Knopf, 1927.

63 Thomas, W.I. & Thomas D.S. *The Child in America: Behavior Problems and Programs*. New York, NY: Knopf, 1928.

US. In Poland, he met his future co-author Florian Znaniecki. Thomas started to pin down and systematize the daily details, everyday observations, and themes of day-to-day communication, and on this material he built the majority of his sociological generalizations.

The analysis of the behavior of social groups — the forms of their adaptation, the optimization and economy of resources in the process of socialization, mutual support, competition, the structure of collective identity, the assortment of social values, the awareness of status and ability to change it, and situational analysis — all these classical sociological terms were introduced by Thomas into scientific circulation through the study of the ethnos.

Just as Sumner formulated very important sociological laws, applicable in the examination of all societies, including complex and modern ones, while rejecting the ethnic phenomena of archaic societies, so too did Znaniecki and Thomas derive a crucial set of sociological instruments, which became the basis of modern Sociology, from the observation of the ethnic group, which became for them the paradigm of all other social groups. For Ethnosociology this is far from accidental, since the ethnos is the simplest form of society, the koineme, which is the paradigm and basic component of more complex societies.

Franz Boas: The Founder of Cultural Anthropology (& His Students/Followers/Successors)

We should consider as the beginning of a full-fledged ethnosociological tradition in the US, the founding of a theoretical school by the outstanding ethnographer, philosopher, and anthropologist, Franz Boas (1858–1942), who emigrated from Germany to the US. There it received the name **"Cultural Anthropology,"** but the German ethnosociologists Thurnwald and Mühlmann unambiguously identified it with Ethnosociology, owing to the shared major theme, methods, principles, starting attitudes, and prioritized approaches to the interpretation of society, the ethnos, culture, and the human.

Boas' worldview took shape under the influence of the German geo-graphic, ethnological, and psychological school (Ratzel, Bastian, Wundt, etc.) and he maintained a love for Germany and fidelity to its culture even in the US (for which he was sometimes blamed). Boas achieved a real revolution in American Anthropology, wherein, prior to his arrival, evolutionary and Social Darwinist approaches dominated, and racial theories, which explained sociological particularities by innate, inherited markers and racial belonging, were popular, and an inflexible conviction in the absolute superiority of modern Western (European and American) society, its technology and values over the rest of the world, reigned. Boas built his scientific program on the denial of all three forms of racism:

- *Evolutionary* or *progressivist*, built on the thesis that complex societies are better than simple ones;

- *Biological*, which explains cultural differences by biological, racial specifics;

- *Eurocentric*, as a kind of European and American ethnocentrism.

Boas advanced a radically new teaching about societies, which maintained the following:[64]

- *The relativity and reversibility* of social processes; in their trans-formations under the influence of social, natural, or geographical factors, societies could become both more complex and simpler;

- *The historicity* of any type of society, whether complex or simple, since behind the apparent constancy of archaic narods is con-cealed an inner dynamic, sometimes less than the historicity of more differentiated social systems;

- The necessity of studying archaic societies only *in field condi-tions*, living with them, carefully gathering data as they present themselves before the researcher, not trying to systematize them

---

64 Boas, F. *The Mind of Primitive Man*. New York: Macmillan, 1938.

a priori, learning the language and living into their worldview and their "life world";

- Cultural Pluralism, i.e., the absence of any basis whatsoever for the hierarchical comparison of cultures and societies: they are all different, but each of them carries its own criteria within itself and must be accepted as it is, even if some of the customs shock the observer;

- A refusal to observe archaic ethnoses as an *object* (with the eyes of the European or American subject) and the demand to participate in them as in a subject (empathy, *Einfühlung*);

- The discovery of the dependence of physical and even racial characteristics on the *surrounding environment*, natural and social;

- Setting high priority on the *linguistic factor* as the generalizing formula of culture.[65]

These principles lay at the basis of Cultural Anthropology, which replaced evolutionism, racial theories, and theories of kinship, which earlier ruled American studies of the ethnos and archaic ("primitive") tribes completely.[66] They were all also shared completely by European ethnosociologists and lay at the basis of ethnosociology as such.

Boas himself followed these rules rigorously, spending much time among the tribes he studied (especially the Eskimo, Inuit, and the Kwakiutl), studying their languages and culture, and penetrating into their life world.[67, 68]

---

65 Boas, F. *Race, Language and Culture*. Toronto: Collier MacMillan, 1940.

66 Ibid. *General Anthropology*. Boston, MA: Heath, 1938.

67 Ibid. *The Central Eskimo*. Lincoln, NE: University of Nebraska Press, 1888.

68 Ibid. *The Social Organization and Secret Societies of Kwakiutl Indian*. Washington, DC: Smithsonian Institution, 1897; Ibid. *Kwakiutl Ethnography*. Chicago, IL: University of Chicago Press, 1966.

Boas supported each of the asserted theses of Cultural Anthropology with serious empirical studies, in the domain of Physical Anthropology (studying the volume and forms of the skulls of infants born to the families of European immigrants in the US before and after a ten-year period of their mothers' dwelling in new circumstances), Linguistics (to him belongs the conjecture that the researcher perceives the sounds of foreign speech based on the phonetic structure of his own language), Archaeology, etc.

Boas' ideas were picked up and developed by the resplendent constellation of his students, among whom are gathered almost all the stars of American Ethnology, Anthropology, Linguistics and Psychology.

Alfred Kroeber: The Cultural Pattern and the Superorganic

One of Boas' first disciples was the anthropologist Alfred Kroeber (1876–1960), the founder of the anthropological school at Berkeley. Kroeber focused his attention on the study of the Native tribes of North America, particularly in California.[69]

Kroeber developed Boas' ideas, applying them to a practical sphere of field studies (empathy, language study, thorough collection of details and initially indecipherable signs, objects and customs, etc.). At the same time, he also actively worked on the theoretical questions of cultural anthropology. He became the founder of *"Cultural Ecology,"* an approach that studied the social context of human interactions with the surrounding natural environment as a unified complex, without specifying what in this unified system is primary and what secondary, which the argument and which the function.

Kroeber continued Boas' line in the study of *Historical Anthropology*, tracing, on the basis of mythological and cultural material, the structure of transformations (migrations, reforms, and other social changes) in

---

69   Kroeber, A.L. (ed.) *Handbook of the Indians of California* / Bureau of American Ethnology. Washington, WA: 1925. Bulletin No. 78.

"primitive" societies as a direct analogue of the historical process of more complex societies.[70]

Kroeber introduced the concept of a *"cultural pattern,"* i.e., a determinate model or an archetype, which comprises the algorithm of society's constant specific characteristics (rites, rituals, processes, ceremonies, situations, etc.), regularly and synchronously replicable in diverse circumstances.

Having focused his principal attention on culture as a "superorganic" phenomenon, Kroeber advanced a holistic model of society, in which the material and spiritual (or rather, social) elements are found together in an inseparable bond.[71, 72]

All of these themes clearly point to the "holistic" tradition of German humanist science, brought to the US by Boas.

Robert Lowie: Historical Particularism

The well-known ethnologist Robert Lowie (1883–1957) was another close disciple of Boas' and a cofounder of the anthropological school at Berkeley. Lowie was the first of Boas' graduate students, who defended his dissertation before him.

Lowie specialized in theories of kinship among archaic ethnoses and developed, as did Kroeber, the practice of historical anthropology. In the sphere of historical anthropology, he formulated the concept of *"historical particularism,"* i.e., of the peculiarity and uniqueness of the historical experience of each ethnos, including those that were earlier considered as altogether without a history and constantly reproductive of one and the same "pattern."[73]

Lower, like Kroeber, conducted field studies among Native Americans (predominantly those of the Crow and plains tribes), but the societies of

70 Ibid. *Anthropology.* New York, NY: Harcourt Brace and Company. 1923.

71 Ibid. *The Superorganic.* Berkeley, CA: University of California Press, 1917.

72 Ibid. *Configurations of Culture Growth.* Berkeley, CA: University of California Press, 1944.

73 Ibid. *Primitive Society.* New York, NY: Knopf, 1920.

South America and Europe also drew his attention.[74, 75] In particular, he devoted a separate study to the Germans, being one of the first to apply the methods of the anthropological and ethnosociological approach (practiced earlier primarily for the study of preliterate societies) to the highly developed narods of Europe, with a highly differentiated and abundantly documented historical culture.[76]

Lowie's significance for Ethnosociology is due to the fact that he focused his attention on transitions from pure archaic societies to cultured societies and to complex societies with a developed religious and political culture. At the same time, he showed both the transformations and continuity of the ethnic element in highly differentiated social ensembles. The scientific and methodological apparatus developed by Lowie allows one to employ ethnosociological principles theoretically to all types of society.[77]

Ruth Benedict: The Personification of a Cultural Pattern

Ruth Benedict (1887–1948), Franz Boas' student, also elaborated the principles of the study of complex cultures by anthropological methods, like Lowie, while continuing to develop and approve of the ethnosociological approach. This found expression in her most famous work, *The Chrysanthemum and the Sword*, written in 1946, immediately after the end of the Second World War and devoted to the ethnosociology of Japanese society.[78]

In her work, Benedict shows how convincing and unexpected in its findings the approach of "cultural pluralism" could be when applied to practical matters. Thus, after the defeat of Japan Americans feared greatly

74 Lowie, R. *The Crow Indians*. New York, NY: Farrar & Rinehart, 1935.

75 Ibid. *Indians of the Plains*. New York, NY: American Museum of Natural History, 1954.

76 Ibid. *German People: A Social Portrait to 1914*. N. Y.: Farrar & Rinehart, 1945.

77 Ibid. *The Origin of the State*. New York, NY: Harcourt, Brace & Co, 1927; Ibid. *Are We Civilized?* New York, NY: Harcourt, Brace & Co., 1929.

78 Benedict, R. F. *The Chrysanthemum and the Sword: Patterns of Japanese Culture*. Boston, MA: Houghton Mifflin Co., 1946.

that the strict and extremely rigid social and cultural structure of Japanese society would become a constant problem for the American occupiers, whose system of values was built not only differently, but in an almost entirely contrary manner. Nevertheless, Benedict shows that Japanese culture and Japanese society appear so strict only from the side, if considered as objects. In them is a complex model of attitudes and patterns, which allowed the Japanese to adapt to the American presence and to flow into Western social standards, reinterpreted in a specifically Japanese way, and even to attain serious successes in the game, according to Western rules. In 1946, such an analysis seemed entirely unrealistic, but a few decades later it came entirely to pass in real life and became a historical fact, which increased the prestige of Cultural Anthropology and Ethnosociology.

Benedict also developed a number of theoretical approaches, the best known of which is *"Psychological Anthropology."* According to Benedict, in each culture one can discover an entirely determinate psychological type, ethnosocial character.[79] This type is standard and acts as the carrier of cultural patterns and their products. The transmission of these patterns occurs through a personified standard.

Abram Kardiner: Basic Personality

Another representative of Boas' school, the sociologist and psychologist Abram Kardiner (1891–1981), turned the concept of a **"basic personality"** into a law. He called the carrier of a cultural pattern a "basic personality," i.e., a sociological type which lies at the basis of the socium and forms its "base."[80]

Kardiner, like Benedict, places before himself the question of the correlation of the collective and the individual in culture and society. And the answer to this question was "basic personality," which, on one hand, carries in itself and relays to others the impersonal cultural pattern, and, on the other hand, individualizes it in its "history." Thus, two dimensions,

79 Benedict, R. F. *Patterns of Culture.* New York, NY: Mentor, 1960.

80 Kardiner, A. *The Individual and His Society.* New York, NY: Columbia University Press, 1939.

the structural (impersonal, immutable, basic) and the individual (histori-cal, personal) can be interpreted simultaneously through the concept of *"cultural personality."*

The sociological concept of the division of social institutions into primary and secondary is also attributed to Kardiner.

Kardiner combined sociology and anthropology with active engage-ments as a psychoanalyst and drew broadly on Freudianism for the resolution of sociological and ethnosociological problems. Kardiner is considered one of the key figures of contemporary psychology.

Ralph Linton: Status and Role

In New York during the 1930s, Ruth Benedict and Abram Kardiner formed the "culture and personality" circle, in the work of which other followers of Boas regularly participated, in particular, the famous sociologist Ralph Linton (1893–1953), who began his career as an archaeologist and ethnog-rapher, engaged in fields studies in the US, Polynesia, and Madagascar.[81]

Linton first expounded on the division, which became a mainstay of Sociology, between the concepts of "status" and "role."[82] *Social status*, as Linton showed, consists of a whole *array* of *roles*, each of which the bearer of status can fulfill with a different degree of perfection. The correlation of status and role is tied with the general problem, shared by the school of Boas as a whole, and by the circle of "culture and personality," of the proportion between the impersonal (structure) and the personal (histori-cal) in society.

Thus, again we find at the basis of the fundamental concepts and the concepts of modern, classic Sociology the ethnos, Ethnology, and Cultural Anthropology (Ethnosociology).

81   Linto, R. *The Tanala: A Hill Tribe of Madagascar*. Chicago, IL: Field Museum of Natural History, 1933.

82   Linton, R. *The Study of Man*. New York, NY: D. Appleton-Century, 1936; Ibid. *The Cultural Background of Personality*. New York, NY: Appleton-Century Crofts, 1945.

Cora Du Bois: The Structure of Modal Personality

One participant of the "cultural and personality" circle was another famous representative of contemporary Anthropology, Sociology, and Ethnography, Cora Du Bois (1903–1991), also a student of Boas. In the spirit of the classical approach of this orientation, Du Bois engaged in ethnographic field studies in Northern California and on the Northeast Pacific coast of America, having released a documented study of the sociological and cultural significance of the "ghost dance" among the Wintu tribe.[83]

Later, under the influence of Kardiner, Du Bois actively began to use psychological and psychoanalytical practices, tests, questionnaires, dream analyses, etc., in her ethnographic and ethnosociological research. Her work in Indonesia was based on this method.[84]

In the theoretical domain, she proposed a nuanced version of Kardiner's "basic personality," which she defined as the "*structure of modal personality.*" This concept was created to make the boundaries of that constant type, within which individual variations in ethnic and social structures are realized, more precise.

Edward Sapir: The Hypothesis of Linguistic Untranslatability

Yet another student of that circle and Boas was the renowned linguist Edward Sapir (1884–1939), who, in the context of the study of the relationship of culture and "basic personality," developed as a priority another orientation outlined by Boas, "**cultural pluralism**," which is embodied in the multitude of human languages.

Sapir identified the culture and language of a society and from all sides approached the axiom of Structural Linguistics (Saussure, Jakobson, Trubetzkoy, etc.), according to which the meaning of utterances is

---

83   Du Bois, C. *Ghost Dance*. Berkeley, CA: University of California Press, 1930.

84   Du Bois, C. *The People of Alor; A Social-Psychological Study of an East Indian Island.* Minneapolis, MN: University of Minnesota Press, 1944.

determined not so much by the correlation of sign and signified (the extensional, a concrete object or phenomenon of the extra-linguistic sphere) as by the inner connection of the sign with other signs in the general structure of the language and the linguistic context.[85] Sapir followed Boas in this, who indicated the fact that the anthropologist's perception of a phoneme of a foreign language passes through the filter of the structure of their own linguistic belongingness. If even the phoneme as the minimal fragment of the auditory expression of language and a material sign is isolated by linguistic perception on the basis of a linguistic pattern peculiar to each language of group of languages, then what is there to say about the perception of the semantic categories that depend entirely on an even deeper and subtler cultural field and context?

This can be traced through the now famous comparison of the names of colors in different languages. In some languages, there are several terms used to describe one shade or another, while others use the same word to describe that which other ethnoses consider unquestionably and obviously different.

Meaning depends on context and on the structure of a language. For this reason, meaning is not common to all humanity, but an ethnically, culturally, socially, and linguistically predetermined phenomenon, belonging only to a concrete semantic and linguistic context.[86]

Sapir formulate this fact as the "untranslatability" of languages. This assertion received the name "*the principal of linguistic relativity*" or the "*Sapir-Whorf Law*" (Benjamin Whorf [1897–1941] was an American linguist and Sapir's collaborator).

From the principle of linguistic relativity issues the impossibility of thinking outside of language. Thought cannot develop without meaning, and meaning is contained in language.

Thus, the pluralism of cultures is corroborated by the pluralism of languages, although the diversity of languages does not allow one to

---

85 Sapir, E. *Selected Writings in Language, Culture and Personality.* Berkeley, CA: University of California Press, 1949.

86 Ibid.

arrange them hierarchically, since to do this one would have to recognize a languages or group of languages more perfect than others, but to do this would be to interpret the "other" through one's "own" lens, i.e., to execute an "ethnocentric act."

We can trace an interesting chain: the concept of a non-hierarchized diversity of cultures (holism) was already previously asserted by Herder and shared by German romantics. Romanticism influenced Organicism, the anthropogeographic approach (Ratzel), and German Ethnology and Ethnopsychology (Lazarus, Wundt). Boas, educated in Germany under the direct impact of these influences, brought this orientation to the US and created a school there, which shaped the look of American, and in many respects, worldwide Anthropology, Ethnology, Sociology, Culturology, and Linguistics over the course of the 20th century. Boas' student Edward Sapir locked onto Herder's intuition, expressing it in his principle of untranslatability as a strictly scientific, linguistic, and sociological law.

Clyde Kluckhohn: The Method of Value Orientations

Rather close in method and theme to the circle of "culture and personality" was another prominent sociologist, colleague of Talcott Parsons and the founder of the Harvard Department of Social Relations Clyde Kluckhohn (1905–1960).

Kluckhohn, as also the majority of cultural anthropologists, followed Boas' rules and undertook a number of ethnographic field expeditions. The result was his studies in the domain of the magical and religious ideas of the Navajo.[87]

At one point, Kluckhohn collaborated closely with Kroeber and acted as his coauthor for the book *Culture: A Critical Review of Concepts and Definitions*.[88]

---

87 Kluckhohn, C. *Navaho Witchcraft*. Boston: Beacon Press, 1944.

88 Kluckhohn, C. & Kroeber A.L. *A Culture: A Critical Review of Concepts and Definitions*. Cambridge, MA: Peabody Museum, 1952.

In the theoretical sphere Kluckhohn proposed that cross-cultural studies should be guided by the method of "*value orientations.*" This method puts forward a classification of cultures according to five main value criteria:[89]

- *The assessment of human nature* (whether good, evil, or mixed);

- *The relations of man to nature* (whether in the submission of man to nature, the submission of nature to man, or their harmonious balance);

- *The understanding of time* (with a special emphasis being placed on the past/tradition, present/enjoyment, or future/posterity/delayed reward);

- *Activity* (being, becoming/inner development, or activity/striving/technique);

- *Social relations* (whether hierarchical, associative/collective-egalitarian or individualistic).

It is easy to demonstrate the potency of these criteria by the example of the analysis of the fundamental ethnosociological moments.

With the help of Klukhohn's criteria it is also possible to describe more subtle differences, or variants of societies in transitional conditions, and separate sociocultural, political, ideological, or religious groups within the framework of one or another society.

---

89 Kluckhohn, C. *Culture and Behavior.* New York, NY: The Free Press of Glencoe, 1962.

Kluckhohn's Criteria / Society	Ethnos	Narod/Laos	Nation	Civil Society
Human Nature	Mixed	Mixed or Evil	Mixed or Evil	Good
The Connection between Man and Nature / Balance	Balance	Balance	Man above Nature	Man above Nature
Time	Present	Past/Tradition	Future/ Progeny or Present/ Enjoyment	Present/ Enjoyment
Activity	Being	Becoming/ Inner Development	Action/ Striving/ Technology	Action/ Striving/ Technology
Social Relations	Egalitarianism	Hierarchy (Caste, Estate)	Hierarchy (Class, Economic)	Individualism

Figure 7. Table of correspondence of Kluckhohn's criteria to the types of society in the ethnosociological series.

Clifford Geertz: Symbolic Anthropology

One of Kluckhohn's pupils was the famous American anthropologist Clifford Geertz (1926–2006), the founder of Symbolic Anthropology.

Geertz participated in field studies on the island of Java, in Bali, and in Morocco. He wrote a few fundamental works of cultural anthropology, devoted to the interpretation of the religious ideas of archaic ethnoses and to the ecological aspect of the economy — in particular, to the problem of the agrarian sector in societies subject to accelerated acculturation and modernization.[90, 91]

In his work, Geertz combines the influence of Boas' school and the "culture and personality" circle, the sociological ideas of Parsons and Weber, the philosophical outlook of the late Wittgenstein, who developed the idea of "language games," and the philosophical theories of Structuralism (Ricoeur). On the basis of these sources, he elaborates a model of "Symbolic Anthropology." The task of the researcher of the cultures of ethnic societies, according to Geertz, is the clarification of their structures and its interpretations, their hermeneutic explanations in terms borrowed from those cultures themselves. Geertz uses the name "*thick description*" to clarify the essence of such a method. It is "thick" in the sense of a refusal to willingly select from the studied ethnic culture fundamental semantic axes, which would sort the accumulated givens according to their relevance or irrelevance in relation to the knowingly specified criteria. The "thick description" of a culture proposes an initial trust in it and a readiness to adjust the sociological and anthropological apparatus in accordance with what the organic bearers of the culture themselves consider important or unimportant. "Thick description" is characteristic for myth, with its synchronism, symbolism, and multidimensionality; "*flat description*" for rational discourse, built on strictly causal ties.

The essence of "*Symbolic Anthropology*" consists in building one's own systems on the basis of what the members themselves of the examined culture consider of primary and secondary importance. This can run counter to the attitudes of the researcher of this or that anthropological school, who is inclined to attribute priority meaning to entirely different factors, but Geertz insists that in every case the value hierarchy of the ethnos be taken into account in the most serious manner. It is easy to recognize the law of William Thomas in this principle: "if society considers something

---

90   Geertz, C. *The Religion of Java*. Glencoe: Free Press, 1960; Ibid. *Islam Observed: Religious Development in Morocco and Indonesia*. New Haven, CT: Yale University Press, 1968.

91   Geertz, C. *Agricultural Involution: The Processes of Ecological Change in Indonesia*. Berkeley, CA: University of California Press, 1963.

great, then it is great." Or Mauss' doctrine of the "total social fact": if in some society something is considered important which is considered by the researcher entirely unimportant (on the basis of the value system of the society to which the researcher belongs), he is obligated to register this importance as "symbolic," to reckon with it, and to take it into account in the construction of his own system of interpretation.

Geertz laid out his foundational ideas in the book "The Interpretation of Cultures."[92] Earlier we saw that the contemporary English sociologist Anthony Smith named a version of the "primordialist approach" after Geertz ("Geertz's Primordialism"), which is the most constructive and optimal model of Ethnosociology as such.

Clark Wissler: Cultural Area

A relatively independent version of Cultural Anthropology was proposed by Clark Wissler (1870–1947), who was the curator of the American Museum of Natural History in New York, though he did, at one time, work together with Franz Boas and was not able to escape his influence entirely. Wissler's works became a source of inspiration for many American and European ethnosociologists.

Wissler devoted a series of works, which received recognition in scientific circles, to the Native peoples of North America.[93]

Wissler's specific contribution was the development of the theory of "cultural areas," with the help of which he proposed to interpret the ethnosociological regionalization of cultures and to establish an asymmetrical correlation between them. Later an analogous approach received the name "mapping," the compilation of conceptual correspondences between diverse pluralities, represented as situated in space ("on a map"). Wissler proposed to analyze cultural areas in a criss-cross manner, establishing different types and forms of analogy between them.

92   Geertz, C. *The Interpretation of Cultures*. New York, NY: Basic Books, 1975.

93   Geertz, C. *The American Indian: An Introduction to the Anthropology of the New World*. New York, NY: Douglas C. McMurtrie, 1917; Ibid. *The Indians of the United States: Four Centuries of Their History and Culture*. New York, NY: Doubleday Doran, 1940.

In the theoretical domain, Wissler insisted on stricter formulations of basic anthropological principles and strove to render Cultural Anthropology a more exact discipline, with the help of the statistical method. He considered culture to be an "obligatory standard," defined as "acquired behavior," and he suggested that it be studied as a "complex of ideas."[94]

Margaret Mead: Children—Capitalists, Materialists, Cynics

It is worth mentioning another group of Boas' followers and students, who made a substantial contribution to Ethnosociology. The brightest figure of contemporary Anthropology was Boas' student Margaret Mead (1901–1978), who developed certain ideas of the circle of "culture and personality." Ruth Benedict, in particular, was a big influence on her.

Mead conducted ethnographic field studies in New Guinea and in Bali, and the books she consequently wrote about them became bestsellers around the world, selling in numbers unthinkable for serious anthropological, scientific works or ethnosociological studies.[95]

In her works, Mead shows the *relativity* of opinions, deeply rooted in modern society, about the status of the child, gender, the processes of socialization, etc., which were considered universal. On the basis of extensive ethnographic and ethnosociological material, Mead shows that in many archaic societies (and even in the majority of them) myths, legends, and stories are the prerogative of adult, socially responsible men, for whom *belief in the supernatural* is an inalienable part of their social status. If an adult, socially responsible man ceases to believe in myths, he loses his status, becomes an outcast and outsider.

Children in archaic societies, on the other hand, display vivid examples of rationalism, skepticism, materialism, and cynicism. Before the passing of the stage of puberty, models of the childish explanation

---

94   Wissler, C. *Man and Culture.* New York, NY: Thomas Y. Crowell, 1923.

95   Mead, M. *Coming of Age in Samoa (1927).* New York, NY: William. Morrow & Company, 1973.

of reasons for phenomena are notable for their crudity and linearity. If in some tribes, adults consider the birth of children the coming into the tribe of the spirits of ancestors, then children, on the contrary, are inclined to ascribe this to the sexual activity of their fathers and mothers on the marriage bed. If adults consider the exchange of objects a symbolic act, necessary for maintaining the balance of the world and signifying that in the ritual or the giving of gifts one must give away as much as (if not more than) one receives, the children of archaic tribes try to amass for themselves as many valuable objects (rocks, boar tusks or dog teeth) as possible and to give away as little as possible, employing for this end rather ingenious tricks, calling to mind in their general features the strategy of modern capitalism, marketing, and even legal procedures, unknown to the world of adults, who are living in accordance with the sacred rules of the "economy of the gift."

Such asymmetry is explained by the fact that children are not yet familiar with culture, and for this reason behave like contemporary "civilized" Europeans.

Gregory Bateson: The Criticism of Monotonic Processes

Margaret Mead's husband Gregory Bateson (1904–1980) was, for a time, another student of Boas', and he too left his mark on Ethnosociology, Linguistics, Philosophy, Psychology, and Psychiatry. He participated in field studies in New Guinea together with Mead, in which he described in detail the initiatory rituals of the tribes of the Iatmul and gave this phenomenon a thorough analysis using the categories of eidos, ethnos, and schismogenesis.[96] He continued his studies in Bali.[97]

---

96 Bateson, G. *Naven: A Survey of the Problems suggested by a Composite Picture of the Culture of a New Guinea Tribe drawn from Three Points of View.* Stanford, CA: Stanford University Press, 1936.

97 Bateson, G. & Mead M. *Balinese Character: A Photographic Analysis.* New York, NY: New York Academy of Sciences, 1942.

Bateson applied his ethnographic knowledge and Boas' scientific program to the domains of psychology and linguistics, advancing the hypothesis that the structure of language almost entirely programs a person's behavior in the social environment. On this principle, he built his *"double bind theory,"* applicable in both psychiatry and in ethnosociological analysis.

The "double bind theory" consists of this: in certain circumstances a man or the social group may receive a linguistic message, containing within itself a contradiction. This contradiction can provoke a significant malfunction of the social system or psychological balance of the person, since it affects the inner, unconscious structures of the psyche, which comprise the basis of the cultural matrix. Hence, Bateson advanced the hypothesis (subsequently completely confirmed) that the speech disorders of parents can serve as the reason for the mental disorders (in particular, schizophrenia) of their children. The receipt of an order formulated in a way that violates the logical structures of language (for instance: "move closer away from me") can in the case of multiple repetitions lead to a serious psychological illness, since the correspondence between grammar, significance, and sense will be shattered.

This becomes a frequent phenomenon on the level of culture, accompanying acculturation. An archaic tribe aggressively attacks one of a higher culture, along with its values, semantic fields, and social codes, which leads to a failure in the functioning of both local and imported social attitudes. Generalizing, it is possible to say that the acceleration of the modernization of archaic or traditional societies in certain cases leads to the establishment of pathological systems of "double binds," to social pathology.

Bateson's ideas concerning *"monotonic processes"* are extremely important. From his point of view, reason functions in the logic of *"monotonicity"*; noticing a tendency towards growth, it automatically prolongs it into infinity, conjecturing by default that growth in the present will continue in the future also. The laws of life, on the other hand, are cyclical and reversible. At some moment, growth ends and depreciation, decline, and decay begin. The system becomes, in turns, more complex and simpler. Thus, reason and its structure enter into contradiction with the peculiar logic of life. This can be traced in both societies and in separate individuals or natural types.

The critique of monotonic processes and the attempt to formulate an approach that would synthesize the principles of rationalism and the vital laws of nature is one of Bateson's main theoretical merits.[98]

Melville Herskovits: The American Negro as the "Basic Personality"

Another student of Boas, Melville Herskovits (1895–1963), focused his field studies on the problem of the Negroes in both North and Central America (the Caribbean region). Herskovits developed the first exhaustive reconstructions of the ethnosociological peculiarities of the Negro population in America, the study of their cultures, customs, and typical social characteristics. Herskovits aimed to recreate and accurately describe the "basic personality" of the Negro as a normative sociological figure.[99]

Herskovits continued the theme of studying Negro societies beyond the borders of America, turning to the study of African societies in Africa itself. Studying this matter, he made a few fundamental discoveries in the area of Economic Anthropology, which first and foremost contemplates the interconnection of ethnic and ethnosociological phenomena with the structure of the economy and economic practices.[100]

The problem of the Negros in the US and in the countries of Central America led Herskovits to the more general theme of social acculturation, the influence of some societies (as a rule, more complex ones) on others (as a rule, simpler ones), with the compulsory displacement of

---

98 Bateson, G. *Mind and Nature: A Necessary Unity (Advances in Systems Theory, Complexity, and the Human Sciences)*. New Jersey, NJ: Hampton Press, 1979.

99 Herskovits, M. J. *American Negro: A Study in Racial Crossing*. New York, NY: Alfred A. Knopf, 1928.

100 Herskovits, M. J. *Economic and The Human Factor in Changing Africa*. New York: Knopf, 1962; Ibid. *The Man and His Works*. New York, NY: Alfred A. Knopf, 1948.

the autochthonous culture by the imposed culture. Herskovits devoted a separate work to this theme as well a joint memorandum, written together with two other outstanding ethnosociologists, Ralph Linton and Robert Redfield.[101, 102]

Robert Redfield: Folk Society

Herskovits and Linton's coauthor Robert Redfield (1897–1958) made a significant contribution to Ethnosociology through his fundamental studies of small agrarian societies.[103] Redfield, like all cultural anthropologists, engaged in field studies. In particular, he researched the culture of Mexico, with an emphasis on the rural population.[104]

The main object of his sociological studies was "peasant culture."[105] Redfield introduced into Ethnosociology the crucial concept "*folk society*." The definition of folk society can be applied to the ethnos with full justification: one can put an equal sign between these two sociological categories.

Redfield describes folk society in the following terms:

- The people composing the folk society look very much alike;

- Their mores and habits are identical;

- All of the members of the folk society possess a strong feeling of belonging to one another;

- A folk society is a small, isolated community, most often illiterate, homogeneous, and with a strong feeling of group solidarity;

101 Herskovits, M. J. *Acculturation: The Study of Culture Contact*. Gloucester, MA: P. Smith, 1958.

102 Redfield, R., Linton R. & Herskovits M.J. *Memorandum for the Study of Acculturation* / American Anthropologist. 1936. Vol. 38. No. 1, p. 149–152.

103 Redfield, R. *The Little Community*. Chicago, IL: University of Chicago, 1956.

104 Redfield, R. *Tepoztlan, A Mexican village: A Study of Folk Life*. Chicago, IL: Chicago University Press, 1930.

105 Redfield, R. *Peasant Society and Culture: An Anthropological Approach to Civilization*. Chicago, IL: University of Chicago Press, 1956.

- There is almost no division of labor (except gender-based) in folk society;
- The subjects and objects of production are families;
- Folk society can be defined as "sacred society."[106]

Redfield follows the fate of folk society in more complex social constructions. They can be preserved as unique enclaves, assimilate entirely, set off into continuous wandering (Romani), end up in slavery and become a "second class narod" (Negros in America), comprise a class of peasants, villagers, the urban underclass, become colonists of new lands, etc.[107]

Paul Radin: The Figure of the Trickster

Extremely important for Cultural Anthropology are the works of yet another student of Boas', Paul Radin (1883–1953), a recognized specialist in the ethnography of the Native tribes of North America, and the author of the bestselling book, *The Trickster*, the preface to which was written by the Swiss psychoanalyist Carl Jung.[108, 109] Radin thoroughly studied the myths, traditions, and rituals of the Winnebago and reconstructed on that basis a general type, met with in the mythologies of the most diverse narods, which he described as the figure of the **trickster**.

The trickster is a cultural hero whose actions are always ambivalent, not given to unambiguous classification along the scale of good and evil, truth and lies, use and harm, and so on. This is a very important figure, since in it we see the matrix of the social culture of society in its primordial

106 Redfield, R. 'Die Folk-Gesellschaft' / Mulmann, W. & Muller, E. (ed.) *Kulturanthropologie*. Koln; Berlin: Kiepenheuer & Witsch, 1966, pp. 327–352.

107 Redfield, R. *The Primitive World and Its Transformations*. Cambridge, MA: Harvard University Press, 1953.

108 Radin, P. *Crashing Thunder: The Autobiography of an American Indian*. New York, NY; London: Appleton and Co., 1926.

109 Radin, P. *The Trickster: A Study in American-Indian Mythology*. London: Routledge & Kegan Paul, 1956.

state, even before it is raised to the level of distinct awareness and the differentiated distribution of socio-formative pairs.

This theme interested Jung, since in his theory the collective unconscious precedes structured moral systems and is always ambivalent in itself. Just as ambivalent is the even deeper structure of the ethnos, the personification of which is the mythological trickster, discovered and conceptualized by Radin.

To Radin belongs also a series of works on the philosophy and religion of simple societies.[110, 111]

Mircea Eliade: Eternal Return

The Romanian historian Mircea Eliade (1907–1986), who lived the second half of his life in the US and fundamentally influenced American Sociology and scientific culture, exerted a tremendous influence on Cultural Anthropology and Ethnosociology.

Even in his early words, Eliade put before himself the task of describing the fundamental differences between archaic and traditional societies and the societies of the Modern era. He studied ancient and modern religions, societies, and cultures, trying to find the most important markers that distinguish contemporary Western culture from the ancient societies of both Europe and also from the East. Eliade came to the conclusion that traditional society, even when it possesses a written culture and highly differentiated rationality, is oriented toward a cyclical model of the understanding of time and on the symmetrical homology of society and the cosmos. Modern societies, on the other hand, are built around the concept of linear, unidirectional time and on the principle of a total asymmetry between the subject (culture) and object (nature).[112] Thus, Eliade

---

110 Radin, P. *Primitive Man as Philosopher*. New York and London: D. Appleton and Company.

111 Radin, P. *Primitive Religion: Its Nature and Origin*. New York, NY: Dover, 1937.

112 Eliade, M. *The Myth of the Eternal Return: Cosmos and History*. Princeton, NJ: Princeton University Press, 2005.

developed criteria that make precise the structure of the relationship between social models and various paradigms.

Eliade devoted a number of books to the study of the mythologies of different narods; his book on the phenomenon of shamanism is widely recognized as a classic.[113, 114]

Eliade's key theme consists of the concept of the "sacred" (in his late period, Durkheim also studied this theme as a priority).[115] It is precisely this factor that comprises the uniqueness of simple societies, of ethnoses. *Sacredness* is the fundamental mark of antiquity and tradition, while *secularity*, the banishing of sacredness, or the "disenchanted world" (Weber), on the other hand, makes up the essence of modernity. At the same time, Weber insists that for the correct understanding of archaic societies and ethnoses it is necessary for the researcher to recognize and become familiar with the "experience of the sacred," without which his observations of institutions, rites, attitudes, statuses, roles, and values of the "primitive" society will not be valid. Eliade himself, like Boas, openly sympathized with archaic ethnoses, believing the experience of the sacred to be that very core pivot whose presence does not simply balance archaic societies with contemporary ones, but makes them more worthy, vital, and well off than the latter.

If, at the start of his scientific career, Eliade was interested above all in sophisticated mystical theology — such as that of the Middle Ages, Hinduism, Buddhism, Hermeticism, etc. — then in his later years he focused all of his attention on the study of the most "primitive" societies, expecting to find in precisely them the keys to the nature of the sacred, which in more complex religious systems is overgrown with a massive quantity of rational and philosophical details. He devoted his last work,

---

113 Eliade, M. *Aspect du mythe. Mircea Eliade. Coll. Idées.* Paris: Gallimard, 1995.

114 Eliade, M. *Shamanism: Archaic Techniques of Ecstasy.* Princeton, NJ: Princeton University Press, 1972.

115 Eliade, M. *The Sacred and the Profane: The Nature of Religion.* New York, NY: Harcourt, Brace & World, 1959.

The Religions of Australia, to the aborigines of that continent and the description of the structure of sacredness in their societies.[116]

Harold Garfinkel: Ethnomethodology & Ethnosociology

Of significant interest is the sociological theory of the contemporary sociologist Harold Garfinkel, which has received the name "Ethnomethodology" but which bears no relation to either the ethnos or to Ethnosociology, although it is extremely interesting in its own right and deserves attention from the point of view of its philosophical phenomenological method.

Garfinkel put before himself a fundamental philosophical and sociological question: where is the rational element of the socium concentrated — in impersonal, common rules and norms or in the particular interests of separate citizens? What is social reason: a pubic dogma or an algorithm for the behavior of separate individuals?

Two main traditions in Sociology answer this question in directly opposite ways. Durkheim and his school (and also classical Sociology on the whole) say that the "collective consciousness" is primary and that society is itself the carrier of rationality, while Weber and "understanding sociology" (including the classic American sociologist, Talcott Parsons) insist that the source of society's rationality is the individual, who seeks the maximum benefit in his egoistic living of the allotted time of life.[117]

Garfinkel passes no ultimate judgement on these questions, but he proposes to approach society from the side of the common person (in the spirit of the sociological Phenomenology of Schutz) and to trace the chain of the rational actions, evaluations, steps, and conclusions of the separate individual or separate group in a concrete situation. From his point of view, rationality is that which is developed by a concrete individual in the process of his search for the optimal paths of solving his short-term

---

116 Eliade, M. *Australian Religions: An Introduction.* Ithaca, NY: Cornell University Press, 1973.

117 Garfinkel, H. *Ethnomethodology's Program: Working out Durkheim's Aphorism.* Lanham, MD: Rowman & Littlefield, 2002.

problems. Each member of a society wants something in each concrete moment of time. Garfinkel asserts that social rationality is formed from these desires and the actions corresponding to them. He calls this approach "*Ethnomethodology*."[118]

The question arises: why did Garfinkel select such a term? The answer is as follows. Classical Sociology, both Durkheim's and Weber's, thinks that the rationality which dominates in society is quite differentiated and "scientific." This means that societies with a developed scientific culture, a high reflection of the correspondence of the subject (proposition) and object (verification), are taken as models. That is to say, by "rationality" is understood, in one way or another, the "scientific rationality" of the Modern Era. But Garfinkel wanted to draw attention to a *different* rationality, to the "*small rationality*" of the average man, who does not feel the slightest need for a "scientific" analysis of his relation to the world and is supplied with the possessing possibilities of consciousness, focused on the realization of intended tasks in a concrete context.[119] Such a society, consisting of empirical individuals, acting rationally in relation to a concrete situation for the sole purpose of satisfying their direct wishes and ambitions is what he called an "ethnos." For Garfinkel, "ethnos" is a synonym of the quality of being unscientific. The study of the small rationalities of concrete individuals (e.g., the sociological analysis of the decisions of jurors, in which Garfinkel engaged during his youth) is the essence of "Ethno"-methodology.

Garfinkel, who named his method of sociological studies (in the spirit of the phenomenological Sociology of Schutz) Ethnomethodology, equated the ethnos to the *unscientific* and *prescientific* type of society. In itself this assertion is entirely correct, since it is precisely the ethnos which is that simple society, untouched by the scientific, rationalistic paradigm of the Modern Era. But the adequacy of this assertion ends here, since the

---

118 Garfinkel, H. *Studies in Ethnomethodology.* Englewood Cliffs, NJ: Prentice-Hall, 1967.

119 Garfinkel, H. *Seeing Sociologically: The Routine Grounds of Social Action.* Boulder, CO: Paradigm Publishers, 2006.

ethnos, besides the fact that it has no scientifically rational dimension, has many other dimensions, none of which Garfinkel was concerned about. He simply dumped into the concept "ethnos," as one would into a garbage bin, all that did not possess the quality of scientific, "subject-object" reflection, and occupied himself intensely with this "garbage," sociologically constructed according to the "residual" principle.

To any specialist familiar with the complex structure of the ethnos, its dynamics, transformations, and inner collisions, such an approach will seem immensely inadequate. But if we take into consideration the historical situation in which Garfinkel was working, everything changes. In the American society of Garfinkel's time, scientific rationality, or more precisely its ideological and propagandistic derivatives, had prevailed so strongly that it seemed self-evident. The authoritative works of cultural anthropologists, available only to the US intellectual elite, remain accessible only to closed academic circles. Any American (or European) commoner, whom Garfinkel would enlist in the "ethnos" in the spirit of his "ethno"-methodology (i.e., into a community of not entirely rational individuals), would have considered himself entirely "scientific," even if he had only read two or three popular science brochures. For this reason, "Ethnomethodology" became a cliché in a society in which the word "ethnos" signified "simplicity" — not something organic and primordial, but "residual" and representing the *refuse* of a highly differentiated society — its fragments — unable to cope with its high level of differentiation.

In other words, as a contemporary sociologist studying the phenomenon on the society of Modernity and Postmodernity, Garfinkel is extremely interesting and relevant, but his "ethno"-methodology has absolutely no relationship to Ethnosociology.

McKim Marriott: American Ethnosociology Today

The most adequate contemporary representative of Ethnosociology in the US is the student and follower of Robert Redfield, the present-day American anthropologist and sociologist McKim Marriott. He himself readily calls his orientation "Ethnosociology," and in this case this designation is entirely justified, since he studies ethnoses (as simple societies, Redfield's "folk society") with sociological methods, relying on Boas' school of Cultural Anthropology (only such an approach should be referred to as "Ethnosociology").

Marriott applied Boas' concept of cultural pluralism to concrete studies of the society of India, starting from the "ethnic" level of separate villages. In the course of meticulous field work he came to the conclusion that to understand the structure of Indian society we must reject European criteria and transition to those formulae, concepts, and categories that the local residents themselves use in their everyday lives. In other words, he proclaimed that *Indian society can be adequately described only by Indian categories* — and that too by beginning with the lowest level (of concrete identity), concrete Indian ethnic villages and settlements.[120, 121]

In his works, Marriott also puts even more serious tasks before himself: he proposes to subject to critical philosophical analysis those methods, with the help of which, Western researchers study non-Western societies as a whole. He traces the dual dichotomies, characteristic of the European consciousness, to which anthropologists and sociologists try in their models to reduce the social categories of studied ethnoses down to and shows that in the majority of archaic cultures, these oppositions are not known, and that the very "map" of society and the world within which they operate are built on other, more complex and "analog" (and not digital) constructs. Marriott insists that anthropology and ethnosociology should actually become multipolar, and Western researchers should voluntarily cease to claim the status of the sole and prioritized subject-observer, subjecting their own culture to an impartial analysis from the position of other societies or from the special "meta-comparative" position, in

---

120 Mariott, M. (ed.) *India through Hindu Categories*. New Delhi/Newbury Park / London: Sage Publications, 1990.

121 Mariott, M. *The Female Family Core Explored Ethnosociologically* / Contributions to Indian Sociology, 1998.

which, during the study of a culture, the researcher and his own culture are necessarily also subjected to analysis.[122]

Marriott's meta-comparative initiative for the philosophical revision of the basic instruments of Anthropology on a new stage and in new conditions brings the fundamental attitudes of Cultural Anthropology and Ethnosociology to their logical limits, going back not only to Boas, but also to Herder.

Ronald Inden: For the Destruction of Colonial Clichés in Ethnosociology

Ronald Inden, another contemporary American ethnosociologist from the University of Chicago, works in this same spirit. Inden specializes in India and, in particular, in those ethnic groups that speak Bengali.[123] After starting with field studies of certain tribes of India, Inden came to a series of general theoretical conclusions concerning the method that the Anthropology and Ethnosociology of the West use when studying other, non-Western societies. From his point of view, up until now, a colonial approach, based on clichés that bear little relation to reality, has dominated the study of India. In his book *Imagining India*, Inden systematizes the most widespread Western clichés and demonstrates their unsoundness.[124]

Thus, he shows that:

- In the eyes of Western researchers, the image of Indian society appears "feminine";

- The social structure is strictly "caste" based;

- The typical landscape is taken to be a "jungle";

- The typical settlement is associated with a "small village";

---

122 Gerow, E. *India As A Philosophical Problem: Mckim Marriott and the Comparative Enterprise* / Journal of the American Oriental Society, 2000, July-Sept.

123 Inden, R. B. (ed.) *Kinship in Bengali Culture*. Chicago, IL: University of Chicago Press, 1977.

124 Inden, R. B. *Imagining India*. Oxford: Basil Blackwell, 1990.

- The collective consciousness is imagined as purely irrational;

- The religious cult is thought of as dominant;

- India as a whole is presented as the antithesis of the West.

Inden carefully takes apart each of these assertions and demonstrates that:

- The gender scenarios in India are more accurately described as "patriarchal," although the form of normative masculinity differs from the European one, and there exist numerous variants and nuances even between Indo-European groups, and all the more so among South Indian ethnoses;

- The caste principle does not operate on the level of official, governmental policy, and on the level of small social and ethnic groups, there exist various forms that mitigate and modify it, so to speak of the dominance of the "caste system" is an outright exaggeration;

- Indian landscapes are extremely diverse; furthermore, not only are jungles not the sole landscape, but not even the predominant one;

- Alongside villages, there exist huge modern megacities in India today;

- The manifold kinds of Indian philosophy are the peak of rationalism, although it differs qualitatively from Western European rationalism, and in contemporary Indian society it is possible to meet with the most diverse forms of thought, including modern and postmodern;

- India's religious landscape is so diverse that it demands special consideration, inasmuch as it is possible to meet both systematized and theologically elaborate, as well as archaic forms, alongside secular thought within the context of one society;

- On the whole, India and its society differ significantly from Western societies. It is not a direct antithesis to them, but, on the contrary, in some of its details—such as its focus on the problem of the "higher I" (ātman) and critical attitude toward the surrounding world (as *māyā*– brings Indians philosophically quite close to European individualism (in its metaphysical presuppositions).

Inden proves that it is necessary to substantially change the attitude of Western researchers to non-Western societies, to reject the predominant standard patterns, and to learn to understand "others" as they understand themselves.

Everything said about India applies in full measure to all other non-Western societies. Thus, contemporary American Ethnosociology in its new phase turns toward the initial program of Boas and German Ethnosociology, which insisted on the rejection of Eurocentrism and called for the researcher to grow deeply accustomed to the studied Ethnosociological system.

Summary of American Cultural Anthropology

If we summarize the general trend of American Cultural Anthropology, we receive an almost finished scientific program of Ethnosociology, which isolates the fundamental moments of this discipline. The orientation that Boas lay in his works was and still is the groundwork for the scientific studies of his school.

Ethnosociology as a science is wholly and completely grounded on the fundamental principles of the scientific conceptions of Boas and his school, which shaped the look of all American anthropology in the 20th century.

Let us reiterate its main provisions:

- A radical rejection of all forms of racism (biological, evolutionary, technological, cultural, etc.);

- A recognition of the differential equality of all types of society (simple and complex, primitive and highly differentiated);

- The comprehension of society and an integral phenomenon, judgment about which can be rendered only from within it;

- The untranslatability of cultures, languages, ethnoses, and societies (meaning is preserved in a linguistic-semantic context).

SECTION THREE
The English School of Ethnosociology, Social Anthropology, Functionalism, Evolutionism

English Evolutionism

Like its American counterpart, English Anthropology first developed on the basis of rectilinear evolutionism. Specifically, it developed from an extreme form of evolutionism called *"Orthogenesis"* (from the Greek roots ὀρθός (*ortho*), "direct, straight, upright, erect," and γένεσις (*genesis*), "origin"). *Orthogenesis asserts that the evolution of living species has a clearly established goal and follows a direct path in its development, from the simple to the complex.* Projecting orthogenesis on society, we get Social Darwinism as the idea that all societies move from archaic and primitive forms in the direction of the contemporary technological and industrial societies of Modernity, although this movement occurs at different speeds in different societies, despite the fact that the difference of speeds is determined only by the influence of barriers and impediments of a natural and social character.

An approach based on Orthogenesis has traditionally been characteristic of the majority of English anthropologists and sociologists.

Earlier we spoke of the theories of Herbert Spencer, who developed "Social Darwinism" on the basis of a radical understanding of evolution. The historical and sociological conceptions of other English anthropologists and sociologists of the end of the 19th century were established in the same spirit.

Edward Tylor: Evolutionary Series of Culture and Animism

Edward Tylor (1832–1917), founder of the evolutionary theory of culture and author of the classic work *Primitive Culture* was among those who take an evolutionary approach.[125] Tylor thought that all societies develop through the "perfection" of social institutions and systems of education. In his opinion, old institutions, customs, and religious beliefs die off in accordance with the degree of a society's "progress" as they lose their functional significance in these societies. Thus, all forms of culture and, in particular, religion met with in archaic societies, which Tylor called "childish," are either the embryos of corresponding instances in contemporary societies, or lack significance altogether.

Tylor drew up genetic series of different aspects of society — institutions, customs, rituals, etc.; at the basis of each were the simplest "primitive" forms, which gradually became more complex until they reached their contemporary variations. According to Tylor, the algorithm of evolution is embedded in the very structure of human behavior; for this reason, different ethnoses passed through the same stages in their development, independently of one another. Objective and entirely concrete group interests push society toward each subsequent stage.

Tylor tried to bring to light the minimal, simplest forms of religious, social, political, and economic institutions in archaic societies, the starting position of the historico-genetic series. Thus, in the area of religion he

---

125 Tylor, E.B. *Primitive Culture*. New York: Harper, 1958.

arrived at the theory of "*animism*," i.e., of vague, primitive notions that the surrounding world is full of "spirits" or "souls," which make it "alive."[126]

James George Frazer: The Symbol of the Sacred King

Another renowned and classic English anthropologist, James George Frazer (1854–1941), who shared the evolutionary approach (he also traced the genetic series and stages of evolution along the line "magic-religion-science"), is of interest, above all, because of the enormous amount of material concerning the magical and religious ideas of archaic societies his work offers, the methodological analysis of which is presented in his famous book *The Golden Bough*.[127] In it, Frazer studies a number of archaic rites connected with the "Year-King" or "Forest-King," drawing material for his analysis from different cultures of the world's ethnoses.

Fraser elaborates on the figure of the "*sacred king*," whose functions had no political dimension but were connected only with the performance of certain rituals (for instance, rainmaking) in European antiquity (Romans, Greeks, Germans), as well as among the archaic narods of today, in Africa, Asia, Latin America, and the Pacific Ocean region. A number of rites, myths, symbols and social institutions that play an important role in ancient societies are built up around the institution of "sacred kingship."

Fraser studied the link between ritual and magical beliefs and convincingly solved a number of riddles from the realm of folklore, which had previously brought anthropologists to a dead-end.

Fraser's book *The Golden Bough* appears in Francis Ford Coppola's film *Apocalypse Now*, in which, on the basis of material from the Vietnam War, the pivotal theme in Fraser's book is illustrated — the "king of the German forest."

---

126 Tylor, E.B. *Researches into the Early History of Mankind and the Development of Civilization*. London: J. Murray, 1865.

127 Frazer, J.G. *The Golden Bough: A Study in Magic and Religion*. London: Macmillan and Co, 1900.

Also of great importance are Fraser's studies of the archaic layers of the Bible, which he worked out and systematized in his book Folklore in the Old Testament.[128]

Bronisław Malinowski: Functionalism and Social Anthropology

A turn in English anthropology occurred together with the influence of the Polish emigrant Bronisław Malinowski (1884–1942), who radically changed the field in England, similar to the way Franz Boas abruptly changed the development of American Anthropology. It is customary to call Malinowski's school "*Social Anthropology*," but in its own fundamental parameters it is practically identical with the German Ethnosociology of Thurnwald and Mühlmann, and the Cultural Anthropology of Boas and his students.

Malinowski rejected Evolutionism and Orthogenesis, insisted on the priority of field studies (he introduced the concept of "participant observation"), denied the racial or genetic factor as a meaningful form of social explanation, refused to hierarchize society on an evolutionary or racial basis — he came forward, practically analogously, with the scientific program of Thurnwald and Boas.

Malinowski's field studies are devoted primarily to the Pacific Ocean region and Melanesia and remain to this day the most authoritative studies of the archaic societies of that part of the Earth.[129, 130]

Malinowski called his method "*Functionalism*." Malinowski essentially proposed to explain any cultural and social phenomenon (rite, symbol,

128 Frazer, J.G. *Folklore in the Old Testament: Studies in Comparative Religion Legend and Law*. London: Random House, 1968.

129 Malinowski, B. *Argonauts of the Western Pacific: An Account of Native Enterprise and Adventure in the Archipelagoes of Melanesian New Guinea*. London: G. Routledge & Sons, 1922.

130 Malinowski, B. *The Sexual Life of Savages in North-Western Melanesia*. New York, NY: Halcyon House, 1929; Ibid. *Coral Gardens and Their Magic: A Study of the Methods of Tilling the Soil and of Agricultural Rites in the Trobriand Islands*. New York, NY: American Book Co., 1935.

custom, institution, etc.) through its function, which must be considered first and foremost, in contrast to the form, name, origin, etc. Function comprises the semantics of culture, Malinowski asserted.[131]

The plurality of societies, languages, symbols, and cultural complexes should *not*, according to Malinowski, be understood as different stages of evolution (contrary to what the evolutionists claimed), *nor* as the interweaving routes of dissemination of "cultural circles" (contrary to the Diffusionists). We owe this manifest to the fact that in different situations, different societies will respond differently to the same challenges. If we re-establish the structure of the challenge and the structure of the response (the function), then we will substantially reduce the volume of disconnected ethnographic material and understand the logic of researched societies. Malinowski applied this principle to the study of the religious worldviews of primitive narods, and also to the area of kinship. In the sphere of the studies of sexual life and the organization of the system of kinship among the tribes of the Pacific Ocean region (in particular, the inhabitants of the Trobriand Islands), Malinowski applied some of Freud's ideas, thereby introducing Psychoanalysis into Social Anthropology.

Malinowski thought that the task of anthropology was to save the diversity of human cultures from Westernization and disappearance under the conditions of the planetary domination of the West. The processes of acculturation swiftly destroy the independence of archaic narods and thereby rob humanity, depriving it of linguistic, ethnic, and cultural riches. An anthropologist should, at least, preserve the memory of this diversity, and, at most, draw attention to the worth and uniqueness of each ethnic society, stopping the process of their destruction.

Alfred Radcliffe-Brown: Social Structures

Along with Malinowski, the English scholar Alfred Radcliffe-Brown (1881–1955) made a tremendous contribution to the establishment of Social Anthropology. He collected ethnographic material from the Andaman

---

131 Malinowsky, B. *A Scientific Theory of Culture and Other Essays*. New York: Oxford University Press, 1960.

Islands and in African societies, later setting out the material he gathered in his expeditions in such classic works as *The Andaman Islanders, African Systems of Kinship and Marriage,* and others.[132, 133]

Like Malinowski, Radcliffe-Brown rejected Evolutionism and emphasized the study of social functions. Durkheim's ideas exerted a sizeable influence on him, and he proposed as the main task the application of the strict criteria of the sociological method to the study of ethnoses and archaic societies. At the same time, he also considered structural comparison, the comparative method, the basic operation that allows one to systematize the chaotic data about primitive societies. Radcliffe-Brown bound Ethnography and Sociology tightly together into a single scientific discipline, Ethnosociology (although he himself did not use this term).

According to Radcliffe-Brown, social relations, the totality of which comprise the social structure, must be placed at the center of attention.[134] The concept of "social structure" is crucial for Social Anthropology as a whole. A *social structure* is a theoretical construct, based on the study, observation, description, and analysis of *social relations*, which are (or represent) the reality of a society. Each society has a unique social structure, which is amenable to internal change, but which preserves at each stage certain immutable features. Social Anthropology is tasked with tracing the changes of the social structure of a society, registering the influence of one social structure on another, and working out different classifications of social structures on the basis of the comparative method.[135]

---

132 Radcliffe-Brown, A.R. *The Andaman Islanders.* Cambridge: Cambridge University Press, 1922.

133 Radcliffe-Brown, A.R. & Forde D. (eds.) *African Systems of Kinship and Marriage.* Oxford: Oxford University Press, 1950.

134 Radcliffe-Brown, A.R. *Structure and Function in Primitive Society.* London: Cohen & West, 1952.

135 Ibid. *Method in Social Anthropology.* Chicago, IL: University of Chicago Press, 1958.

Meyer Fortes: The Sociology of African Tribes

The English anthropologist Meyer Fortes (1906–1983), born in South Africa, was a consistent functionalist and continued the work of Bronisław Malinowski. He developed standard structural models of the classification of African societies, accepted in contemporary Ethnology, in a series of classical works devoted to the ethnosociology of Africa.[136] The most famous of these is *Oedipus and Job in West African Religion.*[137]

Fortes paid special attention to the problem of the sociology of time in archaic ethnoses. His reconstructions of the temporal patterns of archaic narods became classics in Ethnosociology. The studies devoted to this problem were published in the work *Time and Social Structure.*[138]

Like all other social anthropologists, Fortes was convinced that impersonal, super-individual paradigms dominate in the structure of society, predetermining the behavior of the separate members and constantly being reproduced — including through the model of "time closed in on itself."

Edward Evan Evans-Pritchard: The Translation of Cultures

Another well-known British social anthropologist, E. E. Evans Pritchard (1902–1973), collaborated closely with Fortes in his African studies. Together they released the classic work *African Political Systems.*[139] Evans-Pritchard devotes a whole series of works to African ethnoses, in which he demonstrated the effectiveness of a functionalist and structuralist

---

136 Fortes, M. & Evans-Pritchard E. E. (eds.) *African Political Systems.* London & New York: International African Institute, 1940.

137 Fortes, M. *Oedipus and Job in West African Religion.* New York, NY: Cambridge University Press, 1959.

138 Fortes, M. *Time and Social Structure and Other Essays.* London: Athlone, 1970.

139 Fortes, M. & Evans-Pritchard E. E. (eds.) *African Political Systems.* Oxford: Oxford University Press, 1950.

approach.[140] He also gave much attention to Ethno-ecology. Evans-Pritchard reconstructed the basic social and political forms of archaic societies, having built orderly and lucid conceptions and classifications of types using the comparative method from disparate data, seemingly exotic to Europeans.[141] He conducted similar work in explaining the archaic structure of African religions.[142]

Evans-Pritchard cast doubts on whether or not Social Anthropology belonged to the domain of the natural sciences, proposing instead, to refer it to the historical, humanitarian sciences or to that which the German philosopher Dilthey, following Schleiermacher, called the "spiritual sciences" (*Geisteswissenschaften*). Evans-Pritchard also pointed to the fact that the theory of the origin of religion and its interpretation among archaic societies depends to a significant extent on whether the researcher himself is a believer. If he is an atheist, he is inclined to interpret religion psychologically, pragmatically, or sociologically. If he is a believer, he will pay greater attention to the philosophical side and to the forms of comprehending the world and man in archaic religious traditions. Moreover, Evans-Pritchard emphasized (in the spirit of Boas), that the culture of the anthropologist himself can distort entirely the description of the culture he is studying, ascribing to people and groups motivations, impulses, and meanings that have nothing in common with reality.

In his last years, Evans-Pritchard retreated somewhat from the classical Functionalism of Malinowski and Radcliffe-Brown and focused his attention on the problem of the "translation of cultures," reconsidering the generally negative attitude of this school towards Diffusionism. The

---

140 Evans-Pritchard, E. E. *Witchcraft, Oracles and Magic among the Azande*. Oxford: Oxford University Press, 1937; Ibid. *The Nuer: A Description of the Modes of Livelihood and Political Institutions of a Nilotic People*. Oxford: Oxford University Press 1940; Ibid. *Kinship and Marriage among the Nuer*. Oxford: Clarendon Press, 1951; Ibid. *Man and Woman among the Azande*. London: Faber and Faber, 1974.

141 Evans-Pritchard, E. E. *The Comparative Method in Social Anthropology*. London: Athlone Press, 1963.

142 Evans-Pritchard, E. E. *Theories of Primitive Religion*. Oxford: Clarendon, 1965.

conception of the "translation of cultures" can be considered a softened and contemporary form of the "theory of cultural circles."

Max Gluckman: Social Dynamics

The famous British anthropologist Max Gluckman (1911–1975), born, like Fortes, in South Africa, labored in the same spirit as Fortes and Evans-Pritchard and was a key figure in the Manchester school of Social Anthropology. While Fortes laid the foundations of this school, Gluckman further developed his theories, giving them order and a sense of finality.

Gluckman specialized in the ethnoses of Africa, accenting in his studies their legal traditions, the connection of their customs and laws, and the legal significance of their rites and rituals. He studies these themes in his works *Custom and Conflict in Africa, Order and Rebellion in Tribal Africa, Politics, Law, and Ritual in Tribal Society,* and others.[143, 144, 145] Gluckman's main tendency in the theoretical domain was the improvement of Functionalism and Structuralism, which are characteristic of Social Anthropology on the whole, from the perspective of a more meticulous description of the dynamic component and the construction of models of social dynamics.

Edmund Leach: Gumsa/Gumlao

Edmund Leach (1910–1989) was an outstanding British anthropologist, who was formed under the influence of the ideas of Malinowski, but later decided to reconsider the basic points of Functionalism.

Leach predominantly studied the archaic ethnoses of Burma, Sri Lanka, and Ceylon, examining their legal and political systems, and also their social stratification.[146] Based on the example of the populations of two

---

143 Gluckman, M. *Custom and Conflict in Africa.* Oxford: Blackwell, 1966.

144 Ibid. *Order and Rebellion in Tribal Africa.* M. London: Cohen and. West, 1963.

145 Ibid. *Politics, Law and Ritual in Tribal Society.* New York, NY: Mentor, 1968.

146 Leach, Edmund R. *Pul Eliya Village in Ceylon: A Study of Land Tenure and Kinship.* New York, NY: Cambridge University Press, 1961.

villages he studied, Leach formulated a critique of the functionalist theory that all societies tend towards equality. Instead, Leach showed examples of social systems that are constantly found in "unstable equilibrium" with a continuous oscillation of social patterns. This theory received the name *"the model of gumsa/gumlao."*[147]

Two groups of the archaic Kachin ethnos, dwelling in the Burmese countryside, located not far from one another, had two social models of political organization with vividly expressed traits. The system of the *gumsa* was strictly hierarchical and patriarchal, with caste features and a specific language for the aristocracy. The system of the *gumlao*, on the other hand, was radically egalitarian, without any hint of social stratification. In studying their relations, Leach showed that these systems are found in a constant dynamic, provoked in both cases by different reasons: the "feudal" system of the *gumsa* was constantly subject to attacks by crushing elements, which tried to broaden their power and slacken the social harmony, while the egalitarian system of the *gumlao* suffered crisis after crisis owing to its chaotic and disordered organization. According to Leach's conclusion, neither system is immobile nor in equilibrium, but both are constantly modified, right up to the likely change of the social matrix into the directly opposite one, under the impact of inner and historical causes.

This conception proposes the "reversibility" of social phenomena and, in this sense, is fully included in an accurate ethnosociological approach.

On the other hand, in the course of his critical reconsideration of functionalism, Leach suggests transferring attention to the individual and his actions within the ethnos, which, according to Leach, are the reasons for the social dynamic.[148] This point radically contradicts Durkheimian Sociology, Cultural and Social Anthropology, and Ethnosociology and very likely represents the projection of Western individualism onto archaic societies. In this last and most contentious of Leach's

---

147 Leach, E. R. *Political Systems of Highland Burma: A Study of Kachin Social Structure.* Boston, MA: Beacon Press, 1965.

148 Ibid. *Rethinking Anthropology.* London: Athlone, 1961.

conclusions one can see a preparation for the instrumentalist approach in Ethnosociology — applied in an incorrect situation.

Leach's concepts anticipate postmodern theory; in particular, the "sociology of nets" and the "theory of the rational choice of the little actor" (the individual) in the analysis of the structure of social behavior.

Leach is also well known as a critic of the theory of Claude Lévi-Strauss and for his alternative theory of kinship.[149]

Ernst Gellner: From Agraria to Industria

The works of the philosopher Ernst Gellner (1925–1995), who, in the course of his studies, combined the methods of Anthropology, Sociology, and Philosophy, and came to conclusions that are exceedingly important for the entire structure of ethnosociological knowledge are especially worthy of attention.

Gellner engaged in field studies in North Africa and specialized in Islamic society.[150] At Cambridge he was the head of the department of Anthropology, and at the London School of Economics, the head of the Philosophy department.

Gellner was the author of the philosophical work *Words and Things*, in which he subjected to harsh criticism Ludwig Wittgenstein's idea that "meaning" arises from the "language games" of the society to which the discourse belongs.[151, 152] In his book *Plough, Sword, and Book: The Structure of Human History*, he describes his vision of the historical process, in which three social forms are isolated: societies of hunters and gatherers, agrarian societies (*Agraria*), and industrial societies (*Industria*).[153] To each type of society there corresponds its own sociological paradigm, its own type of culture, a collection of meanings and values, its own motivations

---

149 Ibid. *Lévi-Strauss*. London: Fontana/Collins, 1970.

150 Gellner, Ernest. *Saints of the Atlas*. London: Weidenfeld and Nicholson, 1969.

151 Ibid. *Words and Things*. London: Gollancz, 1959.

152 Wittgenstein, L. *Philosophische Untersuchungen*. Frankfurt am Main: Suhrkamp, 2001.

153 Gellner, E. *Plough, Sword and Book: The Structure of Human History*. London: Collins Harvill, 1988.

and anthropological attitudes, etc. Gellner isolates three basic criteria: cognition, coercion, and production. They are directly connected to one another by diverse relations and comprise a unified matrix, all the parameters of which change from society to society.

The specific character of Gellner's approach consists of the fact that he emphasizes the *discontinuity* between these societies, which allows him to consider them as strictly separate sociological concepts. Moreover, Gellner is especially interested in the phase transition from "Agraria" to "Industria," as he calls the ideal models of the societies distinguished by him.

Gellner's view of history is not evolutionary, but does not share the relativism of the functionalist approach of Social and Cultural Anthropology. He attributes to the era of the Enlightenment and its science the status of a "universal" methodology, capable of distinctly and objectively reflecting that which other types of society apprehend subjectively and hence with prejudice. The style of Gellner's books is ideological and aggressive, but extremely clear. Gellner was a firm opponent of the USSR and finished his days as a professor at the Central-European University, founded by the well-known American speculator George Soros.

Gellner is rightfully considered the founder of the *constructivist approach* in ethnosociology and an indisputable authority in the area of the study of nationalism. His major work devoted to the problem of nationalism, *Nations and Nationalism*, is a classic.[154]

Gellner's main idea is that the phenomenon of the "nation" is a by-product of industrial society and was artificially created by the bourgeois for the regulation of politico-social structures under a parliamentary democracy after the destruction of feudal and monarchic class-based regimes (with the peasantry dominant in the sphere of the economy). The concept of the "nation," Gellner shows, arose in the Modern Era under the circumstances of the rapid development of industrial production, the strengthening of the role of cities, the spread of modern scientific ideas, the secularization of the population, and the transition to rationality,

---

154 Gellner, E. *Nations and Nationalism*. Oxford: Blackwell Press, 1983.

characteristic of industrial society.[155] Under the conditions of industrial society, a new model of Social and Political Anthropology formed, based on individual (and not class) identity. This individual identity gradually enveloped more and more layers of society and became the political norm of democracy. At the same time, the mechanisms of class rule fell apart and society began to atomize.

In order to restrain the burgeoning chaos, preserve order, and mobilize the atomized population, the bourgeoisie invented a political instrument, the nation and nation-state, which restrained civil society from dispersion and acted as a surrogate of collective identity, this time artificial and politically imposed. Gellner considers "nationalism," which, in his opinion, is a neutral phenomenon, serving the bourgeoisie in historical conditions for the consolidation of a new form of political power and the execution of necessary reforms of the economy, social interaction, and mass consciousness to be the method of the nation's consolidation.

At the same time, Gellner demonstrates that at the basis of the "nation" and "nationalism" lies the knowingly-false idea of the establishment of a *fictive genealogy of contemporary European bourgeois nations and ancient ethnoses and narods*, belonging to other sociological models. Nations have no relation to ethnoses; they are created under different social and historical conditions and according to a different algorithm.

The difference between nations and rural communities, representing the majority of the population in the Middle Ages, i.e., between "Industria" and "Agraria," consists of the relationship to written culture and language. In "Agraria," book-literacy is the prerogative only of the higher strata, while the masses live in a condition of oral knowledge transmission. For this reason, in "Agraria" there exists a universal language of the nobility, a "koine" (for instance, Latin in the Western Europe of the Middle Ages) and a plurality of ethnic languages and dialects, intrinsic to village areas. In "Industria," on the other hand, education becomes all-national and an

155 Ibid. 'L'avvento del nazionalismo, e la sua interpretazione. I miti della nazione e della classe' / Anderson P. (ed.) *Storia d'Europa*. Turin: Einaudi, 1993.

artificial language is created, knowledge of which is indispensable for all members of society. Gellner calls this language an *"idiom."*[156]

Gellner's analysis of the formation of nations on the basis of poly-ethnic class governments is very important. In these governments, there existed two types of social barriers: inter-class (between the nobility and the commoners) and territorial (between settlements). At the same time the division of labor according to the economic factor was insignificant. In the transition to "Industria," society simultaneously becomes uniform while also dividing itself according to occupations, which, in their turn, are tied to the economic factor, giving rise to the beginning of class differentiation (i.e., social stratification, based on the economic principle). It is precisely at this point that the nation and the phenomenon of nationalism arise.[157] Moreover, Gellner reconstructs the process of the decay and reconfiguration of society in this phase transition as the discovery within the old limits of the government of two types of nationalism, which he calls "Megalomania" and "Ruritania."

Megalomania is the formation of a nation founded on the culture that dominated in the pre-industrial government. In it, the culture and language of the elite are taken as the foundation and reworked in the interests of the third estate. But the formalization of the nation and the nationalism that accompanies it strike a blow to the peripheral regions of the pre-industrial type, which often differ socially and ethnically from the core culture. Thus, the phenomenon of *Ruritania* emerges, i.e., of the "rural" periphery that actively forms national states, which can advance a *counter-project* and try to create a *counter-nation* (for instance, selected from the composition of the new national state). Thus emerges "small nationalism," Ruritania, opposing "big nationalism," Megalomania. This is evident in many examples — in particular, in the fate of the Austro-Hungarian Empire, which fell apart along precisely these lines: Austria became a nation of Megalomania, and Hungary, Yugoslavia, Czechoslovakia, and Romania were the reciprocal counter-projects of Ruritania. Both nationalisms,

---

156 Gellner, E. *Culture, Identity, and Politics.* Cambridge: Cambridge University Press, 1987.

157 Ibid. *Encounters with Nationalism.* Oxford (UK) and Cambridge, MA: Blackwell, 1994.

"big" and "small," have a place only in the transition to "Industria." That is, they are connected with bourgeois reforms, changes of the basic paradigm of society, and are artificial processes, directed by an intellectual and economic elite. In all cases, the "nation" is an artificial construct, created "conceptually" in an empty space.

In its basic features, this analysis is accepted by Ethnosociology and is the main conceptual instrument for the analysis of the nation and nationalism, and of phenomena corresponding to them.

Benedict Anderson: The Nation as an Imagined Community

The ethnosociologist Benedict Anderson continued the use of the constructivist method in the interpretation of the phenomenon of the nation. His book Imagined *Communities: Reflections on the Origin and Spread of Nationalism* became an authoritative work, summarizing (even in its title) the basic provisions of the constructivist approach.[158]

As an ethnographic example, Anderson relies on the ethnoses of Indonesia, which he studied thoroughly from an ethnosociological point of view.[159]

Like Gellner and all other constructivists ("modernists"), Anderson looks at the phenomenon of nations and nationalism as a bourgeois invention and connects this directly with book printing, which created the technological prerequisites for the inculcation of an "idiom" (a national language) on the scale of the whole society. Anderson introduces the term "*print capitalism*," which emphasizes the central significance of book printing for the execution of the phase transition from an agrarian and class-based way of life to a national one.

---

158 Anderson, B. *Imagined Communities: Reflections on the Origin and Spread of Nationalism.* London and New York: Verso, 1991.

159 Ibid. *Language and Power: Exploring Political Cultures in Indonesia.* Ithaca, NY: Cornell University Press, 1990; Ibid. *Language and Power: Exploring Political Cultures in Indonesia.* Ithaca, NY: Cornell University Press, 1990.

Anderson calls nations "imagined communities" and sets himself the question: "What first imagined them?" He gives a historical answer. From his point of view, nations first arise not in Europe itself, but in European colonies, in the US and a few governments of South America. And only then does the type of organization of society along the model of the nation occur in the Old World, which imitates the social-political processes of its trans-Atlantic colonies.[160]

John Breuilly: The Autonomy of the Nation

A follower of Gellner, the historian and ethnosociologist John Breuilly of the London School of Economics also adheres to the constructivist approach. Breuilly thinks that nationalism started to develop in the first phase of the Modern Era and was called upon from the beginning to compensate for the growing alienation between the absolute monarchy (who increasingly began to rely on the third estate) and the peripheral masses, brought out of their customary agrarian life cycle by economic and technological modernization.[161]

Alienation arose as a result of a change of the traditional way of life, and the collapse of Christian values and the class-based order. Absolutism lost its sacred significance and ceased to be seen as legitimate in the eyes of the agrarian masses. At the time of the French Revolution, this circumstance received extreme forms, since social innovations demanded compensating, mobilizing strategies, due to which arose the extreme nationalism of the Jacobins.

Breuilly rejects any connection of nationalism and the nation with the ethno-cultural type and thinks that these phenomena are entirely constructed for the political demands of the government and the intellectuals that serve it.[162]

---

160 Ibid. Imagined Communities: Reflections on the Origin and Spread of Nationalism. Op. cit.

161 Breuilly, J. *Nationalism and the State.* Manchester: Manchester University Press, 1993.

162 Breuilly, J. *Nationalism, Power and Modernity in Nineteenth-Century Germany.* London: German Historical Institute, 2007.

Elie Kedourie: The Eradication of Nationalism

Among contemporary constructivists, it is worth singling out Elie Kedourie (1926–1992). Born in Iraq to a family of Indian traditionalists, he differed radically by his critical views concerning nationalism. He thought that nationalism was the product of disappointed marginals, who elaborated utopian projects on the basis of philosophical research and the study of folklore, recreating an ideal picture of "narodni life," which should have been taken as a model for the construction of a better (more "enlightened") society.

Kedourie thought that Great Britain, which had, in its time, placed its bets on Arab nationalism, had in fact lain a slow-acting landmine in the region, and that rather than controlling the area on the basis of Enlightened and humanistic values, under the aegis of imperial control, it had instead given way for dark fundamentalist passions to devour.

Considering nationalism an artificial phenomenon, Kedourie called for its complete eradication.

Anthony D. Smith: Ethnosymbolism

Among contemporary ethnosociologists, we should highlight especially Anthony D. Smith, professor at the London School of Economics. Smith was Gellner's student, but he somewhat reconsidered Gellner's explanatory model of the phenomenon of the nation. Agreeing with the constructivists that the nation is a contemporary phenomenon of the industrial society of the Modern era, Smith emphasized that at the basis of the nation lies both the technology of the bourgeoisie which has come to power, *and* an appeal to the "ethnos," on the basis of which the nation is created.[163] If Gellner, Anderson, Breuilly or Kedourie assert that the nation is created in an empty space, Smith retorts that it is not entirely empty: the ethnos participates in this process, even if only partially. The nation has a preceding form, the "pre-nation," which has ethnic features.[164]

---

163 Smith, A.D. *Nations and Nationalism in a Global Era.* Cambridge: Polity, 1995.

164 Ibid. *The Ethnic Origins of Nations.* Oxford: Basil Blackwell, 1987.

This is the foundation of Smith's "Ethnosymbolism," which he shared by such contemporary ethnosociologists as Montserrat Guibernau, John Armstrong, John Hutchinson, etc.[165, 166, 167]

Smith defines the ethnosymbolic approach as follows: "For Ethnosymbolism, nationalism draws its force from the myths, memories, traditions, and symbols of an ethnic legacy and ethnic heritage; and this popular "living past" (Smith's emphasis) becomes and can become in the future a basis for its invention and reinterpretation by the modern intelligentsia."

Anthony Giddens: Ethnosociology is a Double Hermeneutic

The well-known English sociologist Anthony Giddens is sometimes mentioned as a representative of Ethnosociology. Giddens' works are mainly devoted to theoretical problems of contemporary Sociology, and in this sphere he is an acknowledged authority. But they have an indirect relationship to the problem of the ethnos or to Social Anthropology, since Giddens was not engaged with this set of problems as a first priority and has no works devoted to archaic societies, ethnoses, or the genesis of the modern nation. Where these themes are considered, they are part of his general sociological approach.[168]

Giddens' acceptance into "Ethnosociology" is based on a paper by the Spanish sociologist Pablo Santoro.[169] Giddens refers only to the Ethnomethodology of Garfinkel, which proposes to combine the

165 Guibernau, M., Hutchinson J. (eds.) *Understanding Nationalism*. London: Polity Press, 2001.

166 Armstrong, J.A. *Nations before Nationalism*. Chapel Hill, NC: University of North Carolina Press, 1982.

167 Hutchinson, J. *Ethnicity*. New York, NY: Oxford University Press, 1996.

168 Giddens, A. *The Constitution of Society: Outline of the Theory of Structuration*. Cambridge: Polity, 1986.

169 Santoro, P. *El momento etnográfico: Giddens, Garfinkel y los problemas de la etnosociología* / Revista española de investigaciones sociológicas. 2003. No. 103, pp. 239–255.

sociological interpretation of society from below, from simple individual units (like Garfinkel and phenomenology), and from above, from the position of the general research structures of classical sociology. He calls this a "*double hermeneutic*." He uses this approach for the study of the problem of self-identity in the societies of Modernity.[170]

Since, as we showed, Ethnomethodology, in itself a productive and important sociological method, has no relation at all to the problem of ethnicity or to the ethnos and its derivatives, the double hermeneutic, in Giddens' understanding, can in no way act as a synonym of Ethnosociology.

Summary of English Social Anthropology, Nation Studies, and Ethnosociology

The anthropological research of the English school, especially beginning with Malinowski and Radcliffe-Browne, when they linked up closely with the functionalist tradition of Durkheim with an attentiveness towards social structures, represents a broad conceptual and domain-specific field, and also a developed scientific program of ethnosociological studies, the fundamental style of which, despite the variety of positions, schools, and authors, corresponds on the whole to the general line of American Cultural Anthropology and German Ethnosociology.

Of special significance is the constructivist approach, started by Ernst Gellner, which introduces into the study of societies a substantial correction, connected with the artificial and pragmatic function of the phenomena of the nation and nationalism as political instruments of class, state, elites, and society.

Smith's Ethnosymbolism extends the zone of the study of the nation with reference to those ethnic elements on which historical nations were artificially constructed.

Thanks to the English school of social anthropologists and ethnosociologists, Ethnosociology as a whole has access to a broad set of methods, approaches, instruments, conceptions, terms, and theories, as well as a

---

170 Giddens, A. *Modernity and Self-Identity: Self and Society in the Late Modern Age*. Stanford, CA: Stanford University Press, 1991.

wealth of material in the form of field research into the most diverse ethnic societies and nations, both in Europe and in other parts of the world.

SECTION FOUR

The French School of Ethnosociology, Classical Sociology, Structural Anthropology

Emile Durkheim: Social Facts and the Dichotomy of the Sacred & the Profane

We should count among the direct predecessors of Ethnosociology in France first and foremost that classic of sociology, Emile Durkheim (1858–1917), who transformed sociology into a strict academic science and won recognition for it in France and the rest of continental Europe. Durkheim founded the regularly published journal *L'Année Sociologique*, in which all of France's prominent sociologists, ethnologists, and anthropologists published their works.

Durkheim first expounded on some fundamental theories of sociology: the "*social fact*," interpreted by him in sociological concepts, rejects the explanation of society and its phenomena through other (physical, biological, etc.) layers of reality. Society is a total phenomenon and bears in itself to the keys to the knowledge both of itself and of everything having a direct and immediate relation to it. Just in the natural sciences there are strict criteria based on the laws of the physical world, so too in the social domain do there exist strict criteria and laws, which Durkheim called upon to discover and study.[171]

---

171 Durkheim, E. *Sotsiologiya. Yeye predmet, metod, prednaznacheniye.* Moscow: Kanon, 1995.

Thus, Durkheim advanced the basic sociological idea of the presence of a "collective consciousness," which influences the individual consciousness of a member of society and is prior in relation to him. The concept of "collective representations," introduced by Durkheim, became another very important term in Sociology.

Examining different types of society, Durkheim proposed to classify them according to their form of *solidarity*: in simple ethnoses this solidarity is *"mechanical"* (i.e., complete and automatic), while in complex ones it is *"organic"* (i.e., it requires the conscious, voluntary act of integration and socialization).

Durkheim's ideas exerted a colossal influence on European science in the 20th century, influencing the establishment of Anthropology (especially English Anthropology), and becoming an integral part of Ethnosociology.

It is significant that in the last few years of his life, Durkheim focused his attention on the problem of "primitive" ethnoses, and although he himself did not participate in field research , his theoretical generalizations possess tremendous worth for Ethnology. Durkheim's last work *Elementary Forms of Religious Life* can well be called a model of ethnosociological research.[172] In this book, Durkheim bases his work on ethnographic studies of the societies of Australian aborigines.

Durkheim's introduction of the dichotomy of the "sacred" and "profane" into models of the study of societies (especially archaic ones) has great significance.[173] With the help of this pair of concepts, where *"sacred"* characterizes separate practices, rituals, institutions, and processes connected with the spiritual, mystical, irrational sides of life, and *"profane"* with the everyday, routine, practical, commonplace sides, it is possible to describe the structure of any society reliably.

---

172 Durkheim, E. *Les formes élémentaires de la vie religieuse.* Paris: Libraire générale française, 1991.

173 Durkheim developed this pair of concepts, which he made sociological concepts, on the basis of the ideas of the Scottish historian of religion, William Roberson Smith. Smith W.R. *Lectures on the Religion of the Semites.* Edinburgh: Douglas, 1880.

It is important to note that within the sacred itself, Durkheim distinguishes two poles: the pure and impure or *"right-hand sacred"* and *"left-hand sacred,"* respectively. The right-hand pole of the sacred characterizes all that is good, light, beneficial, and filled with the highest positive connotations. This recalls the notion of "holiness." However, there exists within the sacred the opposite dimension as well, that which embodies impurity, aggression, horror, and death. This dimension is also seen as something supernatural (in contrast with the profane), filled with higher powers and capabilities, only with a negative connotation. In archaic cultures, "good" and "evil" spirits are held as sacred in equal measure, although one group brings good and the other evil. Remnants of such ancient notions can be met with in the Christian religion, where the existence of both angels and demons is asserted, and where it is also explained that Satan and the demons were originally created by God as angels (belonging to the sacred as a whole), but later by their own will chose evil and became what they are since then (the left-hand pole of the sacred).

If we apply the dualism of the sacred and profane to the chain of societies with which Ethnosociology operates, then we can notice the following:

- In the ethnos, the sacred dominates;

- In the narod, there is a balance between the sacred and profane;

- In the nation, the profane dominates over the sacred;

- In civil society and global society, the sacred is entirely driven out and only the profane remains;

- It is not possible to say anything precise about post-society, but we can suggest hypothetically that in it we will be dealing with the "pseudo-sacred," a simulacrum of the sacred.

Marcel Mauss: Sociology of the Gift

Durkheim's nephew Marcel Mauss (1872–1950) was a student and follower of Durkheim, developing his ideas, but on the whole continuing the orientation on which Durkheim himself focused during the last years of his life. Mauss devoted his research to primitive narods and ethnoses and specialized in the study of their rites, magical practices, social institutions, and economic practice. His works in the domain of **Economic Anthropology**, i.e., in the area of economics, exchange, production, and demand among archaic tribes, became classics of ethnology and laid the foundation for an entire school of economic thought.

His most famous works are *The Gift* and his study on the role of the procedures of gift-giving and return gift-giving in the social structure of primitive societies.[174]

Mauss continued and developed Durkheim's sociological line especially in what concerns the understanding of social phenomena and facts as total. For Mauss, society and the "collective representations" present in it precede both the isolation of separate individuals and the relations between people and nature. Different societies understand status, nature, structure, functions, and even the attributes of a separate personality differently. This means that "personality" is not an empirical fact but a social construct. In the same way, it is inaccurate to consider the surrounding natural world an objective datum, independent of society. Each society understands nature in its own way, in relation to unique "collective representations." Consequently, even the external world is a socially constructed object.

Henri Hubert: The Sociology of Religious Time

Mauss' colleague and coauthor, the French sociologist and anthropologist Henri Hubert (1872–1927) was a specialist of the ethnic culture of Byzantine and the ancient Celts.[175] He was one of the founders of the French sociology of religion.

---

174 Mauss M. *Obshchestva. Obmen. Lichnost.* Moscow: Vostochnaya literature, 1996.

175 Hubert, H. & Mauss M. *Mélanges d'histoire des religions.* Paris: Librairie Félix, 1929; Ibid. *Sacrifice: Its Nature and Functions.* Chicago, IL: University of Chicago Press, 1981; Ibid. *A General Theory of Magic.* London & New York: Routledge, 2001.

Among celtologists, Hubert's works are recognized as classics.[176] They are built on a combination of ethnological and sociological methods, which allow us to look at Hubert as the first French ethnosociologist.

Hubert also systematically occupied himself with the theme of the sociology of time and forms of understanding of time in different religious traditions and archaic societies. He devoted a special essay to this topic, *Essay on Time: A Brief Study of the Representation of Time in Religion and Magic.*[177]

Lucien Lévy-Bruhl: Mystical Participation

If Durkheim and Mauss did not pass any final judgments on progress and evolution in society, emphasizing the functionalist approach and the constancy of social structures, then another French anthropologist and sociologist, Lucien Lévy-Bruhl (1857–1939), familiar to Mauss, set out to describe the social progress and evolution of societies and show people what the main difference between primitive societies ("savages") and contemporary civilization consisted of.

He advanced the general hypothesis that there are two types of thought: "primitive," which is based on the "mystical participation" of the savage with the surrounding world, and "contemporary," based on observance of the laws of logic and the strict differentiation of subject and object (with a transparent and rational procedure for the verification of judgements). Lévy-Bruhl called "primitive" thought "pre-logical" and contemporary thought "logical."[178] If in this case we drop the supposed unconditional superiority of "logic" over "pre-logic," something which seemed self-evident for the evolutionist Lévy-Bruhl, with whom the anthropologists Lévi-Strauss and Evans-Pritchard argued in detail, then we can agree with Lévy-Bruhl's description of the fundamental features of "simple" society,

---

176 Hubert, H. *The History of the Celtic People.* London: K. Paul, Trench, Trubner, 1934.

177 Ibid. 'Étude sommaire de la représentation du temps dans la religion et la magie' / Mauss, M. (ed.). *Mélanges d'histoire des religions.* Paris: Librairie Félix, 1929, pp. 189–229.

178 Lévy-Bruhl, L. Primitive Mentality. London: Allen & Unwin, 1923.

which Ethnosociology equates with the ethnos. "Mystical participation," the absence of a dual "subject-object" topography, the non-observance of Aristotelian laws of logic — all this, indeed, characterizes typically ethnic thought.

Marcel Griaule: Mythology of the Dogon

Marcel Griaule (1898–1956), a specialist of Africa and its ethnic societies, was a key ethnologist and anthropologist of the French school, who carefully studied the mythology and social attitudes of the Dogon tribe of Mali as well as their masks, ritual dances, hunting methods, and art.[179]

Among the Dogon, Griaule discovered extremely original forms in the manufacture of sacred wood statues, replete with incredible refinement. It became clear that this tribe had a developed and complex religious mythology, including various types and series of gods, spirits, and other persons, united by a masterfully elaborated theology.

Griaule set out his theoretical methods for the study of ethnoses in his book *Methods of Ethnography*.[180]

Maurice Leenhardt: Personality and Myth in Archaic Societies

The French missionary and ethnologist Maurice Leenhardt (1878–1954) was engaged in anthropological and sociological field studies in New Caledonia for more than twenty years. Upon returning to Paris, he chaired the department of *Primitive Religions*, which Mauss had chaired before him.

At the center of Leenhardt's attention stood the problem of the relation between myth, personality, and social identity in archaic societies. His main work is devoted to the ethnoses and cultures of Melanesia and to the generalizing figure of *"Do Kamo,"* in which the Melanesians' ideas about "man," "spirit," "god," "life," and "personality" are concentrated and

179 Griaule, M. *Arts de l'Afrique noire*. Paris: Editions du Chêne, 1947.

180 Ibid. Methode de l'Etnographie. Paris: Presses Universitaires de France, 1957.

which Leenhardt interpreted as the totality of super-individual social relations and ties.[181]

Leenhardt's *Do Kamo* corresponds in its general features to that which
Sociology and Anthropology call "personality" and represents a unique
social view associated with values, attitudes, and norms.

Marcel Granet: Chinese Society

Marcel Granet (1884–1940), an outstanding specialist of Chinese culture,
a student of Durkheim, and a colleague of Marcel Mauss, was another
well-known French sociologist and ethnologist. He devoted the majority of his works to the study of Chinese society, its ethnic, cultural, and
political structure. Granet's works on Chinese civilization are to this day
fundamental for the study of China.[182]

Granet combined a linguistic, sociological, and historical approach
of the study of society, proposing to separate the process of sociological
cognition into two main spheres:

1.   The study of religious and mythological ideas;

2.   The thorough analysis of the general legal system, including
systems of kinship, the mode of family life, customs, and government laws.

Granet's essay *Matrimonial Categories and Proximate Relationships in
Ancient China* became the starting point for the eminent anthropologist
and ethnologist Levi Strauss' elaboration of the famous "theory of kinship."

Granet and his studies of Chinese society, for which he tried to cast
aside the entire arsenal of ideas, methods, categories, and axioms customary for the European scholar, greatly influenced the work of another

181 Leenhardt, M. *Do Kamo, la personne et le mythe dans le monde melanesien.* Paris:
Gallimard, 1947.

182 Granet, M. *La pensee chinoise.* Paris, Albin Michel, 1999; Ibid. La Religion des
Chinois. Paris: Gauthier-Villars, 1922; Ibid. *La Civilization Chinoise.* Paris: La
Renaissance du Livre, 1929.

first-rate French sociologist, Louis Dumont, who studied Indian society using the same methods.

Claude Lévi-Strauss: A Key Figure of Ethnosociology

Claude Lévi-Strauss (1908–2009) is a key figure for all of contemporary Anthropology and Ethnosociology. His works have tremendous philosophical significance, and he is rightfully considered the most important figure in structuralism as a philosophical and methodological phenomenon.

Lévi-Strauss' work is multidimensional and multifaceted so we will isolate only those aspects of it that are fundamental for Ethnosociology as a discipline and comprise its theoretical and methodological basis.

Lévi-Strauss applied the method of structural linguistics to primitive, archaic societies. He primarily engaged with the native peoples of North and South America. The Russian linguists, founders of phonology, and outstanding representatives of Structuralism, Roman Jakobson (1896–1982) and Nikolai Trubetzkoy (1890–1938) exerted a big influence on Lévi-Strauss. During the Second World War, Lévi-Strauss emigrated to the US, where he met Jakobson and Boas. It is symbolic that Boas died of a heart attack literally in the arms of Lévi-Strauss. The founder of Structural Anthropology received the baton from the founder of Cultural Anthropology.

In 1973 Lévi-Strauss was made a member of the French Academy.

The Equality of Cultures: Structural Anthropology

At all stages of his work, Lévi-Strauss advanced the idea of the fundamental equality of cultures and insisted on the impossibility and inadequacy of projecting the criteria of one culture onto another.[183] In this matter, he concurred entirely with the starting point of Franz Boas and American Cultural Anthropology. But Lévi-Strauss was the one to grant this

---

183 Lévi-Strauss, C. *Race et histoire: La Question raciale devant la science moderne.* Paris: UNESCO, 1952.

approach the status of a fundamental scientific methodological principle as well as a philosophical and humanistic truth.

A society can be understood only in terms of its own cultural and civilizational context, but immersion into the context of the researched society demands the renunciation of commitment to the context of the society to which the researcher himself belongs. Consequently, we cannot at all *evaluate* societies different from our own. We can only *describe* and *classify* them.

Lévi-Strauss brought to light and harshly rejected all forms of ethno-centrism and racism, involved both in the biological hierarchization of ethnoses and in the forms of Eurocentrism, evolutionism, progressivism, universalism, and the assessment of a civilization in accordance with its technical, economic, or social indicators.

Any assertion containing a direct or indirect indication that one type of society, culture, or social way is better than another is unscientific, ideological, and racist. Lévi-Strauss admitted that infrequently in common speech, journalism, and politics, this principle is not observed, and because of this such discussions lose their objective sense and act as forms of "false consciousness." Lévi-Strauss was convinced that such an approach should be eliminated, since it is incommensurable with the humanistic view of the equality of different cultures, whose differences cannot be hierarchized without bumping up against the ideas of racism, oppression, violence, and the debasement of social, ethnic, and cultural worth. It is not even correct to say that one society is more or less developed than another, since the term "development" is a *value concept* of Western European civilization. Society does not develop — it *lives*. It lives as it thinks it must.

Lévi-Strauss formulated the principles of such an approach in his work "Structural Anthropology." It is Structural Anthropology, which, as a scientific and philosophical orientation, corresponds most precisely to Ethnosociology and overlaps with it in practically in all fundamental parameters.[184]

---

184 Lévi-Strauss, C, Jacobson, C. & Schoepf, B.G. *Structural Anthropology*. New York: Basic Books, 1963.

Binary Code

Methodologically, *"Structural Anthropology"* comes down to the study of the structure of society, which can be thought of in the form of binary opposites.[185] These oppositions do not at all have to be as radical as *is/is not, one/nothing, light/dark*, with which European culture predominantly deals. Archaic societies have more nuanced pairs: *raw/prepared, tillage/ hunting for game*, etc.[186] At the same time, however, one of the classic aspects of archaic culture consists of the *withdrawal* of strict binary opposites and the introduction of new reconciling, mediating term. Lévi-Strauss thought of the figure of the trickster (a coyote or crow) in many Indian myths, studied by Radin, as one such mediating principle.

According to Lévi-Strauss, the detection of binary opposites allows one to interpret myth correctly, distinguishing in it the smallest structural semantic element, the *mytheme.*

Lévi-Strauss' main idea consists of the following: a myth is a completed intellectual matrix, which must be learned through special operations on the basis of mythology (the special logic of myth).

From his point of view, a myth should be studied as a paradigm; the reading of a myth is carried out through periods, like a written score of notes, not like a written text. Only thus can we see and correctly discern the harmony in it. In reading notes we can pay attention first and foremost to the melody unfolding in sequence on the musical line, or else to the harmony, which is considered vertically. At the same time, in the analysis of myth the most important thing is to accurately single out the periods, i.e., those places where a carrying over of the musical sentences notes occurs and a new block of myth begins. This minimal atomic fragment of myth, which is no longer subject to further subdivision and represents a completed element, from which mythological narration is formed, is what Lévi-Strauss calls a *"mytheme."*

---

185 Lévi-Strauss, C. Le *Totémisme aujourd'hui* (1958); english trans. as *Totemism*, by Rodney Needham. Boston: Beacon Press, 1963.

186 Lévi-Strauss, C. *Mythologiques*. Paris: Plons, 1964.

The Elementary Structures of Kinship

In his monumental work *The Elementary Structures of Kinship*, Lévi-Strauss demonstrated that for primordial social systems the exchange of women between clans, phratries, and other groups served as the basis of social structuring and was the main communicational matrix, like the exchange of words in language.[187]

In contrast to the "kinship theories" of other authors, Lévi-Strauss considered neither the family nor the lineage as the basis of the building of the social structure of society, but the *relations between* families and lineages. According to his ideas, at the basis of society lies an operation of *exchange*, which is directed towards the establishment of equilibrium: the giver must receive the equivalent of his gift. The operation of exchange can be likened to *borrowing*: one gives another something on credit, which the other must return.

Words and women act as the top-priority objects of exchange in simple societies. Speech is the exchange of words between people. It is significant that in ordinary forms of communication, intrinsic to all human cultures, the mutual exchange of speech formulas (dialogue) is a law. For instance, in common greetings, the people meeting one another say "Hello!" which must be followed a reciprocal "Hello!" required not by the concrete situation, but by the very nature of speech as exchange. Let us recall that the French ethnologist and anthropologist Marcel Griaule engaged in the meticulous study of the ritual practices of speech among the archaic Dogon.

At the basis of speech lies language, its logic, its structures, and its paradigms, which predetermine by what model and in correlation with what regularities the exchange of speech will occur. They are potential, not visible, and always appear not of themselves, but through the constructing of speech as an actual verbal sequence. Speech is that which is found on the surface; language is that which is concealed within.

---

187 Lévi-Strauss, C. *Les Structures elementaires de la parente*. Paris: PUF, 1949.

The same logic underlies the exchange of women in the structure of matrimonial relations and in the general fabric of kinship and affinity. It is based on the principle of equivalence and follows regulations as unambiguous as speech does. But just the bearer of the language, especially in illiterate societies, very often does not have a notion of the stable and logical grammar that he uses unconsciously, according to linguistics, so too do the structures of matrimonial relations not lie on the surface, but remain potential and concealed, and the clarification of their regularities demands certain efforts.

Lévi-Strauss undertook these efforts, developing, following Mauss, the idea of the "gift," and also the mechanism of exchange of gifts (gift/return gift) as the social basis of society, only applied to the exchange of women, who are the generalization of the "gift" as such, since they concentrate in themselves other forms of exchange, including the exchange of objects and words. The structure of kinship, based on gender exchange, can thus be considered as the "universal grammar of society."

Restricted Exchange

Lévi-Strauss distinguishes two types of exchange of women in primitive societies, i.e., two types of social language of marriage: *"restricted exchange"* and *"generalized exchange."*[188] *Restricted exchange* represents the classic case of the segmentation of a society into two or a multiple of two exogamous phratries. The simplest case: a tribe separated into two halves, which live either on a common territory (for instance, at different ends of a village), or at some distance apart. Between the two phratries, A and B, there occurs an exchange of women. The men (fathers and brothers) give their women (daughters and sisters) to the men of the other tribe to wed, who act in exactly the same way with *their* daughters and sisters. The quantity of exogamous groups can be four, six, and theoretically more, but we nowhere meet with more than eight. Schematically, this can be shown as follows:

---

188 Lévi-Strauss, C. *Les Structures elementaires de la parente.*

A↔B	A↔B	A↔B
	C↔D	C↔D
		E↔F

Figure 8. Type of restricted exchange of women among lineages.

A principle of equivalence is observed in such a model of the organization of marriage. Phratry A gives Phratry B as many women as it receives in exchange. For this reason, Lévi-Strauss says that under conditions of the deindividualization of archaic societies, this can be thought of as a cycle of loans and returns. In the qualitative index of a woman of the tribe, the most important thing is the fact of her belonging to phratry A, B, C, D, etc. Depending on that, and only on that, she is or is not an object of legitimate erotic and social attention, i.e., possessing the social status of wife. In the case of a mismatch she becomes a taboo; she ceases to be an object of exchange. The cruel cults of murdering girls in some primitive tribes, which we recalled earlier, are connected with this, which can often be seen as analogous to the destruction of excessively produced goods, which in certain cases have no chance of finding a consumer. Not every young woman of a child-bearing age is a woman who can marry; she must be a woman — "*nao*" (the opposite of taboo); that is, she must belong to a certain phratry, permitted for the marital union. This is as unchangeable as the construction of speech according to entirely predetermined rules, which no one can change arbitrarily and which change only together with language (i.e., with society as a whole).

In societies of limited exchange, a dual code, which lies at the basis of mythological and religious systems, as well as of social institutions met with in complex and multi-layered societies and cultures, is strictly observed. But it is precisely this type of society that forms the structure of the ethnos, the basic foundation of the model of "kinship-affinity." It most clearly exhibits the line that separates and unites people according to a dual model of one's kin and one's own [TN: affines]. *Kin* relates to Phratry A. *One's own* (or "one's others") relates to Phratry B.

The law of such separation, embodied in the prohibition against incest (by which is most often understood the prohibition of incest between brother and sister, i.e., the prohibition of marital relations in the limits of the same generation), configures the fundamental model of eros, applied to the socium. Affectivity (the feeling of love, affection, tenderness, confidentiality) is divided into two parts: *generic* (nearness to parents, brothers, sisters, and children) and *marital* (realized in erotic relations only with member of the opposite sex and phratry). In both cases, spontaneous affectivity, nearness, and tenderness is limited by structural prohibitions, i.e., by the introduction of distance. Love for one's kinsmen is censored by the taboo of incest; love for a member of the opposite phratry, the fundamental otherness of this phratry, is secured in the very social system of the exogamous groups. This paradigm of the division of affectivity gives rise to the basis of social gender, which is preserved inviolably in the most complex societies. But in a society of direct exchange the socialization of the sexes acts as the most vivid and complete form.

Generalized Exchange

Lévi-Strauss calls the second form of the exchange of women "generalized." Here the equivalence between the gift given and the gift returned is reached not directly, but in a roundabout manner. If, in the first model, there can only be an even number of exogamous phratries, exchanging women strictly "one to one," then in generalized systems, theoretically any number of phratries, unlimited, can participate. Here the exchange is executed in accordance with the following figure:

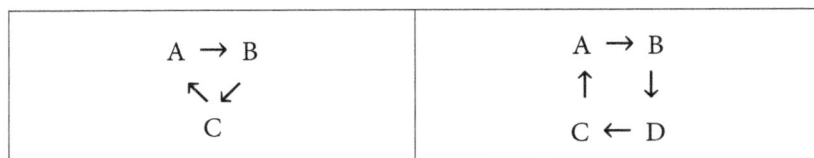

A → B ↖ ↙ C	A → B ↑ ↓ C ← D

Figure 9. Type of generalized exchange of women among lineages.

In this model, women from the exogenous Phratry A are given to Phratry B, from Phratry B to Phratry C, and from Phratry C to Phratry A. The number of elements can theoretically be increased, but has, in practice, an upper limit. In this situation, the spectrum of the relations of affinity, which doubles, is substantially broadened. Now the members of two phratries at once become one's own ("one's others"): the one, to which the women are given, and the one from which they are taken.

The general balance remains the same; the circulation of women aims at full equilibrium: a lineage gives away as many women as it receives. But this time, it does not receive them immediately from the place to which it gave its own away, but through an intermediary. In the case of the number of dimensions exceeding three phratries, groups arise, which, while participating in the exchange, no longer enter into the system of direct affinity. They are "others," but no longer "one's others."

At the same time, generalized systems do not differ principally from direct systems, since a strict ordering of women — "nao" and basic social taboos are preserved.

The Atomic Structure of Gender Relations and their Scale

Lévi-Strauss singles out the minimal structure that is constantly preserved in all social models of gender exchange.[189] He describes it through a group of four members: husband (father) — wife (mother) — son — brother of the wife (uncle). Six axes of relation are theoretically possible between them:

— husband — wife
— mother — son
— father — son
— sister — brother
— uncle — cousin
— husband — brother-in-law

189 Lévi-Strauss, C. Les Structures élémentaires de la parenté.

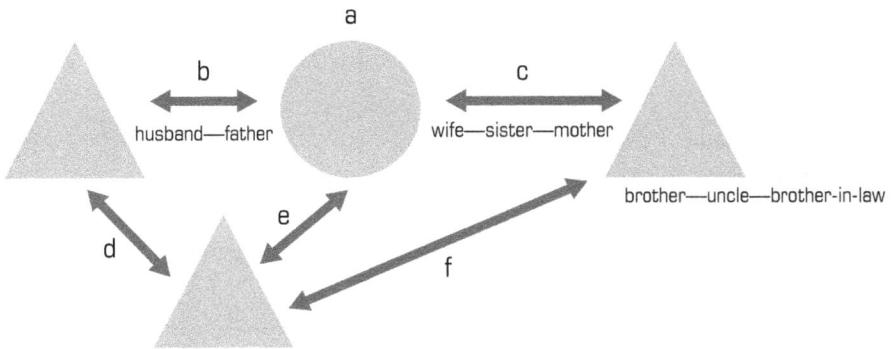

Figure 10. "Atomic structure" of kinship according to Lévi-Strauss.

Relations along the *a* axis are based on *distance* in every society (difference of phratries, "others," affinity in its pure form); relations along the *e* axis are based on *intimacy* in every society (kinship in its pure form); relations along the *b, c, d,* and, *f* axes vary depending on the specific arrangement of each concrete society.

For the study and systematization of these connections, Lévi-Strauss proposes to separate them into two categories: *intimacy/distance. Intimacy* includes tenderness, spontaneity, and nearness. *Distance,* authority, respect, restraint, circumspection, and sometimes hostility. There are no societies in which only one type dominates. If everything were based on distance, it would not possible to continue to a lineage and to start a family; if on intimacy, there would be no order, hierarchy, or observance of taboos (in particular, those concerning incest). Hence, each relation in the atomic structure can be different in different societies; i.e., either intimacy or distance can prevail.

Lévi-Strauss singles out two constants, the relations of mother and son, which are always intimate, and the relations of husband and brother-in-law, which are always based on distance. Thus, only four axes of relation are strictly variable. This variability depends not on how relations in the family take shape, but on the type of society in which the given family finds itself. The structure of ties between husband and wife, father and

son, sister and brother, and uncle and cousin are strictly socially predetermined, and this predetermination serves as the concrete dialect that a
given society speaks. This is reflected on a different level in myths, social
institutions, cultural and stylistic constructs, etc.

Lévi-Strauss isolated a mathematical regularity in the character of
these relations, in the form of reverse similarity:

uncle—nephew	·	father—son
brother—sister	·	husband—wife

Figure 11. Formula of exchange-axes of kinship.

If we know, for example, that among the Circassians, relations between
father and son, and husband and wife, are notable for a certain distance,
then from this it is easy to conclude that the relations between uncle and
cousin, and brother and sister, will be near and intimate. This provides
evidence of a shift of attention to those close by flesh (kin) in the matrilineal kin-group (hence the relations with the uncle), to the detriment of the
erotic impulse, directed outside the lineage.

Another example, from the tribes of the Polynesian Tonga. Ethnologists
relate that in this tribe relations along the lines of father-son and brother-
sister are strictly regulated and made taboo (up to the point that the father
and son cannot stay overnight together in one and the same quarters or
cabin). In this case, the relations between husband and wife and uncle and
cousin will be, on the contrary, much more intimate, since the accent falls
on the socialization of the maternal uncle (not the paternal, since, again,
it is a matrilineal society) and the structure of the marital union along
the line of the spouse (the external impulse in relation to the lineage) is
positively evaluated.

The Maternal and the Paternal in the Socium

Before Lévi-Strauss, the evolutionary perspective on the phases of the sexual development of society were predominant (Morgan, Tylor, Bachofen).

It went as follows: the earliest horde dwelt in a condition of sexual promiscuity, in which there were no regulations on sexual behavior: all members of the horde engaged in sexual relations with each other in a disorderly and chaotic manner. In the next stage, the belongingness of babies to the mother was raised to the status of a social law, since it is obvious that the begotten belongs to the begetter. The existence of matriarchy was assumed on this basis. And, finally, in the last stage the more "attentive" savages learned to trace the fact of paternity, which led to patriarchy.

In the 20th century anthropologists and ethnologists, following Lévi-Strauss, refuted this idea, showing convincingly that a society based on promiscuity never existed, notwithstanding certain special and always strictly ritualized orgiastic rituals, which are met with not only in primitive tribes, but also in highly developed cultures. Moreover, even some species of animals do not have the practice of promiscuity: storks, wolves, ravens, etc.[190] What is taken for matriarchy could well be a form parallel to patriarchy, since in some societies feminoid elements predominate even now and do not give the slightest hint of the evolution of these societies in the direction of classic patriarchy.

Instead of reductionist evolutionary schemes, refuted by ethnosociological and sociological data, Lévi-Strauss proposed the structural classification of kindred ties, based on a fundamental principle: the determination of the belonging of a child to one or another lineage and the location of the child in the space of one of the two phratries.

Lévi-Strauss divided all variations of determination of kinship into four groups: *matrilineal, patrilineal, matrilocal,* and *patrilocal.* The first two types relate to the determination of the belonging of the child to the lineage of the mother or father; the second two, to the location of the child on the territory of the lineage of the mother or father.

Four variants thus emerge:

1. Matrilineal kinship + matrilocal location
2. Matrilineal kinship + patrilocal location

---

190 Lorenz, K. *On Aggression.* New York, NY: Harcourt, Brace & World, 1966.

3.   Patrilineal kinship + matrilocal location

4.   Patrilineal kinship + patrilocal location

Lévi-Strauss called variants 1 and 4 harmonious, and 2 and 3 disharmonious. In cases 1 and 4, the child is located in the lineage to which he belongs and he is raised in it as a "*kindred*," i.e., as part of that kin group from the moment of his appearance in the world right to maturity and the marital period. In cases 2 and 3, on the other hand, the child, after being born, is located in that phatry which is exogenous for him, which puts him the position of a certain alienation from his surroundings, with the exception of the mother (in all cases). None of these versions gives rise either to "matriarchy" or "patriarchy," since they serve to regulate the general balance of the exchange of women on the basis of equilibrium. Theoretically, Lévi-Strauss stipulated, the same process could be described as an "exchange of men," but such an attitude is not recorded in any known societies, since even in sociums with elements formally resembling "matriarchy," the man is not considered a commodity, subject to exchange in the general social system. Neither matrilineality nor matrilocality nor any combination of the two are signs of matriarchy. In the social structure, the mother acts as the carrier of the main factor: belongingness to a lineage, which in itself does not have a gender sign, but merely helps to classify the members of the lineage: that which belongs to A concerns A; that which belongs to B concerns B. The principle of patriarchy and matriarchy plays the same role, but on a different level, on the level of the spatial location of the family or progeny.

In this situation, exchange and equilibrium become the main laws of gender strategies in society.[191]

Cross-Cousin and Parallel-Cousin Systems

Relations with first-cousins have a tremendous significance in the system of kinship. Their example shows that the prohibition on incest does not

---

191 Levy-Strauss, C. *Les Structures élémentaires de la parenté.*

have a physiological or hygienic, but a social character. This is expressed in the division of cousins into *cross* and *parallel*. *Parallel cousins* are the children of the father's brothers or mother's sisters. *Cross cousins* are the children of the father's sisters or mother's brothers. In all forms of determination of belongingness to a lineage, both patrilineal and matrilineal, cross cousins turn out to be members of the opposite lineage in relation to the son or daughter of the given parents.

The majority of archaic societies allow cross-cousin marriages precisely on the basis of social exogeneity, despite the fact that from a physiological point of view cross cousins do not differ from parallel cousins. This refutes the hypothesis of the making taboo of incest due to the observation of the degeneracy of the progeny of incestuous unions.

We stopped to consider Lévi-Strauss' ideas in so much detail precisely because they form the methodological basis of Ethnosociology and comprise its fundamental theoretical base (alongside the theories of Thurnwald, Mauss, the school of Boas, and the Social Anthropology of English Functionalism).

Louis Dumont: Hierarchical Man and Holism

The eminent French sociologist and anthropologist Louis Dumont (1911–1998) made an enormous contribution to Ethnosociology since he applied the sociological method to the study of Indian society and built on this basis profound theoretical models, which enriched Ethnosociology.

Dumont was disciple of Marcel Mauss and continued the main line of French Sociology, which considers society as a "total phenomenon." Evans-Pritchard exerted a significant influence on his enthusiasm for Ethnology.

Dumont's studies of Indian society with increased attention to those categories in which Indians themselves think and act led him to a number of fundamental conclusions. Thus, he described the caste system as a model of the introduction of "transcendence" into the social system, i.e., the assimilation by society of the concept of the "other." In this way, social hierarchy reflects the philosophical dimension of that which lies on the other side and the inclusion of that point which is "beyond the limit" not only in religious and philosophical systems, but in the structure of society as such. Dumont emphasized that social stratification in its extreme form of caste expression (as in Indian society) embodies in itself a certain binary opposition.[192] In particular, such forms as *right/left, Adam/Eve, Father/ King* are built according to a model in which one of the terms of each pair is not simply part of the whole but the whole itself, while the other is only a part or derivative of the whole. In other words, these binary pairs can be drawn up in a general form: *whole/part*. In India, this is expressed by the fact that the caste system proposes that the fullness of society exists in the *Brāhmaṇas*, who occupy themselves with rites and religious ceremonies, as well as religious philosophy. While being only part of the caste system, they are thought of as its essence and purpose, i.e. as the whole . Dumont calls this "Holism." Moreover, Dumont understands hierarchy in a broad (or sociological) sense separately from the problem of power and submission. Thus, in India the highest caste are the *Brāhmaṇas*, whose status is higher than that of warriors and kings (*Kṣatriyas*). At the same time, *Brāhmaṇas* do not possess political and economic power, and in this sense, they depend on *Kṣatriyas*. Hierarchy is higher and deeper than the structure of power relations. It is connected with the concept, very important for traditional society, of the "whole."

Holism expresses the principle of the superiority of the whole to the partial, the individual. Holistic society acts on the premise that society itself as a whole (as the totality, not only of all presenting living persons, but also their ancestors and progeny, as well as their social relations, cults, traditions, rites, symbols, beliefs, etc.) is endowed with the greatest reality. Separate individuals, on the other hand, are real through communion with this whole: their being is dual; on one hand, as a part of the whole they participate in the higher being of the whole; on the other hand, they also have their own being, of a lesser and secondary quality, often identified with the unclean, inauthentic, or illusory (the Indian *māyā*).

---

192 Dumont, L. *Homo hierarchicus: Essai sur le système des castes*. Paris: Gallimard, 1971.

The holistic attitude towards society is characteristic for traditional societies, in which caste structures predominate. Indian society is a model of such societies and can be taken as a paradigm.

According to Dumont, modern Western European society, which is built on a different understanding of the fundamental sociological moments, is on the directly opposite paradigm. All binary oppositions — sex, class, etc. — are thought of as complex agglomerations, as a summation of parts. Standard binarity is expressed by the general formula: *one part/ another part*. Instead of an integrating holism we have individualism, in which each part is thought of as an independent authority. Masses are not removed in the elite, women in men, etc. Dumont calls this paradigm "*individualism*" and considers it the general model of Western and modern society. Dumont comes to this conclusion through the juxtaposition of India's hierarchized caste society and democratic, secular, and individualistic European society. His work *Essays on Individualism*, considered a classic of Sociology and Anthropology, is devoted to this issue.[193]

Dumont paid special attention to Economic Anthropology, started by Mauss, and subjected to profound sociological analysis the processes and institutions of "economic society" and the basic concept of "economic equality," actual equality in sociological theories and the equality of possibilities in liberalism. In his book *Homo Equalis*, which is a symmetrical supplement to the book *Homo Hierarchicus*, Dumont shows that modern Europe, beginning from the Middle Ages, entered into a transition phase from *holism* to *individualism,* i.e., from one type of society to another.[194, 195] The order and caste structure of holistic society creates barriers to the growth of material prosperity of the masses. But the quest by the masses for the unencumbered satisfaction of their interests leads to anarchy and

193 Dumont, L. *Essais sur l'individualisme: Une perspective anthropologique sur l'idéologie moderne.* Paris: Le Seuil, 1983.

194 Ibid. *Homo Æqualis I: genese et epanouissement de l'ideologie economique.* Paris: Gallimard / BSH, 1977; Ibid. *Homo Æqualis II: l'Ideologie allemande.* Paris: Gallimard/ BSH, 1978.

195 Ibid. *Homo hierarchicus: The Caste System and its Implications.* Chicago, IL: University of Chicago Press, 1980.

social materialism. That is why bourgeois revolutions and reforms consist in the transition from politics and religion, which justify stratification and hierarchy, to economics and especially the (materialistic) morals founded on this economics.

Dumont thoroughly investigates the genesis of individualism — as an ideology, methodology, and philosophy. Some traditional societies (for instance, the Indian, early Christian, and part of the European Middle Ages) know the concept of the *"individual outside the world."* This is the ideal of the hermit, the yogi, the monk. Such an individual abandons society (normatively holistic) and the world together with it, *asserting individualism through his withdrawal.* But even those societies that know such a figure and raise him high as an ideal do not reject in all other cases holism and the laws of integrity in all things that concern the remaining sides of life, which the exception of the bracketed sphere of the ascetic. Between the "individual outside the world" and the holism of the rest of society, relations are hierarchical: they do not lie on one place (*either-or*). Being higher and recognized as such, the ascetic or hermit does not try to change society itself and does not interfere in its affairs.

But at a certain moment, a transition occurs from the "individual outside the world" to the *"individual within the world."* This process began to manifest itself in Western Europe together with nominalism, and later with the Reformation (Calvinism) and the metaphysics of Modernity. The individual is acknowledged to be the fundamental reality, and the philosophy and ideology based on individualism begin to enter into direct opposition to traditional society, rooted in holism. Dumont meticulously traces individualism as the basis of modern society in the most diverse manifestations: from Ockham's argument about universals to the pioneers of the economic and political thought of Modernity (Hobbes, Locke, Smith, Rousseau, Hegel, Marx, etc.) and right up to modern neoliberalism (Hayek, Popper, etc.).

According to Dumont, Holism is inseparably connected with hierarchy and traditional society. Individualism is logically associated with equality and modern society.

Dumont considered another important characteristic of the dichotomy between holism and individualism: the distinction between *relations between persons* (holism) / *relations between the individual and nature* (individualism). The transfer of attention from social relations to the relations of the individual with the external world laid the foundation of economics as an autonomous discipline, which primarily studies the relations of man and private property (i.e., privatized by the individual and hence an individualized fragment of the external world).

If we apply Dumont's ideas to Ethnosociology, we get the following picture.

The holistic society described by Dumont relates to what we called the ethnos and narod/laos. For the ethnos, integrity (Holism) is maximal and absolute, and hierarchy is as yet free of stratification and power relation.

The narod/laos is a differentiated, stratified, and polyethnic society, based on the visualization and internalization of the *transcendent* in the form of a socio-political model. It is not by accident that so much attention is paid in this kind of society to religious structures. Here Holism is subject to a certain layering (into castes, estates, etc.) and besides a purely status-based hierarchy (the domination of the sacred, shamanism), a hierarchy of power (a system of subordination and domination) also takes shape.

Individualistic, economic, egalitarian society is civil society, both in its early phase (national states), and in its normatively "ideal" phase (global society). The transition from holistic society (narod) to the individualistic society (civil society) occurred in Europe (and Dumont shows in detail the nuances of this process), but did not occur in India. Hence, we can study *society as narod* not only in history, but in our time as a self-sufficient social and political system, placed alongside modern and civil society.

Moreover, Dumont proposes to reject European Ethnocentrism (he calls it "Sociocentrism") and to recognize the equal rights of holistic and individualistic social models as features of different societies and cultures at different times. If we judge by the length of historical existence and even by the number of modern members, then holistic societies are a much more frequent phenomenon, while the individualism of contemporary Europe will seem like an insignificant, but aggressive and pretentious anomaly. Dumont believes that an authentically sociological and scientific approach is one allows individualistic society to be described in terms of the criteria of Holism while describing holistic society with the help of the apparatus of individualistic ideology and methodology. After thoroughly researching Indian society (holistic, traditional), Dumont himself acted in this way, studying concurrently the man of hierarchy (*Homo hierarchicus*, the norm for traditional society) and the man of equality (*Homo aequalis*, the standard for contemporary Western society).

For Ethnosociology Louis Dumont and his sociological and anthropological theories are of central significance, since they render fundamental the polycentric approach to diverse societies, on which Ethnosociology is based.

Georges Dumézil: Trifunctional Theory

Georges Dumézil (1898–1986), a first-rate historian of religion, a structuralist, and a linguist, can be associated entirely with Ethnosociology, since his works are devoted predominantly to the study of the social stratification of Indo-European narods, including those of the most ancient times. Dumézil was under the influence of the ideas of Durkheim and collaborated closely with Marcel Granet.

Dumézil engaged in ethnographic fieldwork in Turkey and the Caucasus, learning about the ethnic groups of the Turks, Ubykh, Abkhazians, Armenians, and especially the Ossetians, whose ancient culture he was the first to draw to the attention of European scholars.

Dumézil's main ideas received the name "*trifunctional theory*." According to Dumézil, the structure of the Nart Saga, preserved among a number of Caucasian narods and especially the Ossetians, led him to the creation of this theory. Ossetian society, originating in its roots from the Alan, Sarmatians, and Scythians, preserved a trifold structure, characteristic of ancient epics, according to which all members of society are divided into priests, soldiers, and cattle-breeders. This three-part model determines the structure of myths, religious rites, and socio-political arrangements. Starting from the Ossetian model, Dumézil carried out the colossal task of a comparative analysis of the mythologies and religions, along with the socio-political systems of ancient Indo-European ethnoses — Vedic Aryans, ancient Scythians, Sarmatians, Parthians, Romans, Greeks, Slavs, Celts, Germans, Hittites, etc. — and established that the three-part model is met with among practically all these ethnoses. The trifunctional approach was taken as a basis for the interpretation of many rituals, myths, chronicles, and religious doctrines. Thus, a functional connection between Indian *Brāhmaṇas* and Roman *Flamens* was established.[196]

Dumézil devoted separate works to the interpretation of German and ancient Roman mythology from the perspective of the trifunctional theory.[197, 198] The work *The Gods of the Indo-Europeans* summarizes this research.[199]

Dumézil belonged to the structuralist school of anthropology and the history of religion and was inclined to interpret historical chronicles as a form of the unfolding of mythological consciousness.[200] This method received the name *"anti-Euhemerism."*[201] The ancient Greek philosopher Euhemerus had already proposed, in antiquity, the theory that histories and myths about the gods are recollections of real events and exploits, performed by people who acquired in the memory of others exaggerated, fantastic traits. Dumézil not only thought that this was not the case and that the myth was primary, but was also inclined to interpret a history about a series of historical actions as a special version of the exposition of myth in a historical form. He demonstrated this brilliantly in his works

---

196 Dumézil, G. *Flamen-Brahman.* Paris: Geuthner, 1935.

197 Ibid. *Mythes et dieux des Germains — Essai d'interpretation comparative.* Paris: Press Universitaire Francaise, 1939.

198 Ibid. *Jupiter Mars Quirinus.* 4v. Paris: Gallimard, 1941–1948.

199 Ibid. *Les Dieux indo-europeens.* Paris: Press Universitaire Francaise, 1952.

200 Ibid. *Mythe et epopee.* I, II, III. Paris: Quarto Gallimard, 1995.

201 Ibid. *Oubli de l'homme et l'honneur des dieux.* Paris: Gallimard, 1985.

and explained it methodologically in in the comparative work *Man's Forgetting and the Honor of the Gods.*[202]

Dumézil's works are of great importance to Ethnosociology, both from the perspective of their comparative method, and because of the fundamental examination of the process of social stratification in ancient narods. More precisely, the themes he takes up relate to the form of society we call the "narod/laos" in an ethnosociological sense. Social stratification is a phenomenon that characterizes the first derivative of the ethnos, i.e., the narod. The isolation of the three-part model of society can refer only to the narod, since in the ethnos (in its pure form) social equality predominates and stratification is almost entirely absent. For the analysis of the laos and the processes of the appearance of states, religions, and civilizations as forms of the narod's creative work, Dumézil's instruments are optimal.

In his studies of tripartite religious and socio-political systems, Dumézil analyzed extensive mythological and historical material connected with the emergence of the dynasties, countries, and states of the Ancient World. Everywhere he found a constantly repeating theme, fundamental for the moment of the emergence of the narod/laos: war and the subsequent reconciliation between the brave warriors, the newcomers (who lack food, women, and wealth) and the settled, peace-loving local population, occupied with agriculture and possessing, on the contrary, an abundance of wealth and women. In the history of Rome this plot is repeated twice: first, in the case of Aeneas, who arrived from fallen Troy and came across the king of Latins, and later, in the case of Romulus, who entered into conflict (which was later replaced by peace) with the Sabine king, Titus Tatius. In India, among the Germanic narods, in the Ossetian and more broadly North Caucasian Nart Saga, among Iranians, and Greeks — everywhere we come across one and the same picture: the tripartite model is formed from the superimposition of allogeneic ethnoses (with clear nomadic and warlike traits), comprising the basis of the two higher functions (priests and warriors), onto a local population of an

---

202 Ibid.

agrarian type. The third function (predominantly workers-peasants) cor-relates with a specific type of gods, rites, traits, symbols, economic prac-tices, value attitudes, and characteristic features. Thus, Dumézil, aiming to track down far and wide the tripartite system, a feature, in his opinion, of Indo-European ethnoses, himself proved the *composite character* of this system, which consists of two heterogeneous mythological and symbolic complexes, one of which is inherent to warlike nomadic ethnoses and the other to peaceful agrarian ones. The gods and rites of the warriors form the content of the two higher functions; the gods and rites of the farmers, the third, lower function. These aspects render Dumézil's works indispensable for Ethnosociology.

Algirdas Greimas: The Sociology of Meaning and Ethnosemiotic Objects

Lévi-Strauss' pupil Algirdas Greimas (1917–1992), who lived a significant part of his life in France, where he had a scientific career, was a struc-turalist philosopher, ethnologist, historian of religion, and specialist in Lithuanian mythology. Greimas specialized in structural linguistics and became the founder of (together with Roland Barthes) of semiotics in France (the Paris school of semiotics).[203]

Greimas occupied himself with the problem of meaning and the formalization of semantic constructs in systems of signs.[204] He primarily applied this model to the analysis of mythologies, as well as literary texts, since, according to his theory, there is no fundamental difference between the structure of myth and the structure of contemporary literary, philo-sophical, or journalistic texts: they are resolved into a series of constant semantic and functional elements, in which there is revealed the figure of the *actant* (the acting person), his attributes, and actions, as well as a fixed number of possible relationships to other actants. He was influenced by the Soviet scholar Vladimir Propp's structuralist analysis of tales, myths,

---

203 Greimas, A. J. *Semantique structurale: recherche et methode.* Paris: Larousse, 1966.

204 Ibid. *Du sens.* Paris: Éditions du Seuil, 1983.

and epics and by his model of detecting the constant semantic and functionalist structures of Russian fairy tales.

Greimas engaged in the reconstruction of Lithuanian folk mythology
and devoted a separate work to this topic, *Of Gods and Men: Studies in
Lithuanian Mythology*.[205]

In 1971 at the First International Congress for Ethnosociology he presented the paper *Reflections on Ethnosemiotic Objects*.[206] Ethnosemiotic
objects, according to Greimas, are myths, legends, traditions, and tales,
which are distinguished by the fact that they do not center on the individual, as in Western European literature or in the autobiographical
tradition of letters in the Modern Era, but on a system of semantic structures consisting of relations, functions, and ties. The term "ethnosemiotic
object" is very significant for Ethnosociology, since it describes the ethnos
as a semantic and meaning-constituting phenomenon. Emphasis of the
impersonal structure of this object agrees with the main characteristic of
the ethnos as a simple society with the maximal power of non-individual
collective identity. Greimas' definition shows that the ethnos can be considered as that which makes signs (words, figures, sounds, gestures, rituals) intelligible.

André Leroi-Gourhan: Technique and Ethnicity

Mauss' pupil and Griaule's successor at the Sorbonne, the French sociologist and anthropologist André Leroi-Gourhan (1911–1986) held evolutionary, materialistic positions and set at the center of his studies the problem
of technique and its influence on the transformation of different types of
society. His ethnological field studies were devoted to the archeology of
the northern zone of the Pacific Ocean.[207] Leroi-Gourhan's ideas exerted

205 Ibid. *Des dieux et des hommes: etudes de mythologie lithuanienne*. Paris: Presse
    Universitaire Francaise, 1985.

206 Ibid. 'Reflexions sur les objets ethno-semiotiques' / Actes du 1er Congres d' ethnolo-
    gie europeenne. Paris: Maisonneuve & Larose, 1973, pp. 63–72.

207 Leroi-Gourhan, A. *Archeologie du Pacifique nord*. Paris: Institut d'Ethnologie, 1946.

a significant influence on the post-structuralist philosophers: Derrida, Deleuze, and Guattari.

In his works, Leroi-Gourhan correlates two fundamental elements, of principal importance for the establishment of society: technique and the ethnos. Leroi-Gourhan introduces the concept of *"technical tendencies,"* which, in his opinion, are connected with the objective and universal moment of transition from a quadruped animal to a vertical position.[208] Owing to this transition, "yesterday's monkeys" have their hands freed and increased attention is drawn to the face, which promotes the development of technical instruments, which find themselves in the hands "freed" from walking (Deleuze calls this "deterritorialization"), and the emergence of speech associated with a qualitative leap in the reinforcement of the role of the face [TN: in Russian, the same word means person and face] and one of its main organs, the mouth.[209] Thus, language and technique prove to be closely connected and represent two sides of the technical tendencies.

According to Leroi-Gourhan, technical tendencies are universal for all humanity as a species. But they reveal themselves in a concrete ethnic environment. Consequently, the expression of universality is always particular, specific, and ethnic. Technique is something common, expressing itself through the ethnos as something particular.

The ethnos is the concretization of technique. The ethnos, according to Leroi-Gourhan, dwells in two environments simultaneously: an external one (natural, climatic, geographical) and an inner one (cultural, comprising the structure of the "common past"). Between the ethnos and the environment (both varieties) is an *"interposed membrane"* or *"artificial envelope."*[210] This just is the technical tendency as a universal, placed into the structure of the ethnos. The ethnos begins to apply this "membrane," at first to the inner environment (to society itself), and then also to the external one, transforming its structure.

---

208 Ibid. *L'Homme et la matiere.* Paris: Albin Michel, 1943.

209 Deleuze, G. & Guattari F. *L'Anti-Oedipe.* Paris: Les Editions de Minui, 1972.

210 Leroi-Gourhan, A. *Milieu et techniques.* Paris: Albin Michel, 1945.

Step by step, ethnic societies transform in the direction of the development of technique, which increases their universality. At the limit of the ethnic as concrete must be completely forced out by the technical as universal. The meaning of history consists of this: the technical tendency gravitates towards autonomy and the replacement, by itself, of ethnic humanity. The limit of such a tendency is visualized conceptually in post-modernity and post-society. That is why Leroi-Gourhan's ideas were picked up by the postmodern philosophers.

If we leave aside the topic of evolution, man's origin from four-legged animals, and other forms of "progressivist" technological racism, characteristic of Leroi-Gourhan, then we can successfully apply his *ethnotechnological theory* to Ethnosociology.

The ethnos, as Leroi-Gourhan understands it, is the simplest society, maximally local and particular, i.e., minimally technical. We call this the "koineme."

From this fundamental simplicity, we can lay down more and more complex derivatives. Complexity, differentiation, complexity and its degrees are the main indicators of the difference of the narod, nation, civil and global society, and finally, post-society from the ethnos. If we apply Leroi-Gourhan's terminology, then we can identify the complexity and the process of complication, the raising of the level of differentiation, with the technical tendency and consider *"technique"* as a measure of determination of the sociological character of the society we are examining. The German ethnosociologists, chiefly Richard Thurnwald, acted approximately thus in their description of the process of the social transformations of ethnic society. But Thurnwald and Mühlmann ended their analysis at the level of the narod or laos. Thanks to Leroi-Gourhan, we can extend this logic to more complex, contemporary societies, right up to postmodernity.

The further society is from the ethnos, the more technical, universal, and effective it is, and the less human, cultural, and ecological. It proves to be a separate "membrane" from nature, culture, and their balanced synthesis, which comprises the essence of the ethnic habitation of being.

Roger Bastide: The Ethnosociological Labelling of Brazilian Society

The French sociologist Roger Bastide (1989–1974), who specialized in the detailed study of the societies of Brazil, made a serious contribution to Ethnosociology. From 1962 to 1974 he headed the journal *L'Année Sociologique*, founded by Durkheim. Moreover, he was the founder of the sociological tradition in Brazil itself, where he laid the basis for the Faculty of Sociology at the University of Sao Paulo.

Bastide studied the complex structure of contemporary Brazilian society, in which he traced the processes of acculturation, which, beginning with a core of Whites of Portuguese descent, spread to all other ethnic and social groups, refracting fantastically at each stage and begetting various forms of syncretism — Catholic European Portuguese culture crossed with the religious cults and magical rites of the local Native tribes, or the rituals and practices of the black population, delivered from Western Africa.

Bastide thought that Brazilian society was a unique example of the imposition of social stratification onto ethnic stratification. White Portuguese Catholics are the highest class in Brazil and are associated with the figures of the man/master; they are most often, large, average, and small landowners, under whose submission were found, up to the most recent times, mercenaries and hired hands (predominantly Natives), and black slaves entirely deprived of rights.[211]

The black-skinned population, descendants of imported slaves from Africa, stands at the lowest level. However, Bastide noted, the Black population of Brazil and Latin America present on the whole a phenomenon entirely different, from an ethnosociological perspective, from that of the Black population in the US. North American farmers consistently and systematically separated the black-skinned slaves, brought in from the same place, over different estates, in order not to allow any communication between them and not to give grounds for rebellion and revolt. Slaves on the same plantation in the US almost always belonged to different ethnic groups, which caused them, over the course of a few generations,

---

211 Bastide, R. *Images du nordeste mystique en noir et blanc*. Paris: Pandora éditions, 1978.

to forget their language, culture, rites, etc.; i.e., to lose their ethnic features and transition under compulsion to the English language (the language of the master), absorbing their masters' culture. This was a strict form of acculturation, which destroyed the very core of the ethnos. In Brazil and Latin America, groups of imported slaves were most often settled together, which softened the acculturation and allowed them to preserve — albeit in part — ethnic, cultural, and religious attributes.[212]

Nevertheless, the lowest social class in Brazil was, in any case, clearly marked by skin color.

Natives, Mulattos, and Metis were spread throughout the middle stratum. They occupied the middle place, having preserved after colonization a certain degree of independence or else, by moving away to the inaccessible zones of the jungles of the Amazon and its inflows, they were saved by the practice of ethnic conservation.

Thus, Brazil's social strata proved to be ethnically indexed, which is a graphic illustration of Ethnosociology as such.

Bastide added to his studies the psychoanalytical method. He considered the situation, typical for Brazil, in which a White Portuguese landowner has a White Catholic wife, a group of Native mistresses, and a concubine of Negro women. Thus, a gender hierarchy is added to the social and ethnic ones. Bastide traces the self-consciousness of the numerous groups of bastard children, who are born owing to extramarital colonial practices, which comprise an imposing percent of the contemporary Brazilian population. The social identification of the bastard children plainly demonstrates the settled attitudes towards a group of values (White, male, Portuguese, proprietor, master) and anti-values (Black, woman, Native, slave, pauper).[213]

---

212 Bastide, R. *L'Ethnohistoire du nègre brésilien.* Paris: Bastidiana, 1993.

213 Ibid. *Psychanalyse du Cafuné.* Paris: Editions Bastidiana, 1996.

Gilbert Durand: The Anthropological Structures of the Imagination

The contemporary French sociologist Gilbert Durand, a pupil and successor of Roger Bastide and the philosopher Gaston Bachelard (1884–1962), develops Jung's ideas as applied to society and social structures. In his main work *The Anthropological Structures of the Imagination* he proposes an original development of Jung's theory of the collective unconscious, which Durand himself calls the *"imagination"* (*imaginaire*), distinguishing within it different modes, responsible for certain social phenomena, institutes, and processes.[214] Society is conceived of as a projection of the imagination in the combination of a few of its modes.[215]

Durand isolates one "diurnal" mode and two "nocturnal" modes (the *mystical* and the *dramatic*). All myths, legends, religious rites, and social arrangements reflect one or another of the modes of the imagination or their combination. In his works, Durand describes the symbolic arrays that correspond to these modes and identifies them both in myths and in contemporary literature, philosophy, etc. For Durand, the modes of the *"imaginaire"* are active in both archaic societies (directly) and in complex, differentiated societies (indirectly).

The *"diurnal"* mode (ancient, bright) is responsible for the creation of vertical hierarchies and symmetries of "up-down." Many religions and cultures, at the centre of which lie the worship of the sky, light, sun, and corresponding heavenly figures, are based on this. In social structures this corresponds to social hierarchy, power, politics, and patriarchy; in the domain of culture, to rationalism, will, and logos. In this mode, binarity, opposition, and polarity dominate in an intensified and irremovable form. This is the mode of differentiation, distinction, division.[216]

The mode of the *"mystical nocturne"* (the first nocturnal regime) is the complete opposite of the diurnal mode. In it, oppositions are removed;

---

214 Durand, G. *Les Structures anthropologiques de l'imaginaire*. Paris: Borda, 1969.

215 Dugin, A. G. *Sociology of the Imagination*. Moscow: Academic Project, 2010.

216 Ibid. pp. 91–99.

the symbolism of night, mother, unity, peace, and calm predominate. It is the symmetry of center and periphery. The themes of water, earth, calm, shelter, food, comfort, and sleep are associated with it. In differentiated societies, this mode corresponds to privacy, home, kitchen, family, woman, children, fertility, and the peaceful rhythm of toil.[217]

The mode of the *"dramatic nocturne"* (the second nocturnal mode) is built on the integration of binary opposites, which are admitted, but overcome in a synthesis, in order to make room for a new pair. This is a dialectical mode. Its symbols are marriage, the symmetry of right and left, the gender pair, and unstable and dynamic balance. Various twin myths, constructed on the principle of opposition/supplementation (complementarity), correspond to it. Erotic cultural motifs, and everything associated with marriage, are found under the sign of this mode. Various cyclical forms pertain to it.[218]

Durand's reconstruction allows one to study social and political institutions, economic practices, myths, rites, symbols, and dreams — including psychic illnesses, which are also classified according to the modes, with the diurnal being responsible for the family of paranoid disorders, the mystical nocturne for schizophrenia and epilepsy, and the dramatic nocturne for cyclothymia and cyclophrenia — all with the same method.[219]

Durand himself did not apply his sociology of the imagination immediately to the ethnos, but he based his theories on abundant ethnographic and ethnological material. We provided examples of the constructiveness of his method as applied to the ethnos and Ethnosociology in the books *Sociology of the Imagination* and *Mythos and Logos*.[220, 221]

---

217 Ibid. pp. 100–108.

218 Ibid. pp. 109–114.

219 Ibid.

220 Ibid. pp. 313–358.

221 Ibid. *Logos and Mythos: Sociology of Depths*. Moscow: Academic Project, 2010.

Pierre Bourdieu: Engaged Ethnosociology

The well-known French Marxist sociologist Pierre Bourdieu (1930–2002) sometimes used the term "Ethnosociology" in his works. In the context of the discipline of Anthropology, he wrote numerous works critical of structuralism, to which he opposed the "dynamic" approach of "practice and strategy," aiming to depart from the constancy of structures and functions that comprise the essence of cultural, social, and structural anthropology, as well as the ethnosociological approach as a whole.[222] Bourdieu tried to overcome the dualism of *Structuralism/Constructivism*, suggesting the hybrid term "*constructivist Structuralism*."[223]

Bourdieu's attitude towards the ethnos is maintained in a Marxist spirit; by it he understands a primitive society finding itself in the early stages of social development. In the spirit of Marxism, he also criticizes the capitalist exploitation, lying at the basis of colonial practices. On this foundation, in the early stage of his work, Bourdieu promoted "*engaged Ethnosociology*," i.e., the active participation of left intellectuals-sociologists in the struggle of European colonies for independence, development, and the building of socialism. Bourdieu was influenced in the elaboration of this model by his own stay in Algeria in the period when a dramatic struggle for the attainment of independence and freedom from French colonial domination was unfolding. Bourdieu studied the ethnic groups of the Berbers and Kabyle.[224]

For the Marxist Bourdieu, Sociology and Ethnology, like any sciences, reflected a class ideology, and hence the majority of European studies of colonial societies were conducted under the weight of bourgeois-colonialist clichés. Bourdieu was calling for the leftist European intelligentsia to take the side of the oppressed colonial masses, which acted as the social synonym of the "world proletariat."

---

222 Bourdieu, P. *L'Esquisse d'une théorie de la pratique*. Genève: Droz, 1972.

223 Ibid. *Choses dites*. Paris: Minuit, 1987.

224 Ibid. *Algérie 60: structures économiques et structures temporelles*. Paris: Minuit, 1977.

Bourdieu introduced a few new concepts into Anthropology that can be somewhat significant for Ethnosociology. Thus, he developed sociologically the term earlier used by philosophers (in particular, medieval nominalists and scholastics like Thomas Aquinas, and Husserl in the modern era), proposing to consider it as a kind of third unit between rigidly established impersonal social structures (with which the classical functionalist theory of Durkheim and the structuralists dealt) and the subjective interests, wishes, and impulses of the individual. A "*habitus*" is a form of consciousness, containing within itself a set of schemata, sympathies, tastes, and dispositions. The main difference between a habitus and a structure consists, to a large extent, of its individuated and dynamic character. Bourdieu develops these ideas in more detail in his so-called "sociology of taste."[225]

Bourdieu also often employed the concept of a "*field*" in an attempt to replace the more rigidly hierarchized concept of "class." In complex societies, he thought, there are a few social fields which are not related hierarchically and are relatively autonomous. He considered as such fields the areas of politics, law, education, art, and economics. Each field is differently structured sociologically and develops in accordance with its own regularities. In simple societies, among the Kabyles, whom Bourdieu studied in North Africa, fields tend toward combination in one field. Contemporary bourgeois societies, on the other hand, distance them from one another and create the preconditions for various algorithms of stratification in each of them. A recognized artist differs from a beginner not like rich from poor, but like commander and subordinate.

The unified or differentiated character of social fields can be applied in Ethnosociology for the analysis of criteria of difference of the ethnos from its derivatives.

Summary: Ethno-Analysis and Post-Ethnic Analysis

If we unite the four basic scientific traditions we have considered, we get a fundamental theoretical and methodological apparatus for the

---

225 Ibid. *La Distinction; Critique sociale du jugement.* Paris: Minuit, 1979.

construction of a general ethnosociological discipline. The specific character of this discipline consists of the fact that it holds the simple society (koineme), thought of as the ethnos, to be the foundation of sociological analysis (for all types of society!) and further builds its analysis on the study of both the simplest form and its more differentiated derivatives. At the same time, it is the ethnos (archaic society, the primitive form, society, *Gemeinschaft*, community, folk-society) that serves as a benchmark and model for comparison. The ethnos is taken as an "ideal type" (Weber) or "normative type" (Sombart), with the help of which and through comparison with which, any society, however complex, is studied.

Moreover, the correlation of the ethnos and its derivatives is carried out in two main directions: along the lines of similarity and difference.

If we consider the complex and differentiated society as a derivative of the ethnos (the line of *similarity*), then we can find in complex society traces of the ethnos, ethnic dimensions, or analogues of the phenomena met with in the ethnos. We can call this the "*ethno-analysis*" of complex societies.

On the other hand, we can raise the question: how does complex society differ from simple society and in what does the difference between narod/laos, nation, civil society, and ethnos consist? This is analysis along the line of *difference*, which is called upon for the study of complex societies to the extent that they are not the ethnos or are post-ethnic. We can call this approach "*post-ethnic analysis*" or the study of the orders of ethnic derivatives.

In both cases, it is necessary for us to have knowledge, classificational models, analytic instruments, typologies, taxonomies, etc., relating to simple societies (Anthropology, Ethnology, Ethnography, Religious Studies) and the same in the case of complex societies (Sociology in the proper sense of the word). Ethnosociology exists at the intersection of these two sets. Even a brief survey of authors and orientations shows how well-founded and solid its theoretical foundation is and how gripping and profound the history of its scientific establishment is.

CHAPTER FIVE

Ethnosociology in Russia

SECTION ONE
Prehistory of Russian Ethnology

The Origin of Russian Historical Science and Ethnography

Interest in what we today call "the ethnic problematic" was in evidence from the very moment of the emergence of Russian science. In the 18th century, the founder of Moscow State University Mikhail Vasilyevich Lomonosov (1711–1765), Fedor Ivanovich Miller (1705–1783), who stood at the wellsprings of Russian historical science, August Schlözer (1735–1809), Vasily Nikitich Tatischev (1686–1750), the founder of Russian Ethnography, Ivan Nikitich Boltin (1735–1792); Mikhail Mikhailovich Shcherbatov (1733–1790), Nicolay Mikhailovich Karamzin (1766–1826), and many others who were interested in the origin of the Slavic narod, antiquities, and other ethnic groups and tribes, advanced hypotheses about the nature of the ethnonym "Russian," tried to systematize information about those ethnoses which populate and populated Russia from antiquity. They collected, processed, systematized, and published ancient Russian chronicles, annals, and other materials of a historical and geographical character. Miller personally participated in an ethnographic expedition to Siberia and gathered much worthy information there about the life of the Russian narod and other ethnoses.

The Early Slavophiles: Kireyevsky, Khomyakov, Aksakov, Samarin

Interest in ethnography in Russia peaked in the 19th century, when interest in the philosophy of history (Hegel) and the influence of the German Romantics on the Russian nobility reached its apogee. This is evidenced most clearly in three phenomena:

- In the tendencies of the Slavophiles;

- In the flowering of the study of Russian folklore and Ethnology;

- In the political movement of *narodnichestvo*.

The first Slavophiles — Kireyevsky (1806–1856), Khomyakov (1804–1860), the Aksakov brothers Konstantin (1817–1860), Ivan (1823–1886), and Samarin (1819–1876), advanced the thesis of Russia's distinctive character, of the distinctive value of Russian Slavic culture, and that its difference from European culture should be considered, not as "backwardness," but as the expression of the peculiarities of the narodni spirit. Essentially, the question was raised whether European society, despite its pretensions to universality, is a local cultural phenomenon, which must be set in an array of different societies, among which the Russo-Slavic Orthodox culture will occupy a worthy place.

To this, as is well-known, responded the Westernizers (Chaadaev [1794–1856], Granovsky [1813–1855], Belinski [1811–1848], and others) whose positions amounted to the idea that Western culture is universal and all of Russia's differences express its "backwardness" and "underdevelopment," that there is nothing distinctive in character about it, or that if there is, it should be discarded as quickly as possible.

In any case, the Slavophiles focused on the question of the fates of narods, the differences among ethnic societies, the distinctive characteristics of culture and values, and, correspondingly, their significance. They called for the systematic study of Slavic ethnoses and Slavic cultures, with the aim of systematizing knowledge of their social arrangement, customs, mores, distinctive psychological characteristics, etc.

Thereby, they laid the prerequisites for the later emergence of ethnology.

The Late Slavophiles: Danilevsky

The second generation of Slavophiles developed and justified the intuitions of the founders of this movement. We should single out among them the three brightest figures: Danilevsky, Leontiev, and Lamansky.

In his principal book "Russia and Europe," Nikolay Yakovlevich Danilevsky (1822–1885) formulates for the first time the theory of the *plurality of civilizations*, which he calls cultural-historical types.[1]

In contrast with Western European thinkers, who considered their own civilization the only one possible, attributing all others to the category of "barbarism," Danilevsky proposed to consider it as *one of the civilizations,* as a "Romano-Germanic" culturo-historical type. At the same time, Danilevsky distinguished a number of other distinct and fully completed cultural-historical types, which were based on entirely different principles, but possessed all the markers of long-term and stable civilizations, having existed over the course of many centuries, preserving their identity, and surviving governments and different ideological formations, epochs of religious revolutions, and changes of value-systems.

Danilevsky singled out ten fully-fledged culturo-historical types (civilizations):

1. The Egyptian;
2. The Chinese;
3. The Assyrian-Babylonian-Phoenician-Chaldean or Ancient Semitic;
4. The Indian;
5. The Iranian;

---

1   Danilevskii, N.I. *Russia and Europe: The Slavic World's Political and Cultural Relations with the Germanic-Roman West.* Moscow: Slavica Pub, 2013.

6.   The Jewish;

7.   The Greek;

8.   The Roman;

9.   The New Semitic or Arab;

10.   The Romano-Germanic, or European.

He thought that in the 19th and 20th centuries a new, eleventh cultural-historical type was forming, the Russo-Slavic, possessing all the basic markers of a civilization.

Danilevsky thought that civilizations pass through stages of becoming, maturation, and old-age, like living beings. The Romano-Germanic civilization, in his opinion, is in the stage of senescence and decline. The Russo-Slavic world, on the other hand, is just coming into force.

In ethnosociological terminology, the concept "cultural-historical type" corresponds to the concept "narod/laos."

Leontiev: Three Types of Society

Konstantin Leontiev (1831–1891) also thought that Russian civilization and Russian culture were something with their "own distinctive character" (*samobitnie*) and that the main peculiarity of Russian history was its *Byzantinism*, i.e., movement in the currents of the Byzantine-Slavic Imperial tradition, which sharply differentiated Russian history from the history of other Slavic narods.[2]

Leontiev developed the teaching about different types of historical development, isolating such types as 1) "initial simplicity," 2) "flowering complexity," and 3) "all-mixing" or "overflow." He thought that Russia was at the final phase of the second stage and that it should be "frozen." The government should be firm "to the point of severity," and people "personally kind to one another."

---

2   Leontiev, K. *Vizantizm i slavyanstvo*. Moscow: Izd-vo Sretenskogo monastyrya, 2010.

He considered most worthy in a civilization the second stage of "flowering complexity." It is possible that Leontiev borrowed this image from Herder, who had compared ethnoses and narods to different plants, flowers, and trees in the garden of paradise.[3] If we apply Leontiev's periodization to Ethnosociology, then "initial simplicity" corresponds to the ethnos, "flowering complexity" to the narod/laos, and "all-mixing" to civil society and global society (allusions to which can be perceived already in bourgeois nations).

Lamansky: Greco-Slavic Civilization and the Middle World

Vladimir Ivanovich Lamansky (1833–1914), the eminent ethnographer, historian, and researcher of Slavic culture, belonged to the generation of late Slavophiles. He was the author of serious works about the culture of the Slavs of Eastern Europe, and also one of the first essays of comparative ethnography and sociology, *The Italian and Slavic Nationalities in their Political and Cultural Relations*, in which he compared the ethnocultural peculiarities of the Slavic and Italian ethnoses.[4]

In his book *The Three Worlds of the Asian-European Mainland*, Lamansky divided the space of Eurasia into three parts: the Romano-Germanic world, the Asian world, and the Greco-Slavic world.[5] The Romano-Germanic corresponded to Western Europe, and the Asian, to the countries of the East, beyond the borders of Russia. He called the Greco-Slavic world the "middle world," thereby anticipating the concept of Eurasia.

---

3   Herder, J.G. *Une autre philosophie de l'histoire*. Paris: Aubier, 1964.

4   Lamanskii, V.I. "Natsional'nosti ital'yanskaya i slavyanskaya v politicheskom i kul" turnom otnosheniyakh / Otechestvennyye zapiski, 1862.

5   Ibid. *Tri mira Aziysko-Yevropeyskogo materika*. Prague, 1916.

Russian Ethnography

Among the Russian ethnographers who made a contribution to the description, systematization, and classification of knowledge concerning the Russian narod and other ethnoses of Russia, we should single out a few of the more eminent names. Such are Sakharov (1807–1863), to whose pen belongs one of the first collections of Russian legends;[6] Pypin (1833–1904), author of the four-volume *History of Russian Ethnography*;[7] the celebrated collector, publisher, and interpreter of Russian stories Afanasyev (1826–1871);[8] the eminent folklorist and ethnographer Miller (1848–1913), a specialist of the Ossetian language and culture;[9] the philosopher and critic Nadezhdin (1804–1856), one of the founders of the Russian geographical society and the author of programmatic ethnographic studies;[10] Buslaev (1818–1897), a specialist of Russian folklore;[11] Snegirev (1797–1868), who collected a wealth of material about Russian holidays;[12] Zelenin (1878–1954), one of the first systematizer of ethnographic science and a forerunner of ethnology; the Slavist, Turkologist, and historian Golubovsky (1857–1907);[13] the outstanding Turkologist and archeolo-

---

6   Sakharov, I. P. *Skazaniya russkogo naroda o semeynoy zhizni svoikh predkov*. SPb: 1836–1837.

7   Pypin, A. *Istoriya russkoy etnografii*. 4 T. SPb: 1890–1892.

8   Afansyev, A. Russkiye zavetnyye skazki. SPb. Moscow, 1995.

9   Vsevolod Miller. *Osetinskiye etyudy*. Moscow: 1881–1887.

10   Nadezhdin, N.I. . Ob etnograficheskom izuchenii narodnosti russkoy. SPb: Russkoye geograficheskoye obshchestvo, 1846.

11   Istoricheskiye ocherki russkoy narodnoy slovesnosti i iskusstva. Moscow: 1861.

12   Snegiryov, I, M. Russkiye prostonarodnyye prazdniki i suyevernyye obryady; Moscow: 1837–1839; Ibid., O lubochnykh kartinkakh russkogo naroda. Moscow: 1844.

13   Golubovskii, P. V.. Istoriya Severskoy zemli do poloviny XIV st. Kiev: 1881. Ibid., Pechenegi, torki i polovtsy do nashestviya tatar: Istoriya yuzhno-russkikh stepey IX–XII st., Kiev: 1884; Ibid. Istoriya Smolenskoy zemli do nachala XV v. Kiev: 1895. Lektsii po drevneyshey russkoy istorii. Kiev, 1904.

gist Radlov (1837–1918);[14] the first-rate Slavist Pogodin (1872–1947);[15] the folklorist Sumtsov (1854–1922);[16] Loboda (1871–1931), a specialist of heroic epics;[17] Dal' (1801–1872), collector of folklore and compiler of a famous dictionary;[18] Byzantologist and ethnographer Speransky (1863–1938);[19] the philosopher Potebnya (1835–1891), who studied the ties between language, thought, and myth;[20] Anichkov (1866–1937), specialist of Russian paganism;[21] the prominent historian and philologist Shakhmatov (1864–1920);[22] the linguist and slavist Sobolevsky (1806–1908);[23] and the ethnographer and paleographer Karsky (1860–1931), a specialist of the White Russian narod.[24]

All of these authors and their works have preserved their worth. The problem is that Soviet Ethnography, which predominated in the 20th century, although it continued to add valuable material concerning the ethnic and historical problem, was constructed on dogmatic ideological principles and hurriedly rejected all those ideas that could not be inscribed in a materialist, Marxist approach in explaining the origin of ethnoses and cultures. Hence, all traces of pre-Soviet ethnographic thought were

14   Radlov, V. V.. Sibirskiye drevnosti' / Materialy po arkheologii Rossii, izdavayemyye Imperatorskoy arkheologicheskoy komissiyey. Sankt-Peterburg 1888; Radloff F.W. Das Schamanemtum und seine Kultus. Leipzig: 1885.

15   Pogodin, A.L. Kratkiy ocherk istorii slavyan. Moscow: Editorial URSS, 2003.

16   Sumtsov, N.F. O svadebnykh obryadakh. Khar'kov: 1881.

17   Loboda, A.M. Russkiy bogatyrskiy epos. Opyt kritiko — bibliograficheskogo obzora trudov po russkomu bogatyrskomu eposu. Kiev: N.T. Korchak-Novitskogo, 1904.

18   Dal, V.I. Poslovitsy russkogo naroda. Moscow: 1862.

19   Speranskii, M.N.. Rukopisnyye sborniki XVIII veka: Materialy dlya istorii russkoy literatury XVIII veka. Moscow, 1963. Ibid., Russkaya ustnaya slovesnost'. Vvedeniye v istoriyu ustnoy russkoy slovesnosti. Ustnaya poeziya povestvovatel'nogo kharaktera: Posobiye k lektsiyam na Vysshikh zhenskikh kursakh v Moskve. Moscow: 1917.

20   Potebnja, A.A. Slovo i mif. Moscow: Pravda, 1989; Ibid., O mificheskom znachenii nekotorykh obryadov i poveriy. Moscow: 1865.

21   Anichkov, Y.V. Yazychestvo i drevnyaya Rus'. Moscow: Indrik, 2003.

22   Shakhmatov, A.A. Drevneyshiye sud'by russkogo plemeni. Prague: 1919.

23   Sobolevsky, A.I. Velikorusskiye narodnyye pesni: 1895–1902.

24   Karsky, Y.F. Belorusy. Moscow: 1955–1956.

subject to "class" revision and reinterpretation. The results of this reinterpretation and "progress" in science were far from always adequate and acceptable. But the natural scientific process was artificially interrupted and distorted. Thus, today it is still a prospect to consider the worth of different ethnographic methods, classifications, or interpretations, characteristic of different authors and schools. It would be entirely unproductive to trust the readings of Russian ethnographers, folklorists, and linguists, which the relevant specialists carried out in the Soviet period. Therefore, in order to constitute a full-fledged ethnosociological discipline, it is advisable to turn directly to the sources of Russian ethnography and ethnology and to isolate without prejudice what is valuable, relevant, and important for a full-fledged restoration of the domestic scientific tradition.

Russian "Narodniks" and their Role in the Establishment of Ethnosociology

The scholars, writers, and social actors in the school of "narodniks" put the theme of the narod and narodni culture at the center of their attention. Among them were sociologists, economists, historians, and political activists, who created at the start of the 20th century the party of socialist-revolutionaries (SRs).

The narodniks, their work, and their historical theories, are important for ethnosociologists in that they tried to impart to the category "narod" a special conceptual, theoretical meaning, and to build on it their historical and social teachings, anticipating in some sense the task of ethnosociology. Moreover, many narodniks were keenly interested in sociology, and the first definition of sociology as such in Russian was given by the narodnik and sociologist Lavrov (1823–1900).

One of the theoreticians and main ideologists of Russian *narodnichestvo* was Herzen (1812–1870), who, having started with Westernism, significantly reconsidered his opinions at the end of his life, on the basis of his experience as an emigrant, and came to be convinced of the peculiar character and peculiar worth of the Russian narod, and especially of the peasant way of life.[25]

Another prominent ideologist of *narodnichestvo* was the economist and sociologist Vorontsov (1847–1918), the ideological inspirer of the group revolving around the journal "New Word." Vorontsov specialized in the history of the Russian peasant community and its economic, social, and ethnic arrangement.[26] In his works, Vorontsov convincingly showed that capitalism did not take shape in Russia and that the economic and social structure optimally intrinsic to Russian society is agrarian and peasant. Vorontsov's works meticulously describe the economic order of Russian peasantry. Vorontsov saw Russia's development and "progress" in the liberation of peasant labor and in the creation of a distinctive version of Russian peasant socialism.

The famous narodnik sociologist and publicist Mikhailovsky (1842–1904) held a similar position concerning capitalism. In his articles, he rigorously opposed Russia's imitation of the European experience. He made the remarkable observation that Marx's theory of the three phases of economic life was a historical conclusion made on the basis of the observation of *European* life, and its applicability is limited to Western society, while Russia, thanks to the specific character of the communal soul of the Russian, could avoid the capitalistic phase and develop according to its own script.[27] Mikhailovsky's ideas are important for Ethnosociology in that he tries to apply sociological methods to the study of the narod.

A pioneer of ethnographic studies in the form of "embedded observation" was the collector of narodni songs and traditions, writer and expert of the peasant worldview, Pavel Ivanovich, Yakushkin (1822–1872), a representative of early *narodnichestvo*, who wandered through Russian

---

25   Herzen, A. From the Other Shore, Translated from the Russian by Moura Budberg and the Russian People and Socialism, Translated from the French by Richard Wollheim. Oxford: Oxford University Press, 1979; Ibid., Polnoye sobraniye sochineniy. tom 6. Moscow: 1954–1965.

26   Vorontsov, V.P. 'Krest'yanskaya obshchina / Itogi ekonomicheskikh issledovaniy Rossii po dannym zemskoy statistiki, tom 1. Moscow: 1892.

27   Mikhaylovsky, N.K. Polnoye sobraniye sochineniy. T. 1–8, 10. SPb: 1906–1914.

villages as an *ophenya* (a travelling merchant) with the goal of the deep study and description of Russian narodni traditions, legends, social peculiarities, and religious and mythological notions.[28]

The eminent Russian ethnographers Peter Savich Efimenko (1835–1908) and his wife, the first female honorary doctor of Russian history, Alexandra Yakovlevna Efimenko (1848–1918), sided closely with the school of *narodnichestvo*.[29] In her works, the latter undertook an analysis of the social forms of life and economic order of White Russians and Ukrainians, and studied the qualities of character and psychological peculiarities of Russian and Ukrainian peasants. She emphasized "the exceptional inclination of the White Russian tribe to collectivism, its creativity in the sphere of social forms."[30]

The economists and historians Posnikov (1846–1922), Sokolovsky (1842–1906), and Kapustin (1828–1891), who were close to the narodniks, made a significant contribution to the study of communal land ownership and the simplest and most ancient forms of peasant life.[31, 32, 33]

Another narodnik, Prugavin (1850–1920), a specialist in the ethnographic and sociological aspects of Russian Old Belief, studied the connection between religious notions and specific forms of folk life.[34]

Some narodniks exiled for their revolutionary activities made a systematic study of the social, religious, and economic aspects of Siberia and the life of Russian settlers, engaging in the collection, description, and systematization of ethnographical material during, and often after their

28 Yakushkin, P.I. Sobraniye narodnykh pesen P. V. Kireyevskogo v 2 t. L: Nauka: 1983–1986.

29 Efimenko, A.Y. Issledovaniya narodnoy zhizni, vyp 1. Moscow: 1884.

30 Ibid.

31 Posnikov, A.S. 'Obshchinnoye zemlevladeniye Vyp 1–2. Yaroslavl': Tip. G.V. Fal'k, 1875–1877.

32 Sokolovskii, P.A. Ocherk istorii sel'skoy obshchiny na Severe Rossii. SPb: 1877.

33 Kapustin, S.Y. 'Ocherki poryadkov pozemel'noy obshchiny v Tobol'skoy gubernii po svedeniyam, sobrannym zapadnosibirskim otdelom Imperatorskogo Russkogo Geograficheskogo obshchestva' / Literaturnyy sbornik. SPb: 1885.

34 Prugavin, A.S. Raskol i sektantstvo v russkoy narodnoy zhizni. Moscow: 1905.

exiles. Among their number were the specialists of the Yakut, shamanism, and Yakut customs, the ethnographers Khudyakov (1842–1876) and Seroshevsky (1858–1945);[35, 36] the researcher of archaic cults among the Sakhalin Nivkhi (the Gilyak), Sternberg (1861–1927);[37] and the discoverer of the language and customs of the Yukagir, Jochelson (1855–1937),[38] and the Chukchi, Bogoraz-Tan (1865–1936).[39]

By their theories and ethnographic studies, the narodniks prepared a fruitful ideational and methodological base for the consideration of the ethnos as the foundation of sociological analysis, in contrast with the Marxists, who operated in their historical analysis predominantly with the concept of the class. It was precisely because of this basic methodological contradiction that the majority of their works were subject to artificial oblivion and suppression in the Soviet period. According to the same principle, we should turn special attention to them during the proper development of the ethnosociological discipline in our time.

Classical Russian Sociologists on Ethnoses

The works of the founder of Russian sociology as a full-fledged academic science were an important source for the establishment of Russian Ethnosociology. We already saw that the Russian narodniks who occupied themselves with sociology (in particular, Vorontsov and Mikhailovsky) paid special attention to ethnography. Other Russian sociologists — Kovalevsky, Sorokin — also paid special attention to ethnic studies in different periods of their work.

The first-rate Russian sociologist Maxim Maximovich Kovalevsky (1851–1916) personally participated in ethnographic expeditions in the

---

35 Chudyakov, I.A. Kratkoye opisaniye Verkhoyanskogo okruga. L: 1969.

36 Sieroszewski, W.L. Yakuty. Opyt etnograficheskogo issledovaniya. T.1. SPb: 1896.

37 Sternberg, L.Y. Pervobytnaya religiya v svete etnografii Leningrad: Izdatel'stvo instituta narodov Severa. TSIK SSSR: 1936.

38 Jochelson, V.I. Materialy po izucheniyu yukagirskogo yazyka i fol'klora. SPb: 1910.

39 Bogoraz, V.G. Materialy po izucheniyu chukotskogo yazyka i fol'klora. SPb: Izdaniye Akademii nauk, 1900.

Caucasus and collaborated closely with the ethnographer Miller. On the basis of the results of his field studies of the ethnoses of the Caucasus, he wrote a number of ethnographic works connected with the study of laws and customs and the correlations between them in the societies of the Caucasus, problems of kinship and the specific character of kin life, and the structure of clans among some small Russian ethnoses.[40, 41, 42]

Kovalevsky was the first person in Russian science to raise the question of the correlation of the methods of Sociology and Ethnography, the interrelationship between these disciplines, and the determination of their principal objects of study.[43]

Kovalevsky's disciple, the outstanding 20th century sociologist Pitirim Sorokin (1889–1968), who was keen in his youth on the ideas of the narodniks (and joined the party of the SRs), began his activities with a study of the ethnic problematic.

Ethnically, Sorokin was a Russified Komi, and it is natural that the peculiarities of the Komi ethnos provoked his spirited interest.

Sorokin wrote a number of ethnographic works about the religious notions of the Komi, advanced in the spirit of the evolutionary approach, which this great sociologist later rejected.[44] In his analysis of the remnants of Totemism, Sorokin, in the spirit of Durkheim, distinguishes two main spaces, the profane and the sacred, on the analysis of which he bases his conceptions.[45]

But for us, what is important is that his interest in the ethnic problematic lies at the basis of his inclination towards Sociology.

40 Kovalevsky, M.M. Zakon i obychay na Kavkaze. Moscow: 1887.

41 Ibid. Rodovoy byt v nastoyashchem, nedavnem i otdalennom proshlom. Moscow: 1905.

42 Ibid. Klan u aborigennykh plemen Rossii / Sotsiologicheskiye issledovaniya. No. 5, 2002, pp. 129–138.

43 Ibid. Etnografiya i sotsiologiya. Moscow: 1904.

44 Sorokin, P.A. 1910.

45 Ibid. K voprosu o pervobytnykh religioznykh verovaniyakh zyryan / Izvestiya obshchestva izucheniya Severnogo kraya. Vyp. 4. 1917.

Sorokin dedicated other works to the Komi ethnos, which concerned their cultural order and marital practices.[46]

Eurasianism as a Humanistic Paradigm: The Plurality of Ethnoses and Cultures

The problem of the ethnos stood at the center of attention of philosophical doctrine of Eurasianism (Trubetzkoy, P. N. Savitsky [1895–1965], G. V. Vernadsky [1877–1973], N. N. Alekseev [1879–1964], etc.)[47].

The Eurasianists based their theories on the conclusions of the late Slavophiles (Danilevsky, Leontiev, Lamansky) and brought their thesis of the "plurality of civilizations," the absence of a universal path of development for all societies and cultures, the rejection of "Romano-Germanic" colonialism, imperialism, and racism to its logical limit. They advanced as an alternative the particular, original Eurasian civilization, for which both the rate of development and the goal and direction of this development arise from the internal structure of Eurasian civilizational values which have their own autonomous history and content.

A very important feature of the Eurasian doctrine was the idea that Russian Eurasian civilization was built not only by Slavs, but also by other ethnic groups, each of which made its contribution to this process, which must be evaluated on its own merits. The Eurasianists particularly emphasized the role of the Steppe ethnoses: the Alan, Turkic peoples, and Mongols, who imparted to Russian civilization an additional social and spatial dimension, having integrated the woodland Slavs and ethnoses of the great steppe into a single world power, that which the Eurasianists themselves called a "government-world" (*gosudarstvo-mir*).

In the context of the Eurasian worldview, the idea of the distinctive character of ethnic cultures as an unconditional primary value and the affirmation of a plurality of societies and civilizations was combined with the revealing of the sociological particularities of different political and

---

46 Ibid. K voprosu ob evolyutsii sem'i i braka u zyryan / Izvestiya Arkhangel' — skogo obshchestva izucheniya Russkogo Severa. No. 1, 5. 1911.

47 Trubetskoy, N.N. *Foundations of Eurasianism.* Moscow: Arktogeia-Center, 2002.

ideological systems and heightened attention towards ethnoses, ethnic values and structures. In its scientific and systematic expression, the Eurasian method can be considered a phenomenon very similar to Ethnosociology. Eurasianism considers society a form of expression of the ethnos and recognizes the plurality of ethnoses as the foundation of a diversity of social and societal [*sotsialnikh i obshchestvennikh*] systems.

The Eurasianists were fierce opponents of all forms of racism — biological as well as technological, cultural, evolutionary, etc., and thus advanced the idea of the complete equality of cultures.

A significant difference between the Eurasianists and the earlier Slavophiles was their benevolent attitude towards the cultures of Russia's small ethnoses and the call to revive and defend their spiritual and social particularities. Prince Nikolai Sergeyevich Trubetskoy advanced the idea of "all-Eurasian nationalism," at the basis of which lay the idea of the conscious solidarity of Russian ethnoses in the fortification and development of the united "big space" of Russia-Eurasia.[48]

In another capacity, that same Prince Trubetskoy was the founder of Phonology and the Prague School of Structural Linguistics, along with Roman Jakobson, where the theoretical bases were laid for the entire orientation of Structuralism in Linguistics. Jakobson, in turn, sharing many of the ideas of Eurasianism, but not participating in it as an organized socio-political movement, exerted decisive influence on the methodology of Claude Lévi-Strauss and on the appearance of structural anthropology (as the French school of Ethnosociology).

The two sides of Trubetskoy's work — Eurasianism and structural linguistics — are rarely considered together (some know Trubetskoy as a Eurasianist, philosopher, ideologist, and social actor, others as an outstanding scientist, a philologist and linguist), but, in fact, both are consequences of his total worldview. Trubetskoy thought of culture, civilization, and the ethnos, on one hand, and language, on the other, as a structure, predetermining the semantic load of all derivative forms. Language

---

48   Trubetskoy, N.N. 'Obshcheyevraziyskiy natsionalizm / *Foundations of Eurasianism.* Moscow: Arktogeia-Center, 2002, pp. 200–207.

carries in itself the meaning of statements. The ethnos carries in itself the meaning of society, its phenomena, institutes, and processes.

It is possible to consider Eurasianism narrowly or broadly. If narrowly, then we are talking about a political trend in the Russian white emigration of the first half of the 20th century, which reached its apogee towards the end of the 1920s, fell into decline in the 1930s (due to the effect of inner contradictions), and disappeared in the 1940s. But Eurasianism can also be understood broadly, as a general world-view and scientific-paradigmatic device for understanding the world as a cultural and ethnic plurality, not having a single universal measure, where the measure of things in each concrete case is not the individual, nor the class, nor the race, but culture and ethnos. In the broad understanding of Eurasianism, structural linguistics is but one of numerous possibilities of the application of the Eurasian method to the scientific sphere. In this broad understanding, Ethnosociology can also be thought of as a scientific orientation in the framework of the Eurasian paradigm of the humanities.

On the Threshold of Russian [Rossiiskii] Ethnosociology

Summarizing our survey, we can trace which elements 20th century Russian Ethnosociology and Ethnology took shape from.

At its basis lies the humanistic paradigm, *asserting the equality and equal worth of ethnoses and cultures*. It is shared by the most diverse ideological orientations: conservative (Slavophiles), revolutionary (Narodniks), and conservative-revolutionary (Eurasianists).

In its fundamental characteristics, this paradigm is identical with the paradigm that lies at the basis of Ethnosociology, as it is broadly understood in the West (including Ethnosociology itself, Cultural Anthropology, Social Anthropology, Structural Anthropology, etc.). Boas, Thurnwald, Malinowski, Mauss, and Lévi-Strauss proceeded from precisely that same idea of the equality and plurality of cultures and the rejection of racism in all its forms (including the evolutionary or technological racism of the early anthropologists). This same principle was insisted upon, in one way or another, by the first Slavophiles (in the particular case of Russian culture), Danilevsky and Leontiev, the Russian narodniks, and, finally, in the most conceptualized and general form, the Eurasianists. It is precisely on the basis of this shared paradigm that we should look for the deep connections of these traditions, which have produced numerous orientations, schools, theories, and concepts.

Through the application of the humanistic paradigm of the "equality of cultures," we should consider and classify the abundant and partially systematized ethnographic material collected by a few generations of Russian researchers on both Slavic ethnic groups (Great Russians, Little Russians, White Russians, as well as the ancient Slavic tribes of Eastern Europe) and other ethnoses of Russia. But in the course of the systematization of this sea of ethnographic data we should carefully check the quality of all the systematizations and taxonomies we already have. The scientific activist, Boas, in the USA, incidentally, started such an undertaking. He was troubled by the fact that the exhibitions of the Smithsonian ethnographic museum were arranged according to the logic of the vulgar evolutionary approach, which gave visitors a false impression of the meaning, significance, and content of the exhibited artifacts. In Ethnography — as in other humanistic and historical sciences — the position of the observer (gatherer, systematiser, organizer of museum exhibits, etc.) plays a decisive role. If the ethnographer does not at all understand the significance of some artifact or phenomenon, it is unlikely that he will mention it in his statements or display it in the exhibition. The same principle concerns the situation when he understands something incorrectly. But from the perspective of Ethnosociology, anyone who is guided by evolutionary theories or projects stereotypes of his culture on the culture he is studying probably misunderstands everything about it.

Consequently, the mass of ethnographic data, collected over more than two centuries in Russia, demands, in the framework of Ethnosociology, fundamental reconsideration, reclassification, and critical re-examination, not on the basis of ideological dogmas, but proceeding from recognition for each ethnos, simple or complex, large or small, of its fundamental right to possess its own, unique cultural sense and structure, and to follow its own path.

It is precisely such an approach, in fact, which became the beginning of Russian Ethnosociology, which is becoming a scientific discipline only now. At the same time, we see the first serious steps of this formation in Ethnology and the structuralist studies that were developed on the periphery of Soviet society, at the center of the scientific sphere of which there dogmatically dominated the evolutionary (orthogenetic), class, and progressivist approach, incompatible with the humanistic paradigm of the equality of cultures and, accordingly, excluding the very possibility of Ethnosociology as a science.

SECTION TWO

The Creation in Russia of Systematized Ethnology as a Science

The Role of Sergei Mikhailovich Shirokogoroff in the Creation of Ethnology

The elaboration of the first theoretical positions of ethnology as an independent science, which can be considered the beginning of Ethnosociology proper, was the work of the outstanding Russian scientist, sociologist, ethnographer, and ethnologist Sergei Mikhailovich Shirokogoroff (1887–1939).[49] Shirokogoroff was the first to introduce into scientific use the concept of the "ethnos," which was adopted both in Russian-speaking science and in the West. It is significant that the eminent German ethnosociologist Wilhelm Emil Mühlmann denoted Shirokogoroff, whom he considered his teacher and inspiration, as the

---

49 Ob'yektivnyy i vzveshennyy obzornyy material o biografii i ideyakh S.M. Shirokogorova. Revunenkova, E.V., Reshetov, A.M. Shirokogoroff, S.M. / Etnograficheskoye obozreniye, No. 3. 2003, pp. 100–119.

founder of "Ethnosociology."[50] Shirokogoroff's ideas also exerted a decisive influence on another eminent ethnologist, Lev Nikolaevich Gumilev, and although Gumilev formally assessed Shirokogoroff critically, his basic approaches to the ethnos as a system (and indeed the very concept of the "ethnos") were something he borrowed principally from Shirokogoroff.[51]

Shirokogoroff received an education in philology at the Sorbonne in France. When he returned to Russia, he set off on an ethnographic expedition to the Far East to study one of the oldest ethnoses of Eurasia, the Tungus (Evenki). In 1922, he was sent on a scientific mission to China, from which he never returned, because of the establishment of Soviet rule in the Far East. From then on, he lived in China until he died, continuing to engage in scientific activity and publishing his works in foreign languages, including Chinese.

In China, he researched local ethnic groups and produced detailed, documented scientific studies about them.

Throughout his entire life, Shirokogoroff was helped by his wife Elizabeth Nikolaevna, who shared her husband's scientific interests and actively helped him establish contacts with the ethnic groups he was researching.

The Introduction of the Concept of the "Ethnos" and Ethnology as a Science

Shirokogoroff's principal accomplishment was the introduction of the concept of the "ethnos" as a separate sociological and scientific category, on which he offered to build, as a broad scientific program, a new discipline, "Ethnology." We have repeatedly mentioned Shirokogoroff's definition of the ethnos, but will recall it once more: "The ethnos is a group of people who speak one language, acknowledge a common origin, and

---

50   Johansen, U. Vliyaniye Sergeya Mikhaylovicha Shirokogorova na nemetskuyu etnologiyu / Etnograficheskoye obozreniye, No. 1. 2002, pp. 139–143.

51   Gumilev, L.N. *Ethnogenesis and the Biopsphere*. Moscow: Progress Publishing, 1990, pp. 69–71.

possess a complex of customs and ways of life preserved and sanctioned by traditions and differing from the customs of other groups."[52]

It is important that Shirokogoroff isolated another fundamental marker of the ethnos: *endogamy*, i.e., the legitimate possibility of entering into a marriage within the group. We saw with Lévi-Strauss the great significance of the principle of inter-lineage relations for the structure of society.

Contained within the principle of endogamy is the fact that the ethnos consists as a minimum of two exogamous groups (lineages), which distinguishes it qualitatively from a broadened notion of lineage.

Shirokogoroff, on his own account, came across the idea of the "ethnos" in 1912, after observing in his field studies among the diverse tribes of the Far East (Tungus, Manchurian, Oroqen, Ulch, Nivkh, etc.) that all the societies he was encountering, whatever their cultural or linguistic differences, possessed a number of stable and constantly recurring markers, met with in any society, whether archaic or modern. Thus, the idea of the "ethnos" emerged as a scientific concept, generalizing certain anthropological, cultural, and social features.

Social Organization

Vitally important in considering the problem of the ethnos is Shirokogoroff's understanding of "*social organization*," which is a "complex of ethnographic elements, regulating the functioning of society as a constant conglomerate of people who form, in turn, a complex with a certain inner equilibrium, giving the ethnic unit a chance to reproduce itself and preserve its economic system, material culture, and mental and psychical activity, i.e., to ensure the continuity of existence of the ethnic unit in its integrity."[53]

---

52 Shirokogoroff, S.M. Etnos: Issledovaniye osnovnykh printsipov izmeneniya etnicheskikh i etnograficheskikh yavleniy. Moscow: Kafedra sotsiologii mezhdunarodnykh otnosheniy sotsiologicheskogo fakul'teta MGU, 2010, p. 16.

53 Shirokogoroff, S.M. *Social Organization of Northern Tungus with Introductory Chapters concerning Geographical Distribution and History of these Groups.* Shanghai, 1929, p. 5.

This definition forms the core of Ethnosociology. Most important in it is the definition of society ("social organization") through the ethnos. At the same time, Shirokogoroff purposely speaks not of "*ethnic*" but of "*social*" organization and describes it in terms of "ethnographic elements," "ethnic units," etc. Society, according to Shirokogoroff, is in the first place the ethnos. We called this kind of identification the "koineme." Essentially, this is nothing other than the development of Shirokogoroff's thoughts and his understanding of "social organization." In the context of Cultural Anthropology, an analogous function is assigned to the concept of "culture," and in Structural Anthropology, to "structure."

Social organization (koineme) is distinguished by a number of characteristics.

It consists of a "complex of ethnographic elements" (Complex-1); which regulate "the functioning of society"; society is defined as a "constant conglomerate of people," which, in its turn, forms a (secondary) complex (Complex-2), the main purpose of which is to preserve "inner equilibrium," which, in its turn, gives the "ethnic unit" (ethnos, society) the possibility to:

- Reproduce itself;

- Preserve (ensure continuity and integrity) itself as:
  — an economic system;
  — a material culture;
  — mental and psychic activity.

We can present this intricate definitional construction in the following way:

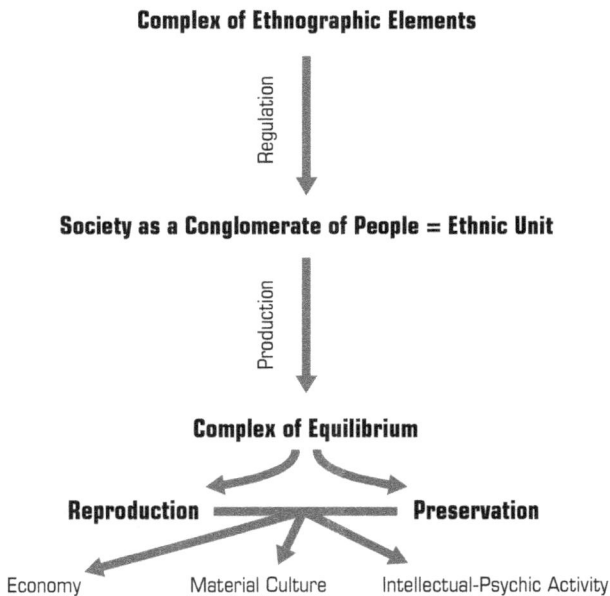

Complex of Ethnographic Elements

Regulation

Society as a Conglomerate of People = Ethnic Unit

Production

Complex of Equilibrium

Reproduction **Preservation**

Economy Material Culture Intellectual-Psychic Activity

Figure 12. Society according to Shirokogoroff.

An analysis of this figure shows that the "ethnographic complex" is an instance preceding all subsequent points and stages and, consequently, comprising the essence of the ethnos. This first complex is the ethnos in its fundamental sense. It precedes a concrete "conglomerate of people" on principle and logically it exists "before" it. We can call this "ethnographic complex" an ethnostatic structure, the ethnos as a constant and invariable (regulating) phenomenon. Both natural and cultural factors are included in this ethnographic complex as a kind of inseparable whole.

Society as a "conglomerate of people" (i.e., a group of people living at a certain time and in a certain space) is located under the determining, regulating influence of the "ethnographic complex." This influence makes a "conglomerate of people" (society) an ethnos. The result of this influence (the content of which is strictly invariable) is the production of a second complex (the complex of equilibrium). In a certain sense, this complex is composed of the reactions of a "conglomerate of people" on its ethnicity. In a normative (normal) case this reaction consists in the direct reconstitution of equilibrium and its instruments, which in their turn will act as an "ethnographic complex" (Complex-1) for the next (generational and historical) conglomerate of people.

Social organization can be considered in different situations. When the ethnos is in a stable and balanced state, Complex-2 coincides with Complex-1 almost entirely. The principles and guidelines accepted in accordance with tradition and the decisions and actions built on their foundations coincide completely and are in a state of strict harmony. People and groups act as the ethnic culture ("ethnographic complex") demands and transmit to the next generation — not only through education or instruction, but through a system of small and great actions, decisions, and deeds — that same ethnic culture. In this case, the gap between Complex-1 and Complex-2 is minimal. The statics of the "ethnographic complex" correspond with consistency to the second complex of equilibrium, which effectively preserves and recreates the main moments of society, ensuring continuity.

But in certain circumstances this process can be *disrupted*. And then the secondary complex (of equilibrium) can *differ* from the first (ethnographic) complex with corresponding changes in the model of equilibrium and transformations of traditions and customs. This is the structural explanation of social and historical changes occurring in ethnoses and consequently in societies.

Later we shall show how this model works and its significance for the study of the transformations of ethnoses and others derivative types of society.

Theory of the Equilibrium of Cultures — The Coefficient of Ethnic Equilibrium

Shirokogoroff formulated the important *law of the equilibrium of cultures*. The main idea consists in observing, on the basis of the field study of ethnoses, the connection between three factors:

1. The quantity of members of an ethnic unit.

2. The territory it inhabits.

3. The level of cultural and technological development.

Shirokogoroff proposed the following formula for the study of these regularities:

$$q/ST=\omega$$

In this formula, q is the quantity of the population of the ethnic group, S is the relative level of culture (according to complexity and technological development), T is the area of territory the ethnos inhabits, and ω is a constant, which Shirokogoroff called the *"coefficient of ethnic equilibrium."*[54]

On the left-hand side of this equation are variables that can take on different values. If we assume that the quantitative composition of the ethnos is constant (the ethnos is not dying out), then the two remaining variables are in an inverse relationship to one another: a decrease in the ethnic territories implies (provokes, demands) an increase in the level of culturo-technological development; expansion in settlement space can lead to a decrease in the culturo-technological level. The actions of this regularity are easy to trace in the examples of urban and rural spaces.

If we assume that the settlement space of the ethnos is fixed by external conditions (geographic, political, etc.), then increase in population is directly proportional to growth in culturo-technological level. To provide for the greater number of people on the same resource base, it is necessary to improve techniques and learn to extract more necessary products with fewer expenditures from the same natural environment.

And, finally, in the case of the maintenance of a constant cultural level, population growth is directly proportional to territorial increase.

Shirokogoroff considers this law universal. In fact, it is entirely applicable when dealing with the ethnos in its pure form, but not with its

---

54 Ibid.

derivatives (the narod, nation, civil society, etc.). It describes entirely adequately the main regularities in changes of the life of an ethnos.

Applying the law to concrete cases, Shirokogoroff notes that, notwithstanding the opinions of evolutionists, cultural level is reversible and is liable to both growth and decline. He adduces as evidence the example of the Tungusic tribes, who in the era of compact settlement in Manchuria possessed iron and copper processing and also the rudiments of the cultivation of cattle and agriculture, and subsequently, being pushed away into the northern Taiga zones, finding themselves in big, open spaces, lost these skills and transitioned to the economic techniques of hunters and gatherers. Thus, the formula of ethnic equilibrium is an obvious confirmation of the more general law the reversibility of social development.

The Ethnos and Cycles

One variant of the general principle of reversibility in Ethnosociology is the idea of the cyclical development of ethnoses. It was formulated by Shirokogoroff, who interpreted the ethnos as a living organism. And as a living organism, the ethnos passes through periods of growth, flourishing, and decline. The different phases depend on many factors, both internal and external, but the simple observation of ethnic processes shows that we can identify fundamentally different conditions in the ethnos, correlating with some degree of "life-forces." This is most often visible in a quantitative indicator: growth in the number of the ethnos' members. In agreement with the law of ethnic equilibrium, this process should automatically result in either increase of the controlled territories or increase in the culturo-technological level. In this way, the formula of ethnic equilibrium acquires an additional dimension. The ethnos' quantity depends on the qualitative parameter "*life-force*." An increase of territories or burst of cultural innovation (if increase of territories is for some reason difficult or impossible) can occur only if the life-forces are present and growing. Then the quantitative increase of the ethnos occurs, together with the processes connected with such growth. At the same time, population growth can be accompanied by either spatial or cultural growth (or by both, but in lesser proportions, if there is the possibility for expansion in both spheres).

The ethnos' decline is expressed in the reduction of the population, but it can also be seen in the decline of the culturo-technical level, if the quantity of the population remains fixed.

The cyclical character of the life of the ethnos was one of the crucial points of Shirokogoroff's Ethnosociology and would subsequently become the main foundation for Gumilev's theory of ethnogenesis.

Ethnoses and Their Environment

Shirokogoroff distinguished three environments in which an ethnos lives. Each of these environments exerts tremendous influence on it. The ethnos works out its strategies, its being, on the assimilation of some of the elements of these environments, rejection of others, and a certain kind of response still to others, and so on.

The initial environment is the natural environment.[55] It is embodied in the variable "T" in the formula of ethnic equilibrium and can be synthesized in the notion of qualitative space.[56] Interaction with the environment — with climate, geography, flora, and fauna — comprises a very important dimension of ethnic being and forms the content of the "ethnographic complex."

The second environment consists of social institutions, culture, technology, and economic mechanisms and is in harmony with the first environment.[57] The structural unity and harmony of the first and second environments, the ecological orientation of culture, is the characteristic distinction of ethnic societies in their most archaic and simplest state. In the formula of ethnic equilibrium, the second environment is the variable "S."

---

55 Shirokogoroff, S.M. Etnos: Issledovaniye osnovnykh printsipov izmeneniya et-nicheskikh i etnograficheskikh yavleniy. p. 47.

56 Dugin, A.G. *Sociology of the Imagination*, pp. 169–186.

57 Shirokogoroff, S.M Etnos: Issledovaniye osnovnykh printsipov izmeneniya et-nicheskikh i etnograficheskikh yavleniy, p. 61.

The third environment is the interethnic environment, i.e., the field in which interactions among ethnoses occurs.[58] The differences among ethnic cultures ("ethnographic complex") give rise to a gap, a differential in this ethnic environment, which is the reason for many social phenomena.

Types of Interethnic Interaction

Shirokogoroff proposed considering three types of ethnic interaction:

Commensalism: from the French *commensal*, "table companion" — a form of symbiosis (cohabitation) of two ethnoses, which interact with one another, where this interaction and exchange are not fundamental for either and where no real harm will be done to either if interaction ceases;

Cooperation: when each of two ethnoses is vitally interested in the other, and both will suffer greatly in the case of a break in ties;

Parasitism: when one ethnos lives at the expense of another; and if their alliance is broken up, the parasite will die, while the host will regain health.

Shirokogoroff describes Commensalism in the following way: he writes,

> The weakest connection between two ethnoses is Commensalism, i.e., when both live on one territory, do not bother each other, and are on the whole good for one another, and when the absence of one does not at all adversely affect the successful life of the other. Thus, for instance, it is entirely possible that a farmer living in a local area without wild animals exists together with a hunter, who nourishes himself with the animals he hunts. Although each of the commensalists can be independent of the other, they can also see a mutual benefit: the hunter can be supplied with the farming products in the case of a temporary bout of hunger, and the farmer can have some of the products of hunting — meat, fur, skin, etc. The Russian settlers of Siberia and the local aboriginals provide an example of such relations, as do the ethnoses of South America, getting along with one another on the same territory: the farmers and hunters of Brazil.[59]

---

58   Ibid. p. 76.

59   Shirokogoroff, S.M. Etnos: Issledovaniye osnovnykh printsipov izmeneniya etnicheskikh i etnograficheskikh yavleniy, p. 95.

Of the other forms of interethnic ties, Shirokogoroff writes as follows:

> Cooperation is a form of relation of two ethnoses in which one cannot live without the other, and both are equally interested in each other's existence. Such relations exist, for instance, among the Indian castes or among conquerors of a noble or chivalric estate (for instance, the Germans) and local populations (Gauls, Slavs). In cases of such cooperation among ethnoses, they select the form of social organization which is equally suitable for both sides. Depending on ethnic stability, the biological or cultural absorption of one ethnos by another can also occur, while the social organization continues to exist. We can see this, for instance, in certain Indian castes and elsewhere; but with transition to another form of social organization through mixing or absorption, the full loss of ethnic peculiarity may occur.[60]

> Ethnic relations can also take a third form of interethnic relations on one territory: parasitism. In this case, one side is the passive element and the other gains as a result. Moreover, the parasitized ethnos can without loss to itself and even with great gain free itself from the parasitizing ethnos, which will then be at risk of dying out completely.[61]

Shirokogoroff emphasizes that all of these kinds of relations can change dynamically in the process of the development of interethnic ties; commensalism can become cooperation, cooperation parasitism, etc.

Ethnoses and War

Another form of ethnic interaction, according to Shirokogoroff, is *war*. This is an extreme but constant form of interaction relations. The ascending ethnos raises under itself a stable or falling ethnos. Since ethnoses on the whole always pulse dynamically, mix in space, alter, transform, and adapt cultural codes, master different types of economic management, acquire new technological skills and lose former ones, war very often flares up among them, alongside the other three types of coexistence.

---

60 Ibid.

61 Ibid. p. 96.

When describing war as an ethnic process, Shirokogoroff (poorly, in our opinion) resorts to the concept of the "biological" in the spirit of "Social Darwinism," even though the entire structure of his ethnology corresponds on the whole much more with a sociological approach. Shirokogoroff writes: "War is the natural aspiration of a (mentally) increasing ethnos, which manifests in this way its biological might. *War is a purely biological function of the ethnos, taking diverse ideological forms, depending on the general cultural condition [of the ethnos].* Finally, since territory has its absolute limit, as does population density (…) *the limitless growth of culture is possible only at the expense of territory,* and, hence, the growth of culture beyond the limits where absolute population density and the use of the entire territory have been reached must inevitably lead humanity to death through the loss of territory and likely its occupation by other animal species."[62]

The Psychomental Complex and Shamanism

We should pay special attention to Shirokogoroff's late research in the sphere of what he called the *"psychomental"* complex, the steady supra-individual structure comprising the paradigm of ethnic being in its spiritual and intellectual dimensions.[63] "Psychomental complex" recalls Frobenius' *"paideuma"* or Joubert and Mauss' "categories of the imagination." We can also compare it to Jung's "collective unconscious," only with the difference that for Shirokogoroff this category has a unique configuration for each ethnos. In this sense, Shirokogoroff fits perfectly into the general program of Ethnosociology and Cultural Anthropology, which insists that it is unscientific and incorrect to evaluate one culture from the position of another culture. Thus, Shirokogoroff writes: "The application of terms from one cultural complex for the interpretation of another cultural complex

---

62   Ibid. p. 91.

63   Shirokogoroff S. M. *Psychomental Complex of the Tungus.* London: K. Paul, 1935.

does not always facilitate understanding of the actually existing functions of the latter."[64]

Shirokogoroff made his main theoretical generalizations concerning the "psychomental complex" as one of the major categories for the study of the ethnos in his last book, *The Psychomental Complex of the Tungus*. In it, he presents a monumental description of the ethnic world-picture of the Tungus, including a detailed exposition of their rites, myths, economic practices, productive technologies, and interactions with all three environments, natural, cultural, and interethnic.

He pays special attention to the phenomenon of shamanism as a central element of ethnic existence. It was Shirokogoroff who drew the attention of ethnologists and anthropologists to the fundamental social function of the shaman in archaic societies, in which the shaman fulfills key vital operations necessary for the maintenance of ethnic existence and transmission of the "ethnographic complex." Shirokogoroff's book was received in Europe as a real breakthrough. Mühlmann, for instance, wrote about it as follows: "As soon as the book *The Psychomental Complex of the Tungus* was released in 1935, it became clear to me that by this work Shirokogoroff had shattered the limits of Ethnography (in the previous understanding of this word) and placed himself among the leading theoreticians of Ethnology."[65] In it, Shirokogoroff asserts in particular that the shaman's trance cannot be considered a psychic illness, first because in the culture of the Tungus and other archaic tribes there is no strict equivalent to the concept of "psychic illness." Second, the shaman is characterized by the fact that he controls himself, his actions and his state even in the trance condition; i.e., in being otherwise than usual, his psychic condition composes a kind of norm. Third, among the representatives of archaic narods, one does meet with phenomena that indeed call to mind the psychic disturbances of people of complex societies, but the latter sort of people very rarely become shamans.

64 Ibid. p. 268.

65 Mühlmann, W., Shirokogoroff S. M. Nekrolog (s prilozheniyem pisem, fotografii i bibliografii) / Etnograficheskoye obozreniye, No. 1, 2002, p. 146.

Following Shirokogoroff and relying in many ways on his studies of shamanism among the narods of Siberia and the Far East, the historian of religion, Mircea Eliade wrote his classical work *Shamanism: The Archaic Practices of Ecstasy*.[66]

Shirokogoroff's Formulation of the Main Points of the Study of Ethnoses

Let us cite the end of Shirokogoroff's programmatic book, where he laid out the principles of Ethnology systematically for the first time.[67] "The development of the ethnos does not take place through the complication of each phenomenon, but through the adjustment of the whole complex of phenomena — ethnographic, psychic (physiological), etc., with the aim of preserving the ethnos; as a result, alongside the development (complication) of certain phenomena a reduction can also occur."[68] This thesis is extremely important, since it clearly formulates *the law of social reversibility*, on which Ethnosociology is built.

"Ethnoses adapt to the environment in two ways: first, by changing their needs or their organs and peculiar characteristics; second, by changing the environment itself."[69] Here he anticipates the concepts of anthropologists and sociologists (Leroi Gourhan in particular) about the dual code of social relations toward the surrounding space and about the "production of space" (Lefebvre's theory).[70]

"The ethnos' movement during settlement and its being always flow along the path of least resistance. Moreover, one of the forces is the ethnos itself, which in deciding (and this is each time a fact it is aware of in part or in whole) is connected with external conditions (the environment), the

---

66   Eliade, M. *Shamanism: Archaic Techniques of Ecstasy*. Princeton, NJ: Princeton University Press, 1972.

67   Shirokogoroff, S.M. *Etnos: Issledovaniye osnovnykh printsipov izmeneniya etnicheskikh i etnograficheskikh yavleniy*.

68   Ibid. p. 117.

69   Ibid. p. 118.

70   Lefebvre, H. *La production de l'espace*. Paris: Anthropos, 2000.

sum of knowledge (culture) and character (biological might)."[71] Here it is necessary to pay attention to the fact that the initiative in the historical decision is ascribed precisely to the ethnos, which contrasts with the class-based or technological approaches of other scientific paradigms.

"The ethnos' awareness of its relations to the environment, together with its awareness of the process of movement in settlement and existence, comprises the content of the spiritual culture of the ethnos, whose development depends above all on the quantity of material received for observation, which in its turn is conditioned upon the degree of complexity of relations and the intensity of the process of movement."[72] This point suggests that we consider the ethnos as a mobile dynamic unit, forming its "ethnographic complex" historically in the process of movement.

Later, Shirokogoroff makes a futurological prediction on the basis of the ethnographic method:

"Man's future, to the extent that it can be seen in the movements of ethnoses, has a certain limit, with approximation towards which either the further development (complication) of culture must cease, or a reduction of territories must occur, which is equivalent in either case to the death of ethnoses, and thereby also the contemporary species of man. By analogy with the other animal species, we can surmise that: (1) the contemporary species of man must have a lesser duration of existence than other species and (2) its end must come as a result of the impossibility of adapting to conditions of the primary environment, which have a tendency to change; (3) the immediate expression of the end of man will likely be manifest in the hypertrophy of his cultural and intellectual development, suppressing the natural performance of his biological functions; (4) the form in which this suppression will take place, one might think, will be man's interference in the regulation of his self-reproduction, i.e., in the conception and birth of progeny. Moreover, physical adaptation to changing organs apparently

---

71 Shirokogoroff, S.M. Etnos: Issledovaniye osnovnykh printsipov izmeneniya etnicheskikh i etnograficheskikh yavleniy, p. 119.

72 Ibid. p. 120.

occurs slower than changes in the organs themselves, and humanity will not have time to adapt physically."[73]

This fragment from 1925 is striking in its relevance. The first point in this prognosis is established by analogy with biological species, which seems doubtful. But then the second point reproduces exactly the position of contemporary ecological movements and groups, which, like Shirokogoroff almost a hundred years ago, predict humanity's death from ecological catastrophes as a result of the inability to adapt to the primary environment. The third point is a prediction about the coming of the information society, in which digital technologies and virtual networks will gradually displace man's organic manifestations, replacing them with simulacra. The figure of the cyborg, depicted in certain postmodern manifestos (in particular, Donna Haraway's) is a stark example of the fact that this prognosis is coming true before our eyes. And finally, the fourth point realistically describes both the "birth control" introduced in China and the progress of genetic engineering.

Shirokogoroff's Ethnology and Ethnosociology

Most of the main points of Shirokogoroff's theory lie at the basis of Ethnosociology as a discipline, which stems directly from Ethnology itself. However, there are a few points that should be clarified.

1. Shirokogoroff considers man a biosocial entity, distinguishing in him natural and cultural elements in the spirit of classical Western dualism, introduced by Descartes, where everything is based on the dichotomy "subject-object." This is the source of the numerous points in Shirokogoroff that can be interpreted biologically. These points do not touch and all the more so do not comprise the essence of his teaching. As we saw, in his definition of the ethnos he does not speak of a common origin, but of "*belief* in a common origin," i.e., of a social or symbolic relation. Nevertheless, the appeal to Biology or Zoology is inadmissible

---

73   Ibid. pp. 120–1.

for Ethnosociology, and those statements or theoretical constructs that can be interpreted in this light should be corrected, interpreted more adequately, or (if they do not admit of either interpretation or correction) rejected. It is precisely here, where the border between ethnology and Ethnosociology lies: Ethnosociology considers man from an anthropological coordinate system and society from a social one. Biology is not drawn in as an independent authority for the explanation of human, cultural, and social phenomena, and the comparison of human and animal communities can only be a metaphor.

2. Shirokogoroff does not recognize a specific conceptual significance behind the term "narod" ("laos"), considering it superfluous. In this way, he misses a very important moment in Ethnosociology: the transition from ethnic society to its derivatives, with the corresponding transformations of social structures. As a result, Shirokogoroff himself often uses the term "ethnos" where he can only be talking about the narod, nation, or even civil society. "Ethnos" and "nation" are often synonyms for him. In consequence, Shirokogoroff applies the method of "Primordialism" where it is not appropriate or only partially appropriate. This terminological and methodological point should be taken into account when considering his works. And here, a correction is called for. In some cases, what he calls the "ethnos" should be referring to the "narod," and sometimes even to the "nation." This is another major difference between Ethnology and Ethnosociology.

3. Shirokogoroff interprets some ethnic phenomena materially, supposing that the multitude of processes in the ethnos can be explained by changes in the surrounding environment as an entirely independent natural phenomenon. Moreover, it is implied that man's prime motivating factor is the search for resources for material survival. Here we again encounter the notion of the

object and objective biological needs as an independent factor influencing the ethnos.

Ethnosociology sets aside this "axiom" of the materialistic worldview, dominating science in the 19th century, as a mere hypothesis, the positive content of which has almost been exhausted. If we are ready to recognize the competence of archaic society and its "ethnographic complex" as equal to others and as an authentic sociological paradigm, then we must admit that the ethnic unit (simple society) knows neither object, nor material, nor material dependence at all, and even the approximate equivalents to these notions are absent from the languages and cultures of ethnoses. If we think that the reason for the migration of some ethnos, for instance, is the desertification of earlier fertile pastures, and we reject the explanation of these tribes themselves (for instance, that an evil spirit, Erlik, was incensed at them for their sacrifices to the heavenly god Tengri) as irrelevant nonsense, we behave no better than colonizers, racists, and imperialists, convinced in our infinite superiority over "barbarians" and "savages." Instead of explaining to the ethnoses he studies who Aristotle and Darwin were, the Ethnosociologist should first learn who Erlik is. Only complete and equitable reciprocity can be the basis for a full-fledged dialogue of cultures, which is the scientific field of Ethnosociology.

Lev Gumilev: A New Stage of Ethnology

The famous Russian history Lev Nikolaevich Gumilev introduced into the development of Ethnology, designated and constituted by Shirokogoroff, numerous entirely new points, elaborated in his own original teaching. Today there are arguments over the extent to which Gumilev followed Shirokogoroff's ideas and approaches and the extent to which he rejected and criticized them. It is not disputed that Gumilev, working in the USSR, knew Shirokogoroff's books, which were inaccessible to the majority of Soviet historians and were practically never mentioned or taken into account. Gumilev not only mentioned Shirokogoroff; an entire series of the most important points of his own doctrine, beginning with the basic term "ethnos," the theory of ethnic cycles, and the idea of the symbiosis of the ethnos with the surrounding environment and ending with his concepts of interethnic processes, is the development or refinement of the Ethnological principles announced by precisely Shirokogoroff, both in the context of Russian-language research and on a global scale. We saw that one of the main theoreticians of the German school of Ethnosociology, in turn, called Shirokogoroff his inspiration and teacher.

Gumilev's theories are a development of Shirkogoroff's ideas, although Gumilev received many aspects critically and tried to overcome and excel them.

We can say that Gumilev's theory is a *superstructure* over Shirokogoroff's teaching. At the same time, we must also take into account the influence on Gumilev of the Eurasian school, which was also entirely closed and inaccessible to the remainder of Soviet scholars.

Gumilev's Definitions of the Ethnos and their Ambiguity

Lev Gumilev's major work is *Ethnogenesis and the Biosphere of the Earth*.[74] In it, Gumilev sets out his notion of the emergence, establishment, and degradation of ethnoses. In this sense, it develops a scientific model that Gumilev himself considered the next stage of the development of ethnology.

We must note at once that the definition Gumilev gave of the ethnos is doubtful and contradictory and falls short of the clarity of Shirokogoroff's formula. In some places, Gumilev says that "the ethnos is not a social phenomenon, because it can exist in several formations."[75] The idea itself is correct, since it shows that the ethnic dimension is present not only in simple societies, but also in complex ones. But if we accept it too literally and deny that the ethnos is one of the forms of society, we will lose scientific precision and will come to a contradiction. True, Gumilev writes

74 Gumilev, L.N. *Ethnogenesis and the Biosphere*. Moscow: Progress Publishers, 1990.

75 Ibid. p. 35.

elsewhere of the ethnos as a "form of collective being, characteristic only of man."[76] This is entirely correct: the form of collective being *is* society and a social phenomenon.

In another place Gumilev defines the ethnos as "a stable and naturally formed collective of people, opposing itself to all such analogous collectives and distinguished by its peculiar stereotypical behavior, which changes regularly in historical time."[77] Here we see the clear influence of Sumner ("we-group," "they-group"), reference to "naturalness" (the primordialist approach), and the regularity (i.e., ordered quality) of historical dimensions (this last point comprises the specific character of the Gumilevian approach).

At the same time, Gumilev is clearly inclined to consider man a biological species. Thus, he asserts that man "as a large predator ... is subject to natural evolution."[78] Gumilev considers many ethnic processes through the prism of evolution and biological materialism. From the point of view of Ethnosociology, this detracts somewhat from the significance of Gumilev's theories, in which it is easy to recognize the evolutionary and biosocial approach, characteristic of the theories of the 19th century which were overcome in German Ethnosociology, Boas' school of Cultural Anthropology, the Social Anthropology of Malinowski and Radcliffe-Brown, and the French Sociology of Mauss and Lévi-Strauss. However, we should not be too strict towards such formulations. Gumilev wrote his scientific works in the Soviet era, when materialistic and evolutionary dogma dominated in science, and he was obliged to take them into account, though all the points of his theory were directed in a completely different direction. So Gumilev's theory of ethnogenesis should be considered in its historical context, and we should try to distinguish in it the most valuable and significant intuitions and insights, setting aside certain definitions, formulations, and methods, which can seem doubtful or opposed to Ethnosociology's main positions. It is much more important to

---

76   Ibid. p. 104.

77   Ibid. p. 135.

78   Ibid. p. 40.

include Gumilev in the Ethnosociological corpus on the basis of the fact that his theories make an authentic and substantial contribution, rather than to exclude him on the basis of some saying or other which does not fit into the Ethnosociological context.

Passionarity and its Variations

The main sense of Gumilev's theory of ethnogenesis in its broad outlines is as follows.

At the basis of all ethnic processes lies *"passionarity."* This is Gumilev's term, formed from the Latin *passio*, which means "passion" and also "affect," "suffering," etc. Gumilev himself underscores the first meaning. "Passionarity" is passion, fervor, abundance of inner energies, the presence of which exceeds the minimum that is necessary for man to support his existence in usual circumstances. Gumilev divides all people into three types: *passionate, harmonious personalities*, and *sub-passionate*, on the basis of which he explains the logic of the development of ethnic processes, which he generalizes under the category of *"ethnogenesis,"* i.e., the process of the emergence and disappearance of the ethnos.

"Passionate" according to Gumilev is one with increased passionarity, whose inner energy, whose "passion," is excessive in relation to the expenditures that are necessary for the collective's usual way of life. The hero, chief, pioneer, and preacher can all be passionate, but so too can the robber, thief, maniac, and destroyer. Passionarity is life energy, taken as a unit: it can be expended towards good, but also towards evil ends. At the same time, it is important that the passionate person is able to challenge death; he does not fear it, since his life energy is excessive, and he himself is ready to project it beyond earthly existence. As a result, the passionate person easily becomes a fanatic and goes first into the battle, not only not avoiding war and risk, but, on the contrary, searching them out, striving for them. According to Gumilev, the level of ethnogenesis depends on the percent of passionarity that accumulates in society.

The *harmonious* person also possesses passionarity, but in limited amount. He does not challenge death and he is not prepared to undertake feats, but he has enough energy to support some level of existence. A society in which this type prevails is in a steady condition. It doesn't develop, but it doesn't degenerate. It is stationary and static.

According to Gumilev, *sub-passionarity* is a deviant type possessing low passionarity, which is not enough for even the support of the usual life cycle. But this deficit of life energy pushes the sub-passionate towards those sources of energy that are excessive, i.e., towards passionate energies. The sub-passionate are often the "retinue" of the passionate, nourishing themselves on borrowed life energy. They increase in periods of the decline and decay of the ethnos. The sub-passionate are cowardly, but mean and resourceful. They are often able to establish control over the harmonic type "in the name of" the passionate. They are nourished on the energies of decay and death. Their prevalence in society is a sign of its collapse and passage out of history.

In his works, Gumilev discusses numerous historical examples of these types, of which every ethnos consists in various proportions.

The Phases of Ethnogenesis

Gumilev's theory of the cycles of ethnogenesis is a major contribution to Ethnosociology. Gumilev thought of the ethnos as a living entity, which runs the whole gamut of life cycles — from birth to maturity, old age, and death. This is an extremely important point, since it directly opposes progress and orthogenesis and introduces nuances into Gumilev's view of evolution. In the history of ethnoses, according to Gumilev, there is no evolution, but there are cycles. Ascent is replaced by decline, and these phases alternate.

At the same time, Gumilev thought that the ethnos' full life-cycle is complete after a period of about 1200 years, although many ethnoses (like people) die earlier to the effect of external factors. Ethnoses that die scatter into their raw constituents, which later become new elements in the process of ethnogenesis. This process continues without end.

Gumilev distinguished the following phases of ethnogenesis: *homeostasis, impetus, ascent, overheating, fissure* or the *inertial phase, obscuration*, and the *memorial stage*.

The process of ethnogenesis begins from a condition of *homeostasis*, i.e., of a complete and steady balance of the ethnos and its surrounding environment. In this condition, the harmonious type prevails, having just the necessary reserve of life forces required for the support of life in the given natural environment.

P_6 n+21 — Sacrifice

P_5 n+15 — Striving for ideal victory

P_4 n+10 — Striving for ideal success

Moment of passionary impetus

Striving for ideal knowledge and beauty

P_3 n+6

The search for success while risking life

P_2 n+3

Striving for accomplishment without risking life

P_1 n+1

The life of a typical inhabitant, adapted to the biocenose of the inhabitant

P_0 n

300   600   900   1200   Years

P_{-1} — Inability to regulate desires

P_{-2} — Inability to satisfy desires

PHASES OF ETHNOGNESIS

Ascent	Acmatic	Fissure	Inertia	Obscuration	Memorial
Concealed : Open					Regeneration : Relict

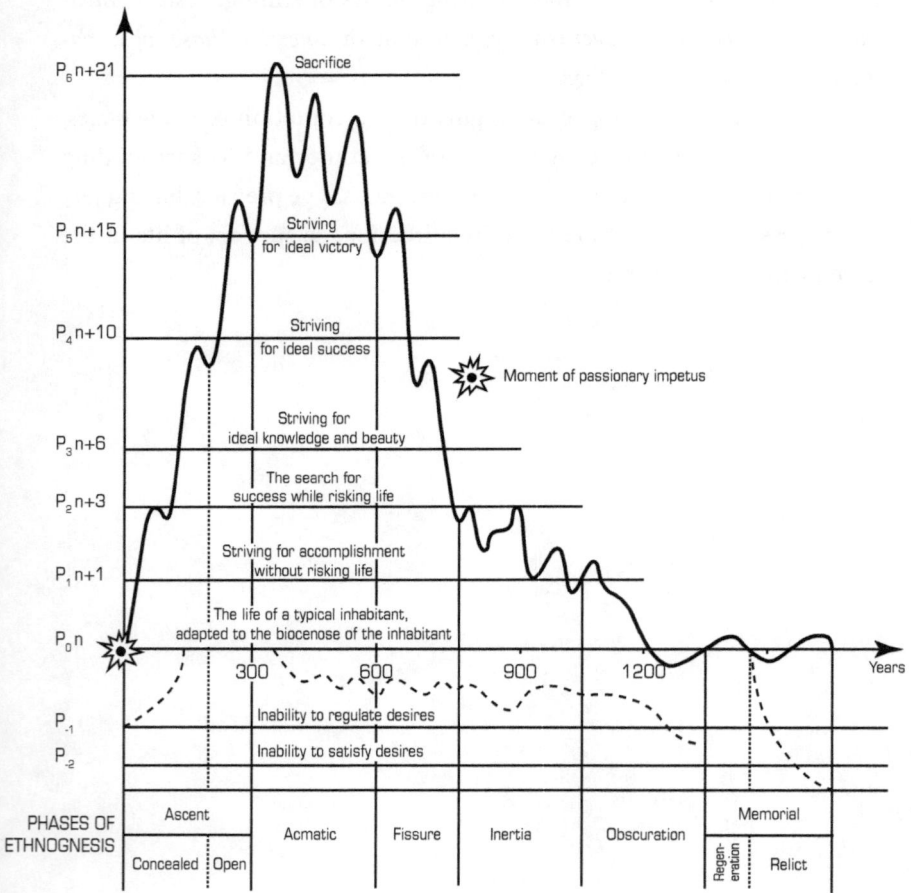

Figure 13. The phases of ethnogenesis, according to Gumilev.[79]

The *impulse* is provoked by a burst of passionarity in the ethnos. In this period, in the ethnic collective existing in equilibrium with the surrounding environment, the quantity of passionate people suddenly increases. Gumilev explained the cause of this mysterious phenomenon through rather extravagant hypotheses — in particular, changes in the cycles of solar activity. He was also amazed by the geometric orderliness of

---

79 Ibid. p. 339.

synchronous outbreaks of passionarity among different ethnoses at the same time and on the same spatial axis. The impulse gives a start to the process of ethnogenesis, as the ethnos comes to movement and the number of the passionate grows, and it is precisely them who impart to the ethnos its heroic impulse, urging towards armed conquests, migrations, and an intensive and active way of life.

In this way, the *overheating* phase is reached. It is the peak of ethnogenesis, when the ethnos reaches the heights of its historical actions — conquests, the acquisition of new territories, and the creation of empires.

At some point, *overheating* occurs, since the number of the passionate and the style of ethnic life dictated by them begins to undermine the stability of the social system. A *fissure* occurs and decline begins.

For a while, the ethnos still preserves its viability, which is realized in the more peaceful spheres of art, culture, and technical development. This is the *inertial phase*. In this period, the sub-passionate type begins to prevail in society, actively corrupting the ethnic system. Slippage downward during this phase leads to the decay of the ethnos and its return to the homeostatic phase. Gumilev called this *"obscuration."* At this point, memories of the ethnos' excellent achievements remain only on the cultural level. This is the *memorial phase*. In some cases, the ethnos disappears altogether, if instead of a new domination of the harmonious type a critical quantity of the sub-passionate is preserved in it from the previous phase.

The Scaling of the Ethnos

Gumilev proposed his own segmentation of the ethnos, an original taxonomy. The ethnos consists of: *consortium, convicinities*, the *subethnos*, the *ethnos*, and the *superethnos*.

"A consortium is a group of people united by one historical fate; it either disintegrates or becomes a convicinity."[80]

---

80 Ibid. p. 339.

"A convicinity is a group of people united by a similar way of life and family ties. Sometimes it becomes a subethnos. It is fixed not by history, but by ethnography."[81]

"The subethnos is an element of the structure of the ethnos, interacting with other elements. During simplification of the ethno-system in its final phase, the number of subethnoses is reduced to one, which becomes a relic."[82]

"The superethnos is a group of ethnoses that has arisen simultaneously in one region and that manifests itself in history as a mosaic totality."[83]

Gumilev thinks of these taxonomic units as incremental stages in the formation of an ethnos. At the basis lies the consortium, a simple group of people united in the name of the solution of some task. The majority of consortia disintegrate without a trace. Only some prove persistent and gradually transform into convicinities, in which the general group project is supplemented by family relations. Next, the convicinities can remain at one level, combining with other convicinities. In certain cases, however, they form into a more organic and steady community, called a subethnos. Subethnoses can unite among themselves without forming another ethnos. In this case, a few subethnoses, preserving their differences, form a kind of cohabitation that Gumilev called *symbiosis*.

From symbiosis, an ethnos is formed. Some ethnoses can live with one another in relative proximity and interdependence without becoming a superethnos. Gumilev calls this *xenia* (from the Greek word for "guest," "foreigner"). They remain "foreign" to one another.

In certain cases, a particular combination of some ethnoses is formed and united in a superethnos. If the combination is harmonious and the ethnoses are complementary (that is, mutually supplementary), then the superethnos can be stable; if the ethnoses are weakly complementary, then they form a "*chimera*," a political structure tending towards decay and degradation.

---

81   Ibid.

82   Ibid.

83   Ibid.

The Unknown History of Eurasia

Gumilev deserves great credit for his historical reconstruction of many
forgotten and poorly studied episodes in the history of the ethnoses of
Eurasia. If the ethnic world of the Mediterranean, Near East, Europe,
China, India, Iran, and other places was studied thoroughly, for a long time,
the narods of the Great Steppe remained on the periphery of ethnographic
and historical interest and were generally classified as barbarian societies
or nomadic empires. In his numerous works dedicated to these ethnoses,
Gumilev shows that in Eurasia we have a wealth of material concerning
the history of the most diverse ethnic groups, which displayed epochs of
greatness and decline, were fascinated by world religions and returned
to forms of archaic polytheism and shamanism, developed originally
political and social systems, produced varied forms of statehood, warred
against one another, suffered dynastic overthrows, exhibited wonders of
heroism and sacrifice as well as the abysses of decline and betrayal.[84] In
other words, the ethnic history of Eurasia, to which world history allots a
paragraph or two, is no less substantial, varied, and saturated with historical events, unexpected turns, take-offs, falls, dramas and worries than the
history of all other far better studied cultures and ethnoses of the world.

In his ethnographic and historical works Gumilev altered the image
of Eurasia, returning to humanity a massive and practically unknown
fragment of ethnic history. This is Gumilev's fundamental contribution
to ethnology.

At the same time, being a follower of the first Eurasianists, Lev Gumilev
consciously strove to demonstrate the prejudiced and selective approach of
Western historical science, which considers worthy of mention only those
events, social forms, and economic systems that resemble and agree with

---

84 Gumilev, L.N. Drevniye tyurki. Moscow: Ayris-press, 2008; Ibid., Tysyacheletiye
    vokrug Kaspiya, Moscow: AST/Kharvest, 2008; Ibid., Chernaya legenda. Moscow:
    Ayris-press, 2008; Ibid., Khunnu. Troyetsarstviye v Kitaye. Khunny v Kitaye.
    Moscow: Ayris-press, 2008; Ibid., Drevnyaya Rus' i Velikaya step'. Moscow: Mysl'.
    1989; Ibid., Poiski vymyshlennogo tsarstva: (Legenda o "Gosudarstve 'presvitera
    Ioanna'"). Moscow: Nauka, 1970.

the history of the West itself. Western historical science is "ethnocentric" and racist at its foundations, and the works of Lev Gumilev, introducing readers to a gigantic field of ethnological and cultural history absolutely unknown to the West, illustrate this fact. In this way, the official (Western) version of history is relativized, and undeservedly forgotten non-Western cultures and ethnoses receive the right to full-fledged historical being in the general context of the history of humanity.

Gumilev's Terminology and the Taxonomy of Ethnosociology: Corrections and Correspondences

Lev Gumilev's ethnology is diverse, multidimensional, and very important for Ethnosociology. At the same time, his methods and terms, the interpretation of certain concepts, and the systematizations and classifications are utterly original and differ substantially from the corresponding terms and classifications of Ethnosociology and Cultural Anthropology. As a result, in studying Gumilev's works there is a risk of confusing, rather than clarifying many ethnosociological models.

Therefore, it makes sense to establish certain connections and bring to light the differences between Gumilev's terminology and the taxonomies of Ethnosociology. Then Gumilev's theories will be able to enrich ethnosociological knowledge, methods, and instruments substantially.

Gumilev's taxonomy of "consortium, convicinity, subethnos, ethnos, superethnos" is highly problematic. The transition from the consortium as a group of citizens to the convicinity as a community connected with family ties and customs is not fixed, since any group whatsoever is produced on the basis of some. The consortium, like the convicinity and subethnos, can be distinguished as a social unit within the ethnos or in the course of ethnic transformations; for instance, as components of the interaction of a few ethnoses or as a result of certain ethnosociological processes (for example, the exclusion from the ethnos of deviants, the autonomization of certain professional groups, etc.). But neither a subethnos nor an ethnos is formed from these groups in result. Every group is obliged to associate in some language and not to think up its own; but this means that any group on the level of the consortium or convicinity already has an ethnic nature. The ethnos precedes it, and is not composed of it.

Doubtful, too, is the fragmentation of the ethnos into the taxa of subethnoses, convicinities, and consortia as an *a posteriori* scaling of the ethnos, since the convicinity as a group of individuals is not the ethnos' basic social group. The minimal inner element of the ethnos is the family and the lineage. The consortium is a very specific phenomenon, which can in no way be regarded as the basic taxon of the ethnos. We will see later why Gumilev isolated precisely the consortium as this basic unit. For now, we should merely note the inapplicability of the structure of Gumilev's scaling of the ethnos as general and accurate model for all cases. It is applicable only to separate historical situations, which we will consider separately.

A second important point: what Ethnosociology regards as the ethnos (koineme, the simplest social form) corresponds in Gumilev's terminology to merely one phase: homeostasis. Ethnosociology conceives of the ethnos as the minimal form of society, found in a static condition and in balance with its environment. In this way, the ethnos as ethnosociology understands it excludes ethnogenesis, leaps of passionarity, and the process of complication and kinetic expansion. The start of ethnogenesis, the impulse of passionarity, is in ethnosociology the transition from the ethnos to its first derivative, the narod, or laos. Hence, what Gumilev himself calls "ethnogenesis" should be called "*laogenesis*," i.e., the process of the formation of the narod from the ethnos. Gumilev himself does not make this distinction, since his approach is a generalized primordial and biological approach, and the fundamental sociological distinction between the ethnos and the narod escapes his attention. The narod and the ethnos are for Gumilev two different phases of the historical existence of one and the same subject, which he calls "ethnos." This is what makes his theory vulnerable to criticism by sociologists. The ethnos in its overheating phase (as Gumilev understands it) and the ethnos in homeostasis (i.e., the ethnos proper, as the simplest society) are entirely different sociological phenomena. There is a connection between them, but it is like the connection between an argument and its function.

The phenomenon of passionarity is the moment of transformation, clearly identified by Gumilev, from the ethnos to the laos. It is an extremely important factor, but its meaning will be fully revealed to us if we specify it in strictly ethnosociological terms. *The presence of a critical mass of passionate persons is a characteristic sign of the narod (laos) and, accordingly, the driving force of laogenesis.* At the same time, the ethnos should be regarded as the minimal association of people of the harmonic type, i.e., as homeostasis.

As for the superethnos, it recalls in many ways the "big narod," which produces grandiose empires, civilizations, and religious cultures; i.e., it is not a qualitatively new derivation from the ethnos, but the maximum scale of a historical construction created by the narod. The narod is by definition always polyethnic to a certain extent.

The nation is an entirely unique historical case, which must be distinguished, as we repeatedly emphasized, from the narod, and all the more so from the ethnos.

So, we should use Gumilev's models in Ethnosociology with great caution, each time checking its terminological and conceptual constructions against the corresponding set of ethnosociological concepts and theories.

Structuralism in the USSR:
Vladimir Yakovlevich Propp

The works of the structuralist school, founded by the eminent Russian scientist, historian, and specialist of the Russian folklore tradition Vladimir Yakovlevich Propp (1895–1970), was another important source of ethnosociological knowledge in the Russian-language context. Propp was influenced by the ideas of the German ethnographer and publisher Émile Nourry (1870–1935), who wrote under the pen name "Pierre Saintyves." Nourry proposed to interpret fairy tales as ancient rituals of initiation, experienced in the imagination. Following Nourry, Propp thought of fairy tales as narratives about ancient, archaic cultures and economic practices and he suggested using the structural method to study them.[85, 86]

The method requires separating a limited number of functional combinations, which reflect the historical content of the corresponding economic and magical rituals, embedded in the strata of much later periods, from the many plots and characters of the tales.

Propp thought that the ancient core of fairy tales was the combination of plots and situations connected with hunting, gathering, and the rites associated with them. He carefully analyzed a voluminous amount of material to separate out this ancient functional core.

The plots of this ancient material are based on the prime rite of death, the resurrection of the hero, and exchange with animals (monsters, fabulous antagonists) of vitally important attributes. According to Propp, the monster must swallow the hero to give him new life and restore the balance between hunters, who kill animals, and animals, symbolically killing the hunters.

Propp also studied other archaic social institutions, the memory of which is captured in fables: male unions (*Männerbunden*) and houses, puberty rites, specific rituals for the children of the tribe's chiefs, the structures and rites of the marriage cycle, and so forth.

A later kind of fairy tale consists of agrarian plots, characteristic of societies less dependent on hunting and gathering, producing food products through agriculture and livestock. In an agrarian context, many old hunters' rites and magic rituals lose their sense and change their significance. Plots, functions, and characters are interpreted in another context, reflecting a new, agrarian social order. For instance, the exchange between culture (man) and nature through the symbolic animal (fish, dragon, monster) eating the hunter, and his later resurrection, in which the animal acts as a complementary partner, is transformed in the agrarian phase

85 Saintyves, P. *Les Contes de Perrault et les récits paralles*. Paris: E. Nourry, 1923; Nourry E. *Corpus du Folklore des Eaux en France et dans les colonies françaises*. Paris: Librairie E. Nourry, 1934.

86 Istoricheskiye korni volshebnoy skazki. L: Izd-vo LGU, 1986.

into a battle against the monster (snake, dragon), which loses its complementary dimension and becomes a radical antagonist, which must be defeated and destroyed.

And finally, the latest kind of fairy tale is the heroic epic, which describes the social models and processes of early statehood with a clearly expressed social stratification, emphasis on the interdependence of estates, and the central position of the individual type of the hero or strongman.[87]

If we ignore the evolutionism and materialism in Propp's explanations for the evolution of the economic structures of archaic societies, his method can be entirely integrated into ethnosociology. The structural and functional analysis of folklore and especially fairy tales is a valuable contribution, since it sheds light on the structure of archaic societies, i.e., on the ethnos, and allows us to reproduce its main sociological parameters.

In their archaic cores (hunting and agrarian), fairy tales relate to the preliterate culture of the ethnos. The heroic epic relates to the first derivation from the ethnos, the narod or laos. Propp's successor, as we have said, was the structural Algirdas Greimas.

Vyacheslav Ivanov, Vladimir Toporov: The Structuralist Study of Philology and Anthropology

The outstanding Russian Soviet philologists, linguists, and culturologists, who often wrote as co-authors, Vyacheslav Vsevolodovich Ivanov and Vladimir Nikolaevich Toporov (1928–2005), are eminent representatives of Russian structuralism. They applied the methodology of Roman Jakobson, Nikolai Trubetskoy, Claude Lévi-Strauss, and Vladimir Propp to the study of mythologies, sacred texts, and different linguistic and philological traditions. In particular, Ivanov and Gamkrelidze wrote a major work on the reconstruction of the Indo-European language and the ancient Indo-European culture, mythology, and social system.[88]

---

87 Propp, V.Y. Russkiy geroicheskiy epos. Moscow: Labirint, 1999.

88 Gamkrelidze, T.V.. Ivanov Vyach. Vs. Indoyevropeyskiy yazyk i indoyevropeytsy. Moscow: 1988.

Ivanov and Toporov co-wrote a series of important books about ancient mythological ideas and linguistic particularities, which made it possible to reconstruct the main parameters of ancient Slavic societies, i.e., to describe the initial forms of Slavic ethnic groups.[89] Toporov's book *The Prehistory of Slavic Literature* is an important work on this topic.[90] For Russian Ethnosociology, these works have fundamental significance, since it is possible on their basis to reconstruct the structure of the ethnos, i.e., to clarify the parameters of the koineme in the history of the transformation of Russians society.

Ivanov and Toporov initiated and contributed to the project of the two-volume *Myths of the Peoples of the World*, which remains the most complete and authoritative encyclopedia on mythologies ever published in Russian.[91]

Ivanov's *Dual Structures in Anthropology* are very significant for understanding the ethnos as a dual phenomenon (the duality of lineages is the most important fact about the endogenous society).[92] This work has special significance for Ethnosociology, because it describes in detail the dual forms in the structure of the ethnos and other, more differentiated social organizations. In particular, Ivanov picks up the idea of the English ethnologist Arthur Hocart about the purely ritualistic functions of royal power in certain archaic societies.[93] Ivanov further develops the idea that the most harmonious types of archaic societies separate status and direct political power, based on violence and direct submission. In these societies, the king enjoys great prestige and the highest status, but

89 Ivanov, V. & Toporov, V.N. Slavyanskiye yazykovyye modeliruyushchiye semioticheskiye sistemy: (Drevniy period). Moscow: Nauka. 1965; Ibid., Issledovaniya v oblasti slavyanskikh drevnostey: (Leksicheskiye i frazeologicheskiye voprosy rekonstruktsii tekstov). Moscow: Nauka, 1974.

90 Toporov, V.N Predystoriya literatury u slavyan: Opyt rekonstruktsii: Vvedeniye k kursu istorii slavyanskikh literatur. Moscow: RGGU, 1998.

91 Ivanov, V. & Toporov, V.N Mify, narodov mira. Entsiklopediya. Moscow: Sovetskaya entsiklopediya, 1980.

92 Ivanov, V. Dual'nyye struktury v antropologii: kurs lektsiy. Moscow: RGGU, 2008.

93 Hocart, A.M. *Kings and Councillors*. Cairo, 1936.

his authoritative rights do not particularly differ from those of the other members of society. The ritual character of royal power, according to Ivanov, precedes its establishment through direct and despotic authority. This idea overturns the usual evolutionary hypotheses that primitive societies are based on the principle of the direct dominance of the leader, the strongest. Ivanov, following Hocart, shows that in many cases, exactly the reverse is true: the statutory superiority and prestige of the king transform into the legitimization of violence as a result of the degeneracy and degradation of the original social systems. Violent rule is a kind of usurpation and deviation.[94]

Ivanov gives dues to the Soviet ethnologist and anthropologist Zolotarev, who built a theory on the basis of the study of dual systems (twin myths, binary oppositions, etc.) in the culture of archaic societies, having great significance for Sociology.[95] Ivanov refers to Zolotarev's unpublished manuscript, which contains the most important conclusions regarding dual structures and their decisive meaning for social orders.[96]

Ivanov's anthropological work *The Science of Man* is a classic. In it, the relevant themes, methods, and theories of contemporary anthropology are laid out in summary from a structuralist perspective.

Ivanov is the head of the Russian School of Anthropology at the Russian State University for the Humanities.

In the Soviet period, Ivanov and Toporov (like Gumilev) were on the periphery of official science, since they championed the structuralist approach, fundamentally different, methodologically and in its ideological prerequisites from Marxism. In our time, the ideas of these eminent scholars should be given their due. Their contribution to Ethnosociology is invaluable.

---

94 Ivanov, V.. Dual'nyye struktury v antropologii: kurs lektsiy. pp. 49–85.

95 Ibid. pp. 86–126.

96 Zolotarev, A.M. Dual'naya organizatsiya pervobytnykh narodov i proiskhozhdeniye dualisticheskikh kosmogoniy (issledovaniye po istorii rodovogo stroya i pervobytnoy mifologii). Rukopis' (zakonchena v 1941). Arkhiv instituta etnografii RAN.

Soviet Ethnography and the History of Ethnoses

Among Soviet ethnographers, we should identify a few outstanding re-searchers, who collected and classified a massive amount of ethnographic and ethnological material.

One eminent figure of Soviet ethnography, who preserved the tradi-tions of the Russian ethnographic school in the Soviet period and thereby ensured partial continuity under conditions of severe ideological dictator-ship, was Sergei Aleksandrovich Tokarev (1899–1985). He began his eth-nographic and anthropological fieldwork among the peoples of Siberia, but later expanded his circle of interests to also include European peoples, Indian ethnoses, and the Australian aborigines.[97] Tokarev familiarized Soviet scholars with the works and ideas of Western anthropologists and ethnographers and wrote general histories of Soviet Ethnography.[98, 99] He paid great attention to the religious ideas of archaic ethnoses.[100] The monumental encyclopedia *The Ethnography of the Peoples of the USSR* was released under his direction.[101]

The eminent historian and ethnographer, Boris Alexandrovich Rybakov (1908–2001), former director of the Institute of Archeology at the Academy of Sciences of the USSR, devoted his scientific activity to the study of ancient Russian society, its social order and religious ideas. He wrote the classic works on the study of the Slavic ethnos, *The Chronicles and Bylinas of Ancient Rus, The Paganism of the Ancient Slavs,* and *The Paganism of Ancient Rus,* among others.[102, 103, 104] His works are fundamen-tal for the study of the structure of Russian society's ancient roots.

---

97 Tokarev, S.A. Obshchestvennyy stroy yakutov. Moscow: Yakutskoye gos. izd-vo, 1945.

98 Ibid. Istoki etnograficheskoy nauki. Moscow : Nauka, 1978; Ibid., Istoriya zarubezh-noy etnografii. Moscow: Vysshaya shkola, 1978.

99 Tokarev, S.A. Istoriya russkoy etnografii. Moscow: Nauka, 1966.

100 Ibid. Ranniye formy religii i ikh razvitiye. Moscow: Nauka, 1964.

101 Ibid. Etnografiya narodov SSSR. Moscow: Izd-vo Mosk. un-ta, 1958.

102 Rybakov, B.A. Drevnyaya Rus': Skazaniya. Byliny. Letopisi. Moscow: 1963.

103 Ibid. Yazychestvo drevnikh slavyan. Moscow: Nauka, 1981.

104 Ibid. Yazychestvo drevney Rusi. Moscow: Nauka, 1987.

We find very valuable reconstructions of the ancient stages of Russian history and its ethnic, social, and ethnographic peculiarities in the works of contemporaries Froyanov and Yudin, who became famous in the Soviet period and made a significant contribution to the study of the Russian ethnos.[105] Yudin (1938–1995) was Propp's student and follower and continued the structuralist approach to Russian history. He wrote penetrating works on the reconstruction of the functional meaning of central figures in Russian folklore.[106] Igor Yakovlevich Froyanov is the author of such works on the history of eastern Slavic ethnoses as *Essays on the Social and Political History of Kievan Rus, Ancient Rus: A Study of the History of Social and Political Struggles*, and *Slavery and Tribute Relations among Eastern Slavs*, among others.[107, 108, 109]

We should also mention the excellent anthropologist and ethnologist Arkady Fedorovich Anisimov (1910–1968), who researched the peoples of Eastern Siberia and collected an enormous amount of data on the social arrangements of the Yakut and Evenk ethnoses.[110] Anisimov also wrote general theoretical works on the religious forms and ideas of archaic peoples, on problems of "primordial thinking," and so on.[111]

Ekaterina Dmitrievna Prokofiev (1902–1978) made a major contribution to Russian ethnography in her studies of the social organization of

105 Yudin, Y.I. Ob istoricheskikh osnovakh russkogo bylevogo eposa. SPb: Russkaya literatura, 1983.

106 Yudin, Y.I. Durak, shut, vor i chert. Moscow: Labirint, 2006.

107 Froyanov, I.Y. Kiyevskaya Rus'. Ocherki sotsial'no-politicheskoy istorii. L: 1980.

108 Froyanov, I.Y. Drevnyaya Rus'. Opyt issledovaniya istorii sotsial'noy i politicheskoy bor'by. SPb: 1995.

109 Froyanov, I.Y. SPb: 1996.

110 Anisimov, A.F. Rodovoye obshchestvo evenkov (tungusov). L: Izd-vo In-ta narodov severa TSIK SSSR:1936; Ibid., Religiya evenkov v istoriko-geneticheskom izuchenii i proble — my proiskhozhdeniya pervobytnykh verovaniy. L: Izd-vo AN SSSR, 1958.

111 Anisimov, A.F.. Obshcheye i osobennoye v razvitii obshchestva i religii narodov Sibiri. Leningrad: Nauka, 1969; Ibid., Istoricheskiye osobennosti pervobytnogo myshleniya. Leningrad: Nauka, 1971; Ibid., Kosmologicheskiye predstavleniya narodov severa. L: Nauka, 1959.

the Yakut, Tuva, and Selkup.[112] She collected and classified extensive material on the shamanism of the Siberian ethnoses.

Gavriel Vasilyevich Ksenofontov (1888–1938) studied the Yakut and their social and religious ideas.[113]

Soviet Ethnology: Yulian Vladimirovich Bromley

The academic Yulian Vladimirovich Bromley (1921–1990), director of the Institute of Ethnography at the Academy of Sciences of the USSR, is interesting in that he was practically the only officially-recognized expert in the USSR on ethnoses and ethnology. Bromley wrote a series of scientific monographs devoted to the study of ethnoses, among which a few stand out: *Ethnos and Ethnography, Essays on the Theory of the Ethnos, Contemporary Problems of Ethnography, Ethnosocial Processes*, and also a textbook on Ethnography, for a long time the only permitted reading on this topic.[114, 115, 116, 117, 118]

Bromley was the main opponent of Gumilev's theory of the ethnos. But Bromley's and Gumilev's statuses were incommensurable, since in the Soviet period the free-thinking Gumilev, the son of "enemies of the people," was considered a marginal and "eccentric," while Bromley was fully integrated in the Soviet scientific establishment. Thus, from a moral perspective, Bromley's critique of Gumilev and his ideas, even if there was a grain of truth to it (in particular, in the criticism of his unjustified

---

112 Prokofiev, E.D. K voprosu o sotsial'noy organizatsii sel'kupov. Rod i fratriya. Moscow-L: 1952.

113 Ksenofontov, G.V. Ellayada. Moscow: 1977; Ibid., Istoricheskiy fol'klor evenkov. Moscow-L., 1966; Ibid., Mifologicheskiye skazki i istoricheskiye predaniya entsev. Moscow: 1977.

114 Yulian Bromley. Etnos i Etnographia. Moscow: 1973.

115 Ibid. Ocherki Teorii Ethnosa. Moscow: 1983.

116 Ibid. Sovremennie Problemy Etnografii. Moscow: 1981.

117 Ibid. Etnosotsial'nie protsessy: teoria, istoria, sovremennost. Moscow: Nauka, 1987.

118 Ibid. 'Etnografiya: Uchebnik / Pod red. Yu.B. Bromley i G.E. Markov. Moscow, Vysh. Shkola, 1982.

biologism and the inadequacies of his social approach) resembled not a scientific discussion, but a snitching or kind of repression. Under such circumstances, it is hardly worth considering the substance of the critique.

On the other hand, because of his status, Bromley was obligated to bring his ethnological and anthropological theories in line with the strict dogmas of Marxism. And since the ideas of Marx and Engels about ancient humanity and archaic societies were primarily based on Morgan's evolutionary concepts, the dogmatic approach of Bromley and his school were, to a significant extent, predetermined. Outside the Soviet ideological context, his ideas could hardly be taken seriously, since they have no independent value.

Bromley developed a fanciful terminology, in which he distinguished *ethnikoses* (ethnoses) and *ethnosociological organisms*, i.e., ethnoses attached to politico-economic forms (in Marxist doctrine). Bromley considered the *tribe* (the original communal order), *peoplehood* (the slaveholding and feudal order), and the *nation* (the capitalist and socialist orders) as forms of the ethnosocial organisms.

It was a big problem for Bromley to fit the concepts "nation" and "nationality" into the Soviet reality, where these concepts reflected complex efforts to adopt Marxist theory to Russian history, efforts started by Lenin and continued by Stalin.

According to Marx and the usual use of the term, the "nation" is a form of the bourgeois organized violence in a class government — a political phenomenon. The German Marxist Karl Kautsky defended this position in his time in arguments with the Austrian Marxist Otto Bauer. Bauer objected to Kautsky that it is also possible to understand by "nation" ethnic groups. Bauer described the reality of the collapsing Austro-Hungarian Empire, where separate ethnic groups — Hungarians, Slavs, Romanians — prepared to form their own national governments, but had not yet done so. But Kautsky was proceeding on the basis of relatively mono-ethnic Germany, where the nation was thought of only as common citizenship.

The situation in the Russian Empire during Lenin's time more closely resembled Austro-Hungary. As a result, in the Russian terminology of the Bolsheviks, Bauer's use of the term "nationality," prevailed, meaning both those nations that had already constituted governments and those ethnoses that were only striving to that end. For Lenin, and, it seems, for Stalin, the concept of "nationality" became a means to talk about the fact that Russia had bourgeois relations and nations had appeared but were soon overcome in socialist society and transformed into nationality. So, in the USSR the terms "nation" and "nationality" were extremely fuzzy. They signified a partly ethnocultural and partly political and administrative (national republics) community. This ambiguity impeded the free scientific study of ethnoses and nations in the USSR and affected Bromley's half-formed theories, developed in accordance with official dogma.

The Institutionalization of Ethnosociology Today

In the current stage of Russian science, interest in Ethnosociology is being awakened with new vigor. We see evidence of this in its inclusion in the register of general disciplines and in the federal component for specialization in "Sociology."

Today, there are a few Ethnosociology textbooks and training manuals.

The textbook by Arutyunyan, Drobizheva, and Susokolov, became the model work for the further development of the scientific instruction of Ethnosociology. It was written from different positions and represented the first approach to the study of this discipline. Because the authors held different opinions about the ethnos, the textbook bears the mark of eclecticism. Nevertheless, the merit of this textbook is that it served as a basis for the development of a federal standard and with it, the study of Ethnosociology was introduced into the university system, itself an important scientific event.

The training materials by Mnatsakanyana are built on a narrower foundation, relying on studies of interethnic and international conflict.

We should also mention the training materials of Tatunts, Perepelkina, Sokolovskii (Novosibirsk State University) and Denisova and Radovel' (South Federal University, Rostov-on-Don).[119, 120]

We should state that in contemporary Russia, Ethnosociology was not established correctly, although its presence among generally required disciplines confirms its importance. In this case, the fact of institutionalization anticipates the full-fledged and final formation of a scientific discipline, which is a stimulus to its development and to creative understanding.

119 Perepelkin, L.S., Sokolovsky. S.V. Etnosotsiologia. Novosibirsk, 1995.
120 Denisov, G.S. Radovel, M.R. Etnosotsiologia. Rostov-on-Don: OOO "TsVVR," 2000.

OTHER BOOKS PUBLISHED BY ARKTOS

VIRGINIA ABERNETHY	*Born Abroad*
SRI DHARMA PRAVARTAKA ACHARYA	*The Dharma Manifesto*
JOAKIM ANDERSEN	*Rising from the Ruins*
WINSTON C. BANKS	*Excessive Immigration*
ALAIN DE BENOIST	*Beyond Human Rights*
	Carl Schmitt Today
	The Ideology of Sameness
	The Indo-Europeans
	Manifesto for a European Renaissance
	On the Brink of the Abyss
	The Problem of Democracy
	Runes and the Origins of Writing
	View from the Right (vol. 1–3)
ARMAND BERGER	*Tolkien, Europe, and Tradition*
ARTHUR MOELLER VAN DEN BRUCK	*Germany's Third Empire*
MATT BATTAGLIOLI	*The Consequences of Equality*
KERRY BOLTON	*The Perversion of Normality*
	Revolution from Above
	Yockey: A Fascist Odyssey
ISAC BOMAN	*Money Power*
CHARLES WILLIAM DAILEY	*The Serpent Symbol in Tradition*
RICARDO DUCHESNE	*Faustian Man in a Multicultural Age*
ALEXANDER DUGIN	*Ethnos and Society*
	Ethnosociology
	Eurasian Mission
	The Fourth Political Theory
	The Great Awakening vs the Great Reset
	Last War of the World-Island
	Political Platonism
	Putin vs Putin
	The Rise of the Fourth Political Theory
	Templars of the Proletariat
	The Theory of a Multipolar World
EDWARD DUTTON	*Race Differences in Ethnocentrism*
MARK DYAL	*Hated and Proud*
CLARE ELLIS	*The Blackening of Europe*
KOENRAAD ELST	*Return of the Swastika*
JULIUS EVOLA	*The Bow and the Club*
	Fascism Viewed from the Right
	A Handbook for Right-Wing Youth
	Metaphysics of Power
	Metaphysics of War
	The Myth of the Blood
	Notes on the Third Reich
	Pagan Imperialism
	Recognitions
	A Traditionalist Confronts Fascism

OTHER BOOKS PUBLISHED BY ARKTOS

GUILLAUME FAYE	Archeofuturism
	Archeofuturism 2.0
	The Colonisation of Europe
	Convergence of Catastrophes
	Ethnic Apocalypse
	A Global Coup
	Prelude to War
	Sex and Deviance
	Understanding Islam
	Why We Fight
DANIEL S. FORREST	Suprahumanism
ANDREW FRASER	Dissident Dispatches
	Reinventing Aristocracy in the Age of Woke Capital
	The WASP Question
GÉNÉRATION IDENTITAIRE	We are Generation Identity
PETER GOODCHILD	The Taxi Driver from Baghdad
	The Western Path
PAUL GOTTFRIED	War and Democracy
PETR HAMPL	Breached Enclosure
CONSTANTIN VON HOFFMEISTER	Esoteric Trumpism
PORUS HOMI HAVEWALA	The Saga of the Aryan Race
LARS HOLGER HOLM	Hiding in Broad Daylight
	Homo Maximus
	Incidents of Travel in Latin America
	The Owls of Afrasiab
RICHARD HOUCK	Liberalism Unmasked
INSTITUT ILIADE	For a European Awakening
A. J. ILLINGWORTH	Political Justice
ALEXANDER JACOB	De Naturae Natura
JASON REZA JORJANI	Artemis Unveiled
	Closer Encounters
	Erosohpia
	Faustian Futurist
	Iranian Leviathan
	Lovers of Sophia
	Novel Folklore
	Prometheism
	Promethean Pirate
	Prometheus and Atlas
	Psychotron
	Uber Man
	World State of Emergency
HENRIK JONASSON	Sigmund
EDGAR JULIUS JUNG	The Significance of the German Revolution
RUUBEN KAALEP & AUGUST MEISTER	Rebirth of Europe

OTHER BOOKS PUBLISHED BY ARKTOS

OTHER BOOKS PUBLISHED BY ARKTOS

STEVEN J. ROSEN	*The Agni and the Ecstasy*
	The Jedi in the Lotus
NICHOLAS ROONEY	*Talking to the Wolf*
RICHARD RUDGLEY	*Barbarians*
	Essential Substances
	Wildest Dreams
ERNST VON SALOMON	*It Cannot Be Stormed*
	The Outlaws
WERNER SOMBART	*Traders and Heroes*
PIERO SAN GIORGIO	*CBRN*
	Giuseppe
	Survive the Economic Collapse
SRI SRI RAVI SHANKAR	*Celebrating Silence*
	Know Your Child
	Management Mantras
	Patanjali Yoga Sutras
	Secrets of Relationships
GEORGE T. SHAW (ED.)	*A Fair Hearing*
FENEK SOLÈRE	*Kraal*
	Reconquista
OSWALD SPENGLER	*The Decline of the West*
	Man and Technics
RICHARD STOREY	*The Uniqueness of Western Law*
TOMISLAV SUNIC	*Against Democracy and Equality*
	Homo Americanus
	Postmortem Report
	Titans are in Town
ASKR SVARTE	*Gods in the Abyss*
HANS-JÜRGEN SYBERBERG	*On the Fortunes and Misfortunes*
	of Art in Post-War Germany
ABIR TAHA	*Defining Terrorism*
	The Epic of Arya (2nd ed.)
	Nietzsche's Coming God, or the
	Redemption of the Divine
	Verses of Light
JEAN THIRIART	*Europe: An Empire of 400 Million*
BAL GANGADHAR TILAK	*The Arctic Home in the Vedas*
DOMINIQUE VENNER	*For a Positive Critique*
	The Shock of History
HANS VOGEL	*How Europe Became American*
MARKUS WILLINGER	*A Europe of Nations*
	Generation Identity
ALEXANDER WOLFHEZE	*Alba Rosa*
	Rupes Nigra

www.ingramcontent.com/pod-product-compliance
Lightning Source LLC
Chambersburg PA
CBHW020656270326
41928CB00005B/153